# TO THE EAST A PHOENIX

Nigel Cameron

# TO
# THE EAST
# A PHOENIX

Photographs by BRIAN BRAKE

HUTCHINSON OF LONDON

HUTCHINSON & CO. (*Publishers*) LTD
*178–202 Great Portland Street, London, W.1*

London Melbourne Sydney
Auckland Bombay Toronto
Johannesburg New York

*First published 1960*

*This book has been set in Fournier type face. It has
been printed in Great Britain by The Anchor Press,
Ltd., in Tiptree, Essex, on Antique Wove paper
and bound by Taylor Garnett Evans & Co., Ltd.,
in Watford, Herts*

# Contents

# Photographs

FOLLOW PAGE 208

ACKNOWLEDGEMENTS

I would like to thank Messrs. John Murray for permission to quote from *Aden to the Hadhramaut* by Van der Meulen, and Messrs. Michael Joseph for 'The Divani Shamsi Tabriz' by Jalalu 'Ddin Rumi, translated by Reynold Nicholson, from *Another World Than This*.

# Explanation

An imaginary traveller went with me on the journey. To explain him you have to embody him, which is not what happened. He remained a sort of ambulant lay figure on which you could hang whatever cap you might be wearing at the moment, from whose other head it surveyed you from time to time. He was insubstantial but very practical, stepping out of you draped in the mantle which from place to place and from emotion to emotion encumbered your more objective view. As you registered the sight and sound and feel of the world, and struck some sort of attitude before it—there he stood, clothed in your own skin, horribly revealing.

But looking at him you felt a kind of freedom: those garments—the wopsical hats, the posture of a thought that has reacted against some experience as a pendulum reacts at the end of its swing by swinging the other way, those trances and desolate tears—those garments pinched as a crab's new crust must pinch him. The birth of an opinion can be as painful as the birth of a child.

So it was good to be able to set new ideas and outlandish thoughts firmly on the traveller as he split from you like the double image of the drunken eye, and to see how they looked—which was how you looked yourself—without the stiff touch of them on your own soul. When escaping, your escape confronted you; but at one remove. Besotted with love—of person, of thing, even of yourself—the traveller was there, swaddled in your passion, in your idiotic aspirations, in your histrionics.

He was, therefore, a salutary companion: but also friendly. And when those new thoughts, shocks of realization, honeysuckles of nostalgia, and assorted states of possession enveloped you in their blurring waves, the traveller could be sent off to the end of his tether like a docile goat; and you could have a long look at him.

I couldn't help liking him, most of the time. After all he was part of me. And sometimes I relied on him, like a sailor on his compass in the wilderness of the waters; or in the way—back of your mind—you rely on the coming of the morning when sunk in the mysticism of tropic nights with their erotics and dream-wish-doldrums of runaway sensuality.

The traveller was my identical twin: the same, but other. I leaned my sanity on his imaginary shoulder and he saw me through without fatally mocking any essence that might be in me.

We set out in the middle of an English summer and perched for a few days on an island in the Aegean at the beginning of a long journey. Poros is hardly the island you would choose if time allowed a longer stay in that bright-eyed sea; but like all the others it is specific for the malignancy of *angst*. The fatigue of the last few months was a weight we didn't want to carry with us, and a day or two was all we could spare. We wanted to start light on a year and a half of travel—to gather burdens, quite different burdens, as we went.

What were those burdens we hoped to gather? What were we hoping to understand in the East? At that time we didn't see the answer clearly. We knew the East; at least the look and smell of it; and the traveller, given half a chance, would rhapsodize on the beauty of it and on the wonder of its people who were, in some ways, wandering through the time of our own Western beginnings. The East for him had all the joy and freshness of the childhood of the human race. He was going on this journey to renew his delight, to deepen and to expand it.

But when you look at a child with its clear eye and sturdy limbs, its flexible and unblemished skin, when you listen to its open mind running like a spring brook with the free water of uninhibited thoughts and imagery—there is sometimes a stab of a moment when you wonder how that child will grow up. You speculate how the hazards of the world will mould it.

The East is two-thirds of the people of the world. I wondered how they were growing up in the battle of the twentieth century. From the awful distance of occidental sophistication I wanted to try to find out.

So, linked and yet separate, the traveller and I set out to see how it might be in that long, long germination beyond the European flower.

# I. Hadhramaut

You must visualize a whole country without water. Even the air above it through which you are flying is innocent of cloud and almost ignorant of the cooling lash of rain. You must know, or better, vividly remember, a thirst that raved in your throat when the water-hole lay twenty camel-miles away; and the desiccating sun that shines today and every day for a thousand years in senseless passion—you must know that too as a desperate enemy. Otherwise you will never understand the Hadhramaut; for that is what the land is like and that is the condition of the people there.

In temperate places on a winter's night when rain flitters in the wind against the cold window, or on a summer's day when fat wet clouds lounge across the meadows, it is hard to grasp that the lives of a good third of the world's inhabitants are entirely regulated by drought. The mere lack of water has shaped their beliefs and the manner in which their societies and families are knit together. Put some cloth in a box and squash it down tightly and the cloth which is springy will eventually take on the shape of the box, so that when you take it out it will be square for a while until its nature asserts itself. The Arabs are like that, very square and cooped-up in the hot dry box of their history, which is in large part the effect of their environment. It is also the effect of the Prophet Mahomet. But that, like the effect of Christ on Salt Lake City, is another matter. Perhaps neither result was intended by either prophet.

From the midst of the air there is almost nothing: sand, cruel rock, watercourses abandoned like dry twigs here and there, and then sand and radiating haze which is the material of heat. It is exciting to look down from the relaxed comfort of your plane at the dangerous barren stretches of the land, but you are not tempted to take a parachute and investigate. Yet there is something there, for this is the same sweet and implacable land and these Arabs who live there the cousins of people whom Doughty entombed in the majestic catafalque of his prose. They are lean men with wild curly hair, and deathless women, and children who die as germs flourish, multitudinously, in the medieval dirt of their exposed place in the sun. Youth is a

9

flower of languorous beauty; old age seldom comes at all. They are men, these Arabs, like the delicate heroes of Lawrence striding among the seven pillars of a wisdom which is now worn out, if it was ever more than hard desert sense. They are men whose eyes and painted eyelids suggest women of wealthy harems, does' eyes concealing an explosive sense of honour whose detonation is the sudden knife between the ribs of the back. They are cunning men, subtle, exhausting, demanding; their ways of business are tortuous, not specially from rapacity but from the exiguous need to survive in their place and time. Riches here are insurance against death: poverty, threat of actual death.

And the cities of square mud sprouting from the sand, inseparable from their ground like objects in early cubist paintings, and like those paintings urgent in their own more-than-reality, are modern Babylons jostling with the sinewy, equivocal, somehow tender hearts of people not much different from those imagined races who once flourished in the space between the Tigris and the Euphrates.

There is a tremendous glamour and a tremendous gulf between you in your plane with *petits pois* on a plastic tray on your knees, and your literary picture of the people below; and between that picture and the reality. Both the glamour and the gulf, in Aden when you land, are rapidly effaced.

One way and another you seem to find yourself in Aden more often than comfort, pleasure, or enlightenment require. It is disenchanting, in every sense an arid place, a bazaar through whose clamour and shoddiness several hundred thousand lost travellers falter each year on their way somewhere else. It is a place of passing trade, of *entrepôt* business, an ocean pull-up half-way to the Orient; and nowhere at all. Even the picturesque windmills which pumped sea water into patterns of lakes outside the town are almost stilled since India, with Independence, discovered she too could make salt by evaporation.

But the passing trade hardly sees Aden beyond the crescent of shops at the waterfront. The adventurous take a taxi up the burning face of the mountain of rock behind the town and drop down on the other side to Crater, a town built in the basin left when the sea invaded one side of the old volcano. Here live merchants in shuttered houses full of women and children and flies and the vague odour of urine, and here they trade in close-packed rows of shops where Leicas hang by Hong Kong socks and a binocular microscope gleams beside a rabbit made of rabbit fur, and the face-cream has long since liquefied like Arab eyes, but from heat and not from passion. The resolute tripper gets as far as Sheikh Othman, and catches a lungful of its dust and the sight of a resting camel-train from God knows where—somewhere in the romantic interior which exists for him only in books by the fire at home.

Yet if he pressed on a little he would come to the no-man's-land of a jet

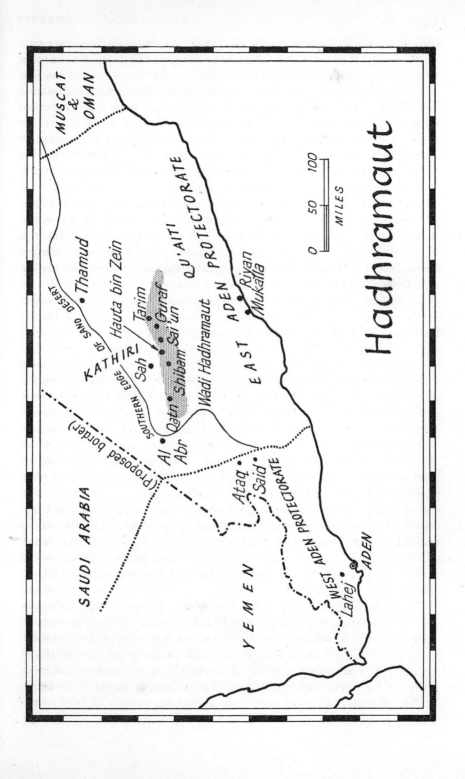

MUSCAT & OMAN

SAUDI ARABIA

YEMEN

DESERT OF SAND

KATHIRI

SOUTHERN EDGE

(Proposed border)

• Thamud

• Hauta bin Zein

• Tarim
• Gurat
• Sai'un
• Shibam
• Qatn
• Sah

Wadi Hadhramaut

QU'AITI PROTECTORATE

EAST ADEN PROTECTORATE

• Riyan
Mukalla

• Al Abr

• Ataq
• Said

WEST ADEN PROTECTORATE

• Lahej
ADEN

Hadhramaut

0      50      100

MILES

crag against the inflamed sun as she sets in her blast furnace beyond the combustible sea; and he would see those aluminium paps of refined oil, ranged in rows there as though some black dinosaur had lain down with its jagged scales breaking the sky and its belly exposed to nourish its revolting young. Even the tall flares roaring as they burn off poisonous gases from the crude oil might be spouts of fire breathed from its improbable nostrils. Across the bay the little line of Aden shops takes on a sweet homely look like a cannibal viewed from the jaws of a tiger. And you hurry away, shaken with the threat in this beauty, back to the comforting grit in Sheikh Othman.

Arab nationalism, which has so disturbed the happy Western balance of power in the Middle East, had just begun to speak in the summer of 1956. At that time people more thoughtful than tourists were not taking too much notice of it. I had arrived from Cairo, where I attended the manifestations of armed strength and popular joy accompanying the exit of the last British troops from the Canal Zone. Shepilov and Sir Brian Robertson (the British representative at the march past) sat side by side, and with them a number of gentlemen from Jordan, Lebanon, Syria, and Saudi Arabia, who, nowadays, would be less inclined to mix. Nasser, a figure like an Arab Clark Gable, handsome, a little fleshy, emanating personal well-being, stood at the salute for four hours while the military parade jangled past. His endurance on that torrid day, when the guests in the stand beside me were visibly wilting, made a strong impression on me. It was obvious that this was a man on the crest of a tremendous wave, the first since the tide of Arab Empire receded ignominiously in the late Middle Ages. The Arab fiend popularly portrayed by journalists was not present. Like the Benign Churchill or the Father-Figure Adenauer it is probably a picture of journalists' minds rather than of any person. Nasser appeared to have a healthy modesty about him. None of the arrogance of the great dictator of the 'thirties showed through that smooth jawline. He looked very much as one might have hoped he would, a man stored with confidence in the inchoate Arab kingdom of which his seizure of power in Egypt was the igniting spark. Shepilov, not far away, spent a lot of time chasing a normally persistent Cairo fly from the pasty acres of his countenance; and Sir Brian Robertson looked the type of man who is always more comfortable in field marshal's uniform—the flies, I think, avoided him.

Yet it was only in Cairo at that time—already, politically, long ago—that Arab nationalism was to be seen. In Aden a mere ten days later everything seemed as it had been for years. So it was surprising to be blinded by tear-gas and to hear shots fired at the back of the police station as the strikers milled around. The strike of employees of a large firm had been going on for weeks, and this was perhaps no more than the culminating incident. But the eruption of violence from the tame workers of Aden struck with disproportionate force. The air was full of nervousness. The first shiver of alarm crept down the ruling spine, and British and Arabs alike were henceforth edgy.

The body of one young man, victim of the bullets fired from the police station the previous day, was attended by a mob of his compatriots as the coffin under a red pall was borne through the streets. I followed them for some way, from the stench of the alleys behind the waterfront. They were a cheerful lot, only slightly conscious of the symbolic nature of the burden they were carrying to the cemetery where on the surface of rock they would place it and cover it with stones. They even laughed as I stood on old crates to take pictures, and seemed genuinely surprised that I should be interested in the funeral. They emptied like a bucket of dye into the channel of shops which border the waterfront, scattering tourists and thumping their fists on the hot paint of parked cars. A little shouting, no police in sight: and it was all over.

But next day a general strike was called and lasted briefly. The Arab newspaper *Al Ba'ath* was officially proscribed for slightly exaggerating the number of dead after the affray at the police station. Its editor, a man of twenty-five, smiled uncertainly at me when I went to see him in his Arab version of an editor's office. I doubt if a European had interviewed him before and his smile concealed both surprise and misgivings. The chaos of cups and scraps of newsprint, old files discarded on chairs, dust on ledges, and makeshift lighting surrounded us both in a friendly way.

We talked around the point for a time like two dogs unsure of each other. I wondered whether he felt political indignation over the events his paper had exaggerated: I speculated how much of him was commerical and how much idealist; how much of him was really dedicated to those ten thousand souls who had no roof over their heads in Aden, and to all the rest of the raggle-taggle population who scratched a living somehow on its super-heated rock. His bland smile did not tell me. Neither did his background—son of a wealthy local bus-owner who disowned him when he took the left in politics and newsprint. But I had the feeling he was testing the strength of the emotions involved, the powers of opposition in Aden. I wondered also if he had realized how deeply he had committed himself to a course which by now has surely landed him in trouble. The naïveté of Arab nationalism, its pathetic simple indignation, is partly its armour and also its vulnerable heart.

There is a small beach called Gold Mohur outside Aden, where only Europeans go to swim. It is a U-shaped bay, whose mouth is screened by a heavy metal net.

Adventurous whites may swim on the safe side of that net within a few feet of the threshing fury of sharks. It is an exciting and generally safe little game, and when I was there the net was still strong. So we all felt very secure.

But after Cairo I was tuned to the right wavelength and I sensed something strange. There was a feeling in Aden—no more than that—of unease. It was difficult to pinpoint what aroused the sensation in me, but it was there. The minor riot did no more than strengthen a feeling already present.

There were portents. A new Political Officer sat in a spacious room in Police Headquarters, a very smooth man with a round baby-face and a cloak-and-dagger mind. Every time I was there a squealer or two sat humbly in the ante-room ready with their bits of tribal information, about to spill the beans of remote little jealousies for a few coins, over-conscious that next door was the lair of the Chief of Police—a man like a jovial farmer, a great bear starred and immaculate and military below his ruddy face. His gin-toned voice boomed every now and then, and his great guffaw of laughter. The Political Officer regarded me with suspicion, so that he kept being very kind and inviting me to his house for meals, and himself coming to drink with me in the hotel. I was unwise enough to tell him I had come direct from Egypt. Maybe that was his worry. Later, in the desert, I realized that he spoke fluent Arabic and understood several of the local dialects, but he consistently refused to utilize this accomplishment in his dealings with the Arabs. Over all he was extremely helpful to me and we established a sort of mutual understanding. But I was amused before I finally left the Hadhramaut to find from him that he knew every one of my movements in detail. He recounted some of them on our last meeting—with a sort of urbane bravado in keeping with the blood and intrigue of his mind, and to prove to me, perhaps, that however little I may have thought of him he was one jump ahead. I allowed him to be satisfied on the last point and we parted on excellent terms.

In the hotel in Aden there were a number of people who appeared to be stranded there for one reason or the other. Amongst them was a Scot from somewhere urban on the west coast—to judge by his arpeggiotic accent. He was a dark little man with a wry little face, and an air of cosmopolitan life of which he was very proud. But his greatest pride was a wife in mid-thirties, a woman of olive creamy skin and indefinable origin. She might have been an Egyptian of a Turkish mother, or a Syrian mixed with Greek. He doted on her, calling her 'my love' at all times, and dressed her in clothes which were chic verging on the garish. She was a buxom lady, nipped in at the ample waist and glittering in gold sandals with tarty heels; but most amiable. The bumptious little Scot had just come from Saudi Arabia and he told a good tale. His wife also knew what was good copy and confided in me a picture of the harem of Saud the King. I took to her and flirted with her, which flattered her husband when it didn't fill him with the acid of distrust. But it mostly inflated his already well-developed ego. With a Presbyterian upbringing and a seductive wife you must have a large ego. It is your vindication.

I sometimes wondered what this clever man did there in Aden.

At the airport at dawn one day the pools of electric light were just dispersing before a grey morning. It was strange, as places are in cold light when you have only seen them in the heat; almost unreal. I cast an eye round for yesterday's silver bullets of jet fighters panting on the tarmac. But there were none. I looked for the buttery fleece of the riding camels of the Aden Protectorate Levies that were prancing and racing with their polychrome saddles and trappings the other noon, for their riders in proud white with their lances flashing and their green sashes flying; but only the creeping mist eddied here and there amongst hangars, and the cold eye of day looked down on deserted places.

Mahomet the driver, who had taken me for a drive in the late night—'for it is your last day in my taxi'—was cold and had wrapped an old scarf round his head like a man with toothache. He was sleepy, too, his brightness of soul only glimmering now and then. He forgot he had put some of the luggage in the boot, he dropped his ignition key in the sand; his goodbyes were listless, and mine were not much better.

One old Dakota stood on the tarmac. It did not look as though it could fly any more. A hum of muted conversation came from the waiting-room, as though a party was dragging on from the previous night. At least a hundred Arabs were there, and a sprinkling of separate Indians. Sitting down at a sticky glass-topped table with a mug of scalding tea I wondered vaguely, and then with some alarm, how many of the company were hoping to board that decrepit Dakota for Mukalla with me. The men were chewing *kat*, a narcotic leaf imported from East Africa, and surreptitiously from Yemen, which keeps the male population of Aden in a state of blessed stupor and swells the government revenues from tax; and the women were seated on ragged bundles. A few poultry and a goat were nosing and children in their best dresses sleepily picked their noses, the little girls with henna patterns on their hands.

In the frenzy of departure, when we all milled round the exit door, it became obvious that a large proportion of the crowd intended to get aboard. Indeed, clutching their tickets, they had every right. So, like a twentieth-century ark, the Dakota filled up with people and animals, greatly outnumbering the primitive seating accommodation. The extras crouched on the cold metal floor and sprawled over the heap of mailbags and crates in the rear, and the poultry clucked in baskets. We took off invoking the Prophet, may his name be praised, and staggered into the space above the town like a wounded bird as one of the women was sick inside her black veil and not a few men greened with fright. It seemed as though for one reason or the other almost everyone regretted the venture: and as we made our way along the coast, apparently unable to gain much height, I too began to wonder if it would not have been better to take the camel which someone had jokingly offered me. But having committed yourself to something which proves ridiculous, I reflected as I smiled to a quavering child by my feet, it is well to accept the consequence with a good grace. We were, as the Faithful realized, in the hands of God—always a risky business.

As the sun got up and the land turned from grey to umber and to orange and yellow, and the sea began to sparkle like a green pearl, private thoughts paled like the electric lights of the airport, and the unmitigated beauty of the scene commanded all attention.

The seaboard of southern Arabia is walled with dark escarpments that tower sometimes six thousand feet in the air, jagged and adamantine, keeping the sand world from the encroaching glances of other lands. Beyond these gaunt ridges standing up from the voyaged sea lies a place rumoured since the time of Pliny and probably before, but still largely unknown. Even today the mapmakers are vague about it and the historians conjectural. And, as I later found, its own memory of the past is restricted to the Muslim era. It is a strong place, a limbo of the terrestrial imagination; and for me, because of that, relentlessly attractive. But certainly in archaic times a lively minor civilization flourished there and left its stones and its inscriptions, long before the fire of the Prophet's words destroyed or effaced it. Once part of the Sabean Queen's domain (the woman we call Sheba) it was the land of frankincense scored by trade routes, thriving almost solely on religion's primeval predilection for a heady smell. Along this southern coast which Marco Polo documents with travellers' tales (for he probably never passed that way) the coastal boats plied laden with spices and with wood from India—for the palm tree is nearly useless for building; and the boats returned from Aden 'where the merchants ship a great number of Arabian horses, which they carry for sale to all the kingdoms and islands of India, obtaining high prices for them, and making large profits'. Chinese pots, whimsical cargoes of incense, and, later, boatloads of pilgrims for Mecca, jewels from Ceylon to adorn the temptress Sheba, were the merchandise that passed along this coast.

This district [says Marco Polo] produces a large quantity of white frankincense of the first quality, which distils, drop by drop, from a certain small tree that resembles the fir. The people occasionally tap the tree, or pare away the bark, and from the incision the frankincense exudes, which afterwards becomes hard. ... There are also many palm trees which produce good dates in abundance.

Mukalla, a white town fringing a bay at the feet of an escarpment, is not one of the old ports, perhaps because it is too exposed to the south-west monsoon to be always a safe anchorage, and the first mention of the town occurs in medieval times. The airstrip lies twenty miles along the coast, to the west towards Shihr the ancient incense port, a stretch of flinty sand and a huddle of huts warping in the sun. In the huts some R.A.F. men were stationed, sighing for the comparative delights of Aden.

'Still, it might be worse,' one of them said. 'I was stuck up in Guraf for three months. In the bloody Wadi—you wait till you get there. That's just too something far from civilization for me.'

'The Wadi Hadhramaut?'

'Yes,' said a Scots boy. 'The bloody Wadi—the hellish Hadhramoot. Just too far from civilization for us!'

It is. And it isn't. It depends on you.

'All the women's veiled. They're no for sale,' he added reflectively.

Europeans abroad make it hard to feel where you are.

Midday. Through the stone waste of a minor wadi which leads to Mukalla. Lunging over twenty miles of rudimentary track in the jeep. Here and there a boy with goats, a small girl in a dress that is trailing behind and knee-high in front, scraggy dusty sheep grazing at twigs of extreme dryness. You could cast metal in this sand-mould with the furnace of the sky for fire and bellows of the burning wind.

Near the mouth of the wadi we came to a walled house whose garden sprouted palms.

'Oasis!' cried the traveller, joyfully. 'I had begun to think there was no more water in the world.'

It was something like that.

'But you can't have an oasis after only a few miles,' I demurred. 'They have to be at the last gasp when you have been agonized with mirages of water all the day long.'

Yet he persisted, and we looked into the garden where a woman was hauling water from the well. She saw us and stood one second petrified. Then the bucket clanged down into the depths and she ran away indoors. We pushed on to the sea, the traveller only slightly edified.

A strip of what was once tarred road dived under the wheels.

'It gets worse every day,' said the R.A.F. driver, and he swerved to run alongside it.

Round a bend in this road the shattered walls of rock part and the ocean is foaming on smooth beach. Camels sit in orderly rows facing out to sea like sphinxes bordering a processional way. To the right is a small suburb called Shehr and to the left the gates of Mukalla. In the middle is the road, running through the length of a football pitch—a fact ignored by cyclists, drivers, and footballers alike and leading to some temporary difficulties. There was a game on as I passed. A few spectators sat on old oil-drums or stood about on what might have been the limits of the pitch, and the Arab boys were putting up a good imitation of the traditional game in bare feet.

Beyond is the gate of Mukalla, Moorish on one side and Gothic on the other. I never had this satisfactorily explained to me in terms of architecture,

B

but it neatly symbolizes the situation within the town. Mukalla is the head-quarters of the British Adviser to the East Aden Protectorate and also the seat of the Sultan of Qu'aiti. The Sultan's airy palace preens itself with the delicacy of a Japanese temple above the walls on the seaward side of the gates. The sea gently roars at its feet and camels cough and grunt and their drivers sit with them like nurses, feeding them and sometimes patting and stroking their shoddy fur. Caravans from the interior unload here before the equivocal gate, and men and animals wait overnight in the camel park until they are hired to take a return load. Nowadays their burdens are not frankin-cense for Shabwa and the religious consumers of Cairo and the Middle East. The romantic may 'drop tears as fast as the Arabian trees their med'cinable gum', as Shakespeare says, but the caravans load with flowered enamel basins and drums of kerosene these days.

The scene is really no less enchanting because its economics have altered, and no less terrible in human terms. A predynastic camel on a basalt relief is no different from today's camel, and the dirt and poverty and cheerfulness of the Bedouin drivers thrusting greenery and short sticks down the camels' throats is probably little changed.

Through this revelation of a scene we bumped in the jeep and passed through the gates of Mukalla. I had the feeling we were going too fast, of being hurtled over-casually into a place more violently unusual than I could readily understand. The sensations of it came so thick on each other that I could not think, could only take in what I saw at random, and gasp. I wanted to stop and sit down on the road in the shade for a long look.

The Union Jack was flying above some withered trees. Two cannon with which British Residency people garnish their porticoes stood polished by two pillars and one lounging Bedouin soldier in strawberry headcloth and white *futah*. A car was simmering in the shade. No other sign of life.

I got down into the blazing heat and entered the first door I saw. A big man was seated at a table of papers which were weighted with bits of stone. He was writing. In a moment he looked up, surprise turning to cheerful surprise on his face.

'Hullo! Who are you? Are you supposed to be here?' He got up from the battered office table and beamed at me. I introduced myself.

'Oh, yes! We had a letter from the secretariat in Aden about you.'

'And I sent you a cable two days ago,' I said, 'to tell you when I was coming.'

He looked at me, expression unchanged, big smile. 'Well, sit down somewhere. The telegram is coming by camel, I suppose. Look, I've got to get this list straightened out or we shan't know who's going to address the end-of-mourning gathering tomorrow.' He began to tick off names on a long scrawled list. 'Awfully glad to see you,' he said, looking up momen-tarily. It was a perfectly genuine afterthought. I began to take to him

immensely. 'The order is frightfully important, too. All the local high-ups.'
Gentle mockery, the impatient patience of a man who probably liked what
he complained about.

'Time-keeping and detail,' he went on as though we had been together for
weeks, 'are not characteristic of the Arabs—— Is old what's-his-name out
of bed yet?' he shouted over his shoulder to an Arab clerk in the far corner
of the room. 'Though I suppose he'd come anyway . . . not to miss the
fun.'

In scraps I took in the sense of the place, sitting on a wrecked chair amid
the mouldering furnishings. The contrast between this air of gentle decay
and the vitality of Arthur Watts was interesting.

Suddenly he said: 'Trouble is that I can't put you up. And the R.A.'s
got H.E.' (Resident Adviser and His Excellency the Governor of Aden.)
'And I've got someone else staying on me.' He stopped. He had a habit of
concentrating his bright brown eyes on you, sharply focussed, and saying
nothing for a moment. 'So you'll have to go temporarily into the Rest
House. . . . Rather a stables of a place. I'll take you along.'

A loud blast sounded on a whistle. From upstairs, I thought. One of the
Arab soldiers leapt as if a scorpion had stung him, and ran up the stairway
whose bottom steps were whiskered with threadbare carpet.

'But come to lunch with us,' Arthur Watts went on, taking no notice of
the interruption.

I sat passively, allowing what might happen to happen, somehow perfectly at ease. The soldier came down the stairs and spoke a word in the
official ear.

'Look. I'll have to leave you.' He jumped up with his lists. 'Put your
gear here and take a walk around the town. Don't go poking about too near
the mosque and don't for God's sake let it be too obvious that you're taking
photos of the women. See you at twelve.' With a cheerful wave he was
away.

To walk down the street of Mukalla was for me a torture and also a
delight; and the special memory I have of the town is this excruciating joy-
pain of horror and pleasure mixed, which took shape in the few days I spent
there. It was approaching the Id, or Festival of the Prophet's Birthday, and
the town was not quite normal. Its Christmas decorations were up—fresh
blue paint splodged around the windows and doors on the peeling mud
façades; and there was a certain coming and going in connection with the
end of mourning for the late Sultan, complicated by the almost simultaneous
accession of the new.

There is one main street in Mukalla leading straight from the gate,
passing between the Residency (once a Sultan's Palace), and the present
Royal abode. To the left are houses backed by more houses riding on the
skirts of the escarpment directly behind. On stinking moraines of rubble and

garbage hundreds of children play amongst the ruins of old houses and the
scabrous shacks of those who have no house. Conducted by the rascally
Rest House keeper I went one day to see this back of the town. We scrambled
up and down at the level of the main-street roofs, stumbling over inde-
scribable ordure and followed by a mob of local children so ragged, so large
of eye, so merry, so pranky, and so alive that it was hard to believe they
came from the pitiable dwellings around me. But they did. With the agility
of goats and a sure knowledge of their terrain they made circles round me
and raced ahead screaming as only Arab children can scream.

'*Nazrani! Nazrani!*' they taunted—first a few bold ones, then all.

A foreigner is too infrequent in Mukalla not to be fair game. *Nazrani*,
unbeliever, I was for them; and nothing else. Nothing at first meeting would
quell their abandoned noise, except the camera pointed at them, which produced a momentary silence, giggling, and rigidity. They followed everywhere on that particular day, completely destroying the normal tenor of
local life, warning everyone of my approach, so that in the end I gave up
and went away. But on subsequent days I had less trouble. However odd, I
had become part of the accustomed scene and as such treated.

On that first morning walking eastwards along the waterfront street
there were few children about and I was not plagued by them. On the left
houses; on the right the unbearable glitter of the sea, where, on rocks beyond
the low sea-wall men were washing in the surf, their dark bodies naked,
bones thin and fragile like birds' bones. Ahead on the left the conical minaret
of the Mosque dominated the town, sugar-white, decorated with Reckitt's
blue; in the shade of its walls many Bedouin sat, camel-drivers, loungers, men
from the tribes of the whole interior area on unknown business of their
own.

They are blue-black men, their naturally dark skin smeared with a
mixture of indigo and sesame oil so that when you shake hands with them or
rub past them you are stained too. The application of this mixture is said to
ward off the heat and also the freezing cold of desert night in winter. They
are wild men with frizzy hair. Whatever they do there is an immense pride
in their bearing, a sort of nobility or haughtiness which does not spoil their
relations with you because they drop easily into familiar speech and are suddenly boys with sweeping dark eyelashes shading their laughing eyes. The
eyes are often rimmed with a thick line of *kohl* which is said to protect them
from infections and from glare, but which in conjunction with the deep
setting of the eyes themselves gives the men a curious dreamy handsomeness. The patrician thinness of noses, the fine bones, the entirely pleasing
swagger of them is striking always, and sometimes arresting so that you
stop and watch as a couple of friends cross the road hand in hand with their
heads in the burning sky. Round their necks they often wear an amulet of
writing from the Koran, and the upper arms are decorated with bangles of

blue-stained silver blooded with a cornelian or two. Bare blue chest seldom well padded with flesh retains a distinct reminder of the rib cage, tapers to slender waist, and hips are draped in the black folds of *futah* or short sarong. There are many ways of draping the Bedouin *futah* so that you have enough leg-room when you stride or climb, so that you have a pouch for your valuables or so that you have a spare length to shawl your shoulders at night. Almost all the tribesmen wear centrally at the waist an extravagant J-shaped knife, called *jambiya*, hilted with semi-precious stones, sheathed in fat wrought silver, filigreed with gold and bedizened with cornelian. With this *jambiya* they shave, eat, cut whatever must be cut; and sometimes kill. I once asked a Bedouin in a distant village near the Yemen border to show me his *jambiya*. Reluctantly he took it from its sheath; and even more reluctantly—only, I felt, because I was accompanied by a local Sheikh—he allowed me to take it and look. I thanked him and returned the gorgeous weapon—not daring to say how much I admired it in case that should cast the evil eye on it so that he would feel compelled to give it to me. Before replacing it in the sheath the Bedouin made a small cut in his finger. When I asked him why he deliberately did that, he said:

'Because our *jambiyas* are useful to us and they must not be unsheathed without a reason.'

The same fellow, a long triangular man with stilt-like legs, wore, as most Bedouin do, a twist of black twine below the knee. 'That is for strength of limb,' he said, 'and the flaps on the top of my sandals are to scare away the scorpions when they come out suddenly from behind the stones.'

At the back of the Mosque, also in its shadow, is a well which feeds the courtyard pool where the Faithful perform their ablutions—hands, feet, mouth and genitals—before entering to pray. It is a finely appointed well, as befits the house of the Prophet; and three men pull water there. In the Hadhramaut the wells are invariably built so that a sloping ramp descends from the lip some ten or twenty feet into the ground on an incline of about one in two or one in three. The bucket, formerly of goatskin but now often fashioned from the orange inner tube of a lorry tyre, is lowered over the pulley by a rope to which the men are attached in loops. Attracted by chanting I stopped to watch as the bucket rose to the edge of the well, met the trip mechanism, and spilled into the channel. Then it began to descend. All at once the three men appeared out of the mouth of the covered ramp, pacing up and chanting with each step. They were blind men, the leader with open cornflower-coloured eyes opaque like marbles. Their shoulders bulged with muscle, their calves were like taut ropes. They paused, sightless, on the brink, filling their lungs with air as the bucket in the depths filled with water: and with a clipped-off exclamation—Hoi!—they leaned back on the rope and strained away down the slope into the dark mouth of the earth. There is nothing in the Arab lands for a blind man to do but beg for the charity of others, and these three men pulling the water for the Mosque for hour upon hour in the great heat of the day probably felt themselves, on the whole, fortunate.

Along the street to the *Suq* where the buildings are close-pressed on either hand and where the air is full of interjections of spices and the grumbling pungency of unknown culinary substances, where the open shops are dark caverns stuffed with improbable treasure—Indian carpets, Indonesian batik sarongs, pots of *kohl*, mysterious pastes, lurid sweets of unparalleled sickly stickiness, bottles of Pepsi-Cola and bits of broken cars; past the blue alley of the tailors where the sewing machines rattle thinly like the sound of many pins falling in arid air, and the cheap cloth is stitched piece to piece and a man sells cheap daggers on the urine-smelling pavement; and on round the dog's-leg bend to the harbour, deafened by the treble scream of a living skeleton hung with dying skin who sells fish under a cloud of flies.

Unbelievably, there is a little of Venice here at the harbour in the meeting of water and sun and stone: in the hulks of pooped galleons, reminiscent of the European mercantile adventure, each with its blazoned cipher IHS on the carved stern, the mingling of spice-crazed medieval Europe and the squalid bewilderment of the subject East is implicit; and over all, over the dirty quay and the ramshackle derrick by a pile of rotting sacks, over the backs of the negro porters bent beneath square cans of the miraculous kerosene—dances the strange elegance of an arcaded row of shops. Just why they should have reminded me forcibly of the rue de Rivoli in Paris I can hardly say. But in this strange setting that arcade had a sort of architectural lightness of dignity more French than anything else. It peters out in a mound boxed over like the hill of Poros with white cubes of houses surmounted by another of the Sultan's former palaces. From there the white crescent of Mukalla recedes into the haze by the distant gate, the solitary white phallus of the Mosque erect against the cliff, which itself is topped by three watch-towers like three remaining teeth.

On the return through the town I isolated the smell of fish and followed it down an alley by the sea. An archway, jammed with women totally extinguished beneath black cloaks that fall from head to feet leaving only a slit for the eyes, admitted me timorously to the fish market, the women taking me in with a second's acute perceptive glance before they jerked away their heads. A little gesture of invitation and you might be slashed with the blood-dripping chopper wielded by the naked man as he severs a great slimy fish. In the confined stone-flagged place the carnage was brisk, the air lanced with customers' voices, clouded with a canopy of gorged flies. Blood and black cloth, pale hands stretching for their purchases, burning eyes deep-set and deep brown peeping like eyes of gazelles; shafts of sun striking down on scales, on flies on scales, on blood on stone, on toes of women bloodstained, on sweat and blood mixed on the chest of a fat fish-monger: and the inflammatory presence of those conoid black women passing through the undressing stares of Arab men. In a corner there was a small soulful boy poking the eyes of a fish-head with his finger.

In the afternoon I slept an hour or two in the Rest House, exhausted, and surprised to be exhausted, by the impact of the morning. I woke and lay listening to the silence that was intensified by the breakers and given volume, as the dark drew on, by soft voices of camel-men speaking to their beasts as they passed. . . .

There are other worlds, other compounds of beauty and bestiality that people make to live in, that people strive to live in when these things have grown haphazard from the greed and loneliness of men. Into one of those worlds, Mukalla, I had fallen by chance in the morning. And lying there in my own sweat on the hard bed with the knowledge of that world existing past the frets of the window I began to be absorbed into its life. I began to feel it, and to forget to know about it.

Then darkness had fallen; the long day came to night with growling of monsoon waves on the foreshore over the road, beyond the wooden arabesques of the solitary window. The hot floor was less hot to the feet and the flies had gone away for a time. Two glasses which had contained sweet tea sat among shaving things and a broken shoelace on the scrubbed wood bench by the white wall. I dressed and went down the mud steps to the road, carrying my wooden key to the wooden lock in my hand, for Arab keys are larger than toothbrushes and rather similar in shape, with wooden bristles, and not handy to keep in pockets. Three reddish lights winked in other houses. The road surface was uncertain under the feet. Grey mist smelling of aromatic salt—of undersea like the mist that is said to hang over the Doldrums in the slack sails of ships—hung over the bay and filled the road. Through it came vague shapes that were camels and men, with no noise, on their bare feet. When they were almost on you the sound of camels' breathing was loud and their sour smell intensified and then dimin-ished as they passed. At the gate the soldiers were almost asleep with arms curled round their rifles, and a single little bulb gave dim light beneath that undecided arch. I passed without challenge, the eyes of the soldiers following me, and stumbled through the shapes of drowsy animals in the camel park. Here and there one coughed in an almost human way and shoved its muzzle along the sand to dislodge a bug. The sea was breaking slowly and the faint wind from it hurried the mist away up the valley in front of me.

The sounds of a violin, delicately ordered cadences of Bach embroider-ing on a theme, moved quick and sprightly, surrealist among the coughs of the camels; and carried magically out on the vapours of the sea. A light squared the void of a window. A short pause in the music: then the terminal variation with slight emphasis and *rallentando*: the final summating note.

Silence falling as magically as the music amid the bronchitis of camels. Near,
a voice complaining as children do: 'Mummy. Can't I stay up to eat to-
night . . . with you and Daddy and the other people? Please, Mummy?'
Silence. The sound of my stumbling on the rock and sand. Then violin
again, a gavotte tripping through the air over the heads of camels, singing
them as if they needed to be sung to sleep; dispersing in the sea: a tiny
passionate European thing in the alien air. And I, half Bedouin in my
thoughts, for the moment wondered. There were two lines running to the
ends of human experience. You don't have time to follow them both.

Towards evening on the following day a great crowd of men and boys
assembled in the courtyard in front of the Sultan's Palace and sat in most
orderly rows on the rush matting which covered the ground facing the
building. There must have been three or four hundred men of Mukalla
there with their shoes beside them; but they were strangely quiet for such
a gathering. The sun was setting over the Palace wall, gilding the ragged
cliff behind the town where, like a black line drawn over its upper border,
the women stood to watch the menfolk gathering. The ground by the wall
of the Palace was covered with carpets thoughtfully brought from the
rooms, and here the great ones of the Qu'aiti State, and the chieftains owing
allegiance to the Sultan, slowly trickled in and sat with their backs to the
wall facing the people of the town. I went along with Arthur Watts and the
other Europeans of the Protecting Power and we were given our places
against the same wall. There was some amusing shuffling for position
amongst various venerable Arabs—the places of greatest honour being
nearest to the centre where a microphone sprung from a sort of lectern by
which the new Sultan would sit. One old man sat very far down the row with
a great humming and hawing as he did so. Various dignitaries came one
after the other to persuade him to move to a higher place: which he eventually did, having made his subtle point that he was the least of all those
present and only moved in order to accede to their courteous wishes.

When it eventually began the ceremony went on for about three hours
as one man after the other came to address the gathering on the virtues and
holiness and lamented passing of the old Sultan. The Poet Laureate gave an
address which, though I knew almost nothing of what he said, was delivered in such musical Arabic, with such fire and poetry and passion, that
the crowd who were getting restive at the back rows, and I who was wondering when the speechifying would end, with one accord settled entranced to
listen to him. He was followed by what for me was the next best thing of the
evening—a boy of about seven or eight in new white clothes who mounted
to the lectern on a box and delivered the speech of his father who was ill and
unable to be present. The aplomb, the intelligence, the command of the
difficult Arab tongue and the clarity of his enunciation were astonishing in
a child of his age. Quite unperturbed by the vast crowd and the presence

of Arab scholars of great local repute, he read fluently from his sheaf of papers, and at the end got down quietly to take his place amongst them.

The next day was full of junketings beginning with diving and swimming and tugs-of-war between boats in the harbour, in the presence of the new Sultan whose Accession Day it was: and ended with the Sultan's Banquet at night. The Resident Adviser, Colonel Boustead, invited me to lunch. In a drawing-room full of crisp chintz, books, and Arab carpets on walls and floors I began to get to know this curious and interesting character. A friendly, abrupt, rather nervous man, he is given to moments of blankness when you have the uncomfortable feeling that either you are boring him inexpressibly or he has just lost the thread of your discourse. In fact neither is the case. In one such moment, as we were talking over drinks before lunch, Brake the photographer was explaining the snow conditions in the New Zealand Alps—a subject which, to the Colonel with his record of several Everest expeditions, seemed to be a good one—suddenly the Colonel's face went blank. He fumbled in his pocket and took out a policeman's whistle and blew a piercing blast. As suddenly his face resumed its interested appearance.

'In some respects the two areas seem to be comparable,' he said as though nothing had happened. And the conversation went on, from his point of view, normally.

My suspicions that we were about to be ejected for boring him were allayed when one of his personal Hadhrami Bedouin Legion guards appeared and was ordered to bring more ice.

After lunch as we were returning to the drawing-room for coffee Colonel Boustead suggested that we might like to photograph his bodyguard, young men of the Bedouin Legion which he was instrumental in forming from recruits from the tribes of the Eastern Protectorate. Two piercing blasts from the whistle. A couple of minutes' delay during which the Colonel seemed to have forgotten completely why we were standing in the quadrangle from which all the rooms of the Residency opened. Then a tumbling on the threadbare stair and six young Arabs spilled out before us, hastily forming a line and fidgeting the pieces of their white dress uniforms into military order.

'There you are,' he said turning to us. 'My Revoltings. Some of them straight from sleep, by the looks of things. . . .'

It is one of his words. Before long we ourselves were greeted as 'My revolting journalists' with a paternal grin. And when, long after, we went to take leave of the Colonel on our way back to Aden, he turned on us severely.

'And who gave *you* permission to leave?' he demanded.

I never quite got used to this shock tactic, and invariably cast my mind back on errors of omission and commission. It was like being back in the Forces. But then that grin from the scarred ageing face would turn the whole

thing into jest and you would be ordered to go in the Colonel's own car to
the airstrip. Easily capable of obtaining absolute attention with a word, the
Colonel treated these Bedouin soldiers rather as you might treat a litter of
favourite puppies. As we talked to them he teased them unmercifully, so
that they were convulsed with childlike laughter. Then at a word they froze
to attention and dismissed, bundling down the stairs, chattering and pushing
each other. After that I got a quivering salute whenever I saw one of these
boys and the remotest twinkle in the eye was answered with a conspiratorial
grin.

I don't think Boustead was conscious of ordering people about. From
boyhood when he joined the Navy, deserted to the Army, and was many
years later officially pardoned on the strength of daring military exploits,
he had been used exclusively to a society where one is ordered or gives
orders. Unmarried, he was shy and, I thought, ill at ease with women. One
day I was *ordered* to come with him to inspect the boys school which he
has set up in Mukalla for orphans of the tribes; there was no question about
it—I had to go. And another day he sent a message that he was going to
drive along the sand for several miles and walk back, and that this would be
interesting for us. Again it was a command. Having dismissed the driver
about five miles from the town he got out and strode off at tremendous pace,
talking all the time. The other members of the party had difficulty in keeping up with his steady four or five miles an hour on sand in the steamy heat
of the monsoon by the shore. And yet another day we were ordered to
attend a meeting of the State Council over which he presides. A dozen or so
Arab dignitaries sat round the oval table with Boustead at the head, and the
meeting proceeded gravely. Out of the corner of my eye I saw the familiar
fumbling in the midst of a speech by the Prime Minister of the Qu'aiti
State—and that whistle-blast sounded out, causing a dormant sentry to
execute a spontaneous levitatory movement at the end of which he was some
inches above the floor and rushing to the Colonel's side.

There is a story—perhaps apocryphal, but in spirit true—of such a
Council Meeting with a similar whistle-blast. The bodyguard was waiting
outside and ignored the first blast. He ignored the second too, and a certain
dissolution began to affect the elderly statesmen round the table. On the
third frenzied shrill the sentry poked his Arab nose round the door and
said coolly:

'Off-side, sir.'

I should have liked to be present.

The characteristic of change in southern Arabia during all time past has
been its exceeding slowness. Through all the millennia since men first came
there, since the ancient Himyaritic civilization gave way to Islam, and during

the centuries since that time, the total amount of change in the way people lived was slight. Remarkably little of the outside world filtered in. The camel was the sole means of communication; the camel plodding haughtily over the unyielding grit of the deserts, stepping with a camel's aloof delicacy through the hot rocks, turning its supercilious head to survey the frenetic activity of men. The camel is an aristocrat, a superb obstinate bastard of a beast. It is fitting that he should be superseded not by the clumsy bumbling of a lorry, but by the unassailable dash of the aeroplane swooping down with fire streaming from its eyes and jets screaming with the madness of speed. The camel is utterly at home with the plane. A prince recognizes a prince.

The Royal Air Force rules the Hadhramaut. An Air Force officer commands the regiment of soldiers stationed in the area, as well as his own men. True, he is under the general orders of the Colonial Office and the Agents which it appoints to 'advise' the sultans and sheikhs with whom Britain has Treaties of Protection. But to some extent where power actually lies, lies also command, direction, persuasive potential.

There is an Arab saying: 'I am a prince. You are a prince. Who shall drive the donkey?' The pride of the tribesmen, which in the midst of the twentieth century is the donkey, is crumbling before the devastating superiority of the plane. So is the old way of life. The Arabs are still princes in the Hadhramaut, but now infinitely petty, hopelessly at the mercy of a military might which, warriors and dealers of the *coup de grâce* themselves, they immediately understand. The lord of Arabia is the aeroplane—at least in the Hadhramaut where there is no overlord whose name is oil.

The traveller and I had little idea of what we were going to see when we took off in the hot-box cabin of the R.A.F. plane to fly to Al Abr. The words 'Desert Fort' echoed blissfully in the traveller's romantic mind. 'Situated near the Yemen and Saudi borders at a well where the trade routes cross'— was dominant in mine. Below, in the scarred rocks of the territory, pathetic little villages clung to the valleys, the scratches of their cultivation minute and hopeless, intolerably futile amongst the roaring lands. We passed the mountain escarpment and came to the wadi country where the land is flat like the mud of a dry river-bed, and cracked and crazed by the heat, leaving canyons between each piece like the pattern of an ill-fitting angular jigsaw puzzle. And this in turn gives way to—

'Look! Desert!' cried the traveller with his nose pressed to the perspex window.

—to desert as he had always thought of it, or almost like. For we were coming to the fringe of the sand desert where photographers love to play with patterns of ripples, with the wind solidified, and the solitary figure trailing a centipede's tracks in the virginity of the boring smoothness of sand. The Rub' al Khali is the sand desert, the emotive core of southern Arabia, the Western romantic's Mecca where his imagination can stretch its

wings and die like a nightingale between the brazen heaven and the griddle
of the earth.

And then we came down past the mud buildings of a village and a trio
of tattered palms, down on to the perfunctory level of the airstrip of Al
Abr where a knot of men stood in the hot wind with their head-cloths
flapping and wind-burned faces and screwed-up sun-struck eyes.

We came down the ladder from the plane on to the griddle into the oven-
air. The wonder of the place engulfed us with its ache of desolation, a pang
of emptiness yearning from horizon to horizon, with the blinking blue disc
of the sun laying fire on your scalp.

'Ay-ee! What a place!' murmured the traveller, as you would mumble
at the altar of your private god in the intensity of his presence.

'More terrible than I knew . . .' he said. 'And the Fort—well!'

The Fort perched on an outcrop of rock, mud whitewashed, incandescent,
with suggested crenelations, loopholes, a gate moorishly arched and filled
with an iron-studded door. . . .

'This is it!' he cried, and I had to restrain him from sitting down in the
shadow of a wing and gazing pop-eyed and rapturous. I had difficulty in
restraining him because I would have liked to do that quite as much as him
at the moment. But Jock—so introduced, whiskey-face suffused, strawberry head-cloth with ends sucked between peeling lips—pounded up to us
and pumped hands and thrust us into his untouchably hot jeep. Three or
four grinning soldiers like the Colonel's Guard piled into the back with
their rifles clattering, their eyeshadow seductive and their thin fingers
terminating in pale violet nails.

'Give you a cold drink in a sec,' said Jock. 'My tent's not too far away.
You ought to get a head-cloth and suck the end. Cools the air when you
breath in. Arabs all do it. Keeps the bloody dust out of your innards too.'

There were two wells sitting on the sand outside the Fort, encumbered
with camels and blue men, and women all black in their falling robes. The
camels were drinking from small tubs of basketry lined with skin, and the
women were hauling the water and filling goatskins, the full ones lying in
piles on the sand, oozing, licked by a dog or two with twitching leg and
eczematous coat.

And the Fort shone there like a miniature castle of icing sugar under an
arc-light, and a few girt Bedouin taggled around the gate.

We drew up with a lurch and went to a tent where a refrigerator that
ran on kerosene sat between two camp beds, and a scrap of mirror hung from
the pole.

The traveller kept his nose pointed like a bow-sprit to the Fort while I
asked about the work and the life of Al Abr.

'I'm just a policeman,' said Jock and downed a whole glass of iced
lemonade. The rumble of his belch coming out of that suffused round face

was oddly reminiscent of England and pubs and Army messes. 'The way to keep order in the desert is to put a soldier or two at the wells. That's Al Abr. A soldier or two at the well. I blow the whistle and the other chap—you'll see him in a minute—shouts for some more bods on the bloody radio when we think we might get trouble. That's it for three or four months until we get a spot of leave in the fleshpots of Aden. Like to see how it works?'

He went to the flaps of the tent and blew a whistle. There was a sudden commotion and a yell or two of alarm in the Fort. The stragglers disappeared inside and utter quiet came down. A few slender black lines which were rifle barrels edged out over the walls and through the loopholes, and a short military bark came faintly over the superheated air.

'That'll larn them,' Jock said, roaring with laughter at the chaos which he doubtless knew reigned inside the Fort at his sudden signal for the alarm. Then he blew another blast and the rifles disappeared and the tops of the walls dotted with surprised black heads, and women at the well who had stopped their water-pulling turned to it again.

'The Colonel was here one time,' said Jock, pouring more iced water on the acid yellow powder he had put in the tumblers. 'And he blew his whistle in the middle of the night for his orderly to get him some more drinking water or something.'

'And . . .' I began to imagine what had happened.

'That's it. The whole booody Fort turned out thinking there was a raid on and one poor clot fell down the stairs and bust his leg.'

I asked about the border question.

'There isn't any border. These damned politicians make me puke. How can you have a border when there's nothing but bloody sand and sun? And these buggers don't give a cuss for a line that someone drew in White-hall, even supposing they knew what a map or an office was.' His appella-tion was one of affection for the Arabs, that genuine fellow-feeling of a man who has lived with them and lived as they do and is no longer quite of his own nationality. I thought it would be good to know one people like Jock knew the Bedouin around him; and I began to have the *angst* of the itinerant. You begin to know—I began to know so often here and there in the world—and then you go away. You touch and you begin to tremble, but you never quite consummate the emotion.

'They come and go,' Jock was saying. 'With their camels and their bags of worthless tricks. They stop at the wells and get the gossip and——'

'And the gen,' the R.A.F. pilot of our plane put in. 'There's not much in the way of trickery that they're not up to.' His was an entirely different attitude.

'Bedouin are Bedouin,' said Jock.

'You can't confine them in borders?' I suggested.

'That's it.'

'You can have a damned good shot at it with a burst or two of cannon-shells from a fighter sortie,' said the R.A.F. pilot decisively.

'You know,' said Jock slyly to me. 'These chaps,' indicating the pilot, 'think they are smart. But I know places where the Arabs have staged a little tribal warfare so that the R.A.F. will come and shoot them up so they can collect those nice brass shells from the cannon. They fetch a few bob apiece in the *Suq*.'

But finally the R.A.F. is master. It is obvious.

We took off with a new passenger, a thin Bedouin boy of maybe eight. He sat on the floor of the aircraft in terror, his matted hair falling in curly hanks about his greying face. He shivered with fright and was sick and very ashamed of being sick, all the way to Sai'un. He was an orphan whom Jock was sending to the Bedouin Boys' School in Mukalla, and at Sai'un he would find another plane to take him. We left him there, his spirits reviving as we got our feet on the good yellow sand of the airstrip and breathed again the hot dry air which had got so cold during the flight.

This was Guraf 'in the bloody Wadi' which the R.A.F. boy at Mukalla had sworn about, and ten or fifteen miles to the west lay Sai'un. Between is the flat bed of the Wadi Hadhramaut intricately patterned with three-inch dykes where the crops are sown when the seasonal *seil* (flood-water from the hills) sweeps down in a brief uncertain vanishing torrent. A scattering of houses stood about, each with its small grove of date-palms hanging with clots of ripe fruit, each with its well striking deep and dark and cool into the tantalizing flood that runs beneath the burned crust of the Wadi. The mighty gush of water which must at one geological time have carved out the Wadi has long ago vanished, and what water there is flows secretly under the feet, down in the vaults of subterranean regions where surely the Arabs ought to have placed some fantasy of an Arab heaven. But they have not; for Islam is not a religion which allows much fantasy—or should it be that the life of Arabia, from which sprang the Prophet and the Word, has always been too hard a place for fantasy? You fancy it was like that when you drive along the Wadi with the hot wind desiccating your skin.

'This is the wind that ripens the dates,' Ralph said. 'They will be happy now. It dropped a week ago and they were afraid their crops would be spoiled.'

Ralph, the local representative of Pax Britannica stationed in Sai'un to advise the Sultan of Kathiri State on whose territory we now found our-selves, came to meet us at the airstrip. A tall thin Scot, rootedly Glaswegian as an Arab is rootedly Arab—even as direly Scots as a Bedouin tribesman is of his tribe and utterly different from all other men—Ralph was glad of company though he would not show it. His Arabic sounded like Scottish English, which is not perhaps very bad Arabic since the vowels of the two languages have a broadness in common.

If the traveller had wanted to live in an Arab house, Arab fashion, his every wish was granted in Sai'un and during the rest of the time in the Wadi. We pulled up at an Arab house of two storeys, mud-plastered and whited with lime which is mixed with sugar and polished with a black stone. A negro 'slave' appeared after some shouting across the yard to women who kept their backs turned, and from the waist of his *futah* he produced a toothbrush key, and unlocked the door. We went up the narrow white stairs to white rooms low and pillared like vaults, where light was modulated by rotting wood screens of intricate beauty filling the windows. Four pillars of immaculate white, each almost a yard in diameter, stood in the room where we slept, effectively concealing any occupant from any other and causing you to walk miles out of your direct way every day. Through the windows was the well with its ramp diving down into the dust and a woman in rags with her girl in rags pulling the rope, creaking the pulley, clank and splash of spilled-out water, clank and hollow clank sinking down the shaft again, bonk as bucket hit water at the bottom; pause: then creak creak, creak, clank, and splash. . . . Minute after minute at the rising of the young gold sun and at the setting of the expended sun in the embers of the Arab universe.

'What you need is a swim,' said Ralph suddenly as we were deploying our belongings about the floor and in the niches set into the walls—for there were no cupboards or other furniture.

I looked at him with the sweat running down my face and said, 'Yes, wouldn't that be the thing?' I saw no point in his remark.

'Well. That's easy.' And he laughed at the astonishment which must have been hanging on my face.

His house was a hundred yards away in a grove of palms growing from a thick silent carpet of dust. We went in. He pushed open a door to the right. 'Take a look. The Arab name for this sort of tank is *jabia*.'

The floor of the large room was water four or five feet deep, a heaven of cool liquid in which I promptly abandoned myself for half an hour, mar-velling at this luxury and prodigal waste of water in a thirsty land. But afterwards I found out that not a drop is lost. Every few days the contents of the *jabias* in the wealthy houses of the Hadhramaut are let out into the fields in irrigation channels; and the women at the wells fill them up again.

On the roof of Ralph's house as night fell we sat drinking. The white town glowed all round, cones of mosques pricking the soft air, the last rays of sun caressing the cliff of the Wadi. In the mid-distance the Kathiri Sultan's confectionery palace stood up fanciful above the roofs of all the houses, multi-storeyed, garnished with pastel blue and orange bands. Clouds gathered and stretched oppressively between the tops of the cliffs, boxing in the cleft of the Wadi; and it was gradually dark with the finality and velvet softness of tropical night. When we walked home to our house with our toothbrush key in hand everything was silent and the dust deadened our footfalls and no respectable Arab was awake.

Very early the next day I took off with the R.A.F. for a village called Ataq which lies in the Western Aden Protectorate. There, in the flat desert near a tall village of the same name, lies another Fort.

'Disappointing,' was the traveller's opinion on catching sight of it from the plane as the sun was rising. 'It looks like a cattle-shed in Scotland, all stone and no whitewash. And look at the regular rows of tents pitched outside it . . . and all those soldiers in shorts. And a tank!'

The R.A.F. Regiment held this fort with a posse of the Aden Protectorate Levies whom we had seen training at the airport in Aden—men from many tribes of the interior.

At Ataq a column of Land Rovers and a couple of armoured track vehicles, not tanks, were waiting for us, and I climbed into one, together with the usual half-dozen Arab soldiers who clattered their rifles and chattered and rubbed their indigo over me and took all my cigarettes as we went along. We were making for a place called Said, hurriedly, for the sun was already hot and soaring up, and the metal sides of the cars too scorching to touch. A mile or two from Ataq, going towards the south, the flat country heaves up into mounds of coal-like rock which lately had afforded ample cover for snipers from two opposing tribes who were in petty dispute. One of the curiosities of Arab warfare is that these fierce men are the worst shots in the world. This they admit to themselves. But their intelligence system is good and they have word of you before you come their way. A twig or some small stone of light colour is placed on the track where you must pass and in the waiting time they align rifles on the object and practise firing until their aim is correct. The rifle can then be left in position, and when the target arrives all that has to be done is to pull the trigger.

With this happy piece of knowledge in mind I sat scanning the glinting black rock for the alien glint of rifle—an activity, considered logically, which was mere timidity since I was sitting in a fast buggy with track vehicles before and behind me swivelling their cannon to right and to left. But the scent of danger releases a little adrenalin into the sluggish blood and releases, too, a silly little dramatic impulse in the imbalance of your psychological motivation; the result is a small thrill, probably unjustified by facts.

At Said there is a piece of flattish ground where a small airstrip was being constructed; it was this that the technical people of the party were going to inspect. Not a soul was there when we arrived, and the R.A.F. boys who drove us and manned the cannon emerged from their incarceration in the heat of the metal boxes and made tea immediately; which was not unwelcome. Shortly a tall well-stuffed figure came along bearing his rifle on his shoulder and girt with several hundred cartridges around the waist and in the cross-band over his other shoulder. He wore a green turban and a red *futah*, heavy sandals, and the usual extravagant *jambiya*. Accompanying him was his son. The son of the sheikh is no mean thing in parochial deserts; so this young man, with his trappings almost as military and gaudy as his father, wore an expression of tremendous importance. They took us to the outskirts of their village whose camel-coloured walls and upspringing houses attracted me intensely, but on my remarking that I had heard the best *jambiya*-makers in all the Hadhramaut lived in the village, the Sheikh said:

'No, you are mistaken, we have no such men.'

It was a clear intimation that he did not wish me to explore, so I had to content myself with looking at the outside of the place and playing with a crowd of ragged angels under the delicate shade of a huge *ilb* tree. The son took us to his house on the outskirts—rushing up before us to make sure the women were out of sight—and gave us tea very affably. He sat on the floor and took a circular woven band, placing it round the back of his shoulders and behind the knees so that he could lean back supported by it.

'The Arab's chair,' he said, noticing that I watched him. And when we were going away he sent an urchin running for one to give me.

The Sheikh was very pleased with the airstrip on his territory. His trouble was that he was bottled up between two more powerful tribes and could not get his caravans out towards Aden. Once the strip is built and operating, the trouble will vanish and he will even be able to send his products by air. As he talked of this I was once again struck by the turn of events which replaces the camel by the plane—even in this little green valley of millet with its mud village and its lop-sided tomb of the local holy man, the *qubba* or dome on it sadly asymmetrical.

Eventually we left the Sheikh and his son and their fierce guard (who had picketed the convoy at a discreet distance) and wound up the gully to the flat top of the escarpment; and returned through the place of ambushes to Ataq in a cloud of dust like engine smoke. And roaring up in the plane again, we came to Sai'un with something of the feeling of coming home. I questioned myself about this, and the traveller ribbed me unmercifully on the subject, for he knew I had had it in Mukalla too.

'I'm supposed to be the romantic,' he teased, 'and you the——'

'Sane observer,' I said before he could define me as anything worse.

'And we are absolutely at one, nevertheless, on this.'

'Perhaps the very lack of possessions has something to do with it,' I suggested. 'We aren't encumbered with the *lares* and *penates* in tangible form. We can be ourselves completely within the bare walls of our house and we don't know how to emulate our neighbours for they're so different that we don't understand their way of life . . . something like that.'

c

'You will analyse the feeling until it disappears,' he warned.

'Then it will not have been anything at all if it vanishes at scrutiny.'

'That's where you are always wrong,' the traveller replied severely. 'You don't allow for being human. Maybe this feeling of being at home is nothing very much but a pleasant dream, a compound of fine motes of perception, as you would undoubtedly say. But they are not for analysis but for experience. From the feeling you can go on to another feeling, and putting many together arrive at something like your human picture of being in the Hadhramaut.'

'And after that I can think of the logic of the place and the sordid details like the slops emptying out into the middle of the streets?' The rapture of the physical world around me, its penetrating otherness, was too seductive not to absorb headlong, and, for the time, I let myself wallow in it, thoughtless, impressionable as the tape which mindlessly spins through the recorder, taking the slightest impulse into its hungry molecules.

Breakfast in the house at Sai'un was served by a cadaverous negro, the descendant of slaves whom the Hadhrami Arabs used to import from the coast of Africa. He wore a checked *futah* and an amulet and understood nothing. The silence with which he arrived on his great feet, grinning hopefully and a trifle bewildered, with a couple of plates each morning always caused me some astonishment. The plates contained fried eggs whose toughness was only outdone by the *chapatties* accompanying them, and the coffee was a strange turbid liquid outstanding in sweetness and nothing else. Nothing we could do would substitute a more local meal for this unholy mess, so we bore with it as guests should. This was the Sultan's house and we did not wish to offend him.

It is the fate, and sometimes the joy, of the journalistic voyager to find himself attending a host of ceremonies in many lands. The fatality is the process of ordinary life which ceremonies, by their nature, obscure: the joy is somewhat in the quality of the revel which, again in its very nature, expresses the spirit of the participants, and, by reflection, their more ordinary usages. But it requires experience of many junketings—greater than I had at that time—to see much more than the surface texture.

The *ziara*, or village fair, at Hauta bin Zein, a village midway between Sai'un and Shibam in the Wadi, was so local and unpretentious that I think I benefited greatly from seeing it and from wandering in its dust and heat for several hours. With Ralph I had gone to lunch with the *Gaim* or local governor of the village in his house—an excellent meal of the typical Hadhrami cooking which owes something to Indonesia where so many Hadhrami men went to make their fortune in the old Dutch days. The whisperings of the women who had cooked, and of the small boys who served, made an undercurrent of doubt, curiosity, and occasional hilarity just beyond the carved wooden pillars of the doorway as we sat eating. A huge black negro stood over us naked and herculean, his muscles rippling as he fanned us from his height. It was some time before I could catch his eye and smile, for he expected that we should ignore him and was absorbed like a factory worker in the mechanical process, thinking his own thoughts. But when our eyes met he repaid me with a smile which lit his whole face with sudden pleasure.

The *ziara* marked the anniversary of a local holy man's death and was in full swing in the square after lunch. All the outlying farmers and their wives and dependents had flocked into Hauta for the day as they do anywhere else in the world, attracted by the unusual range of gauds and the opportunity to meet and exchange the backlog of gossip. The slight relaxation of taboos, and the number of people crowded together round the stalls, made it easier to observe the women, though of course they still kept closely veiled. But the peasant women who work in the fields in their tall conical basketry hats are more free in this respect and are not usually veiled. You tend to think of them automatically, in the context of strict purdah around you, as rather coarser just because they are not subject to the outrageous norm of modesty imposed on women in general.

During the afternoon the crowd deserted the market place and drifted off to the nearby cemetery where the holy man's tomb raised its delightful pink dome from the scattered burial mounds of lesser people, each grave marked by upright stones, two for a woman and three for a man, none for a child. And there, after prayers, a procession formed, the village elder or *mansab* riding a white donkey at its head, a band of men dancing along and playing tambourines and a croaky flute; and they slowly came back to the village. A circle formed, all men, the women standing on walls at a distance. The dancers twirled and hopped in a half-wild little jig, old men and young vying with each other, dancing mostly in pairs with short swords brandishing to the sad and jerky tune. The sellers of goatskins came and joined the crowd, their new inflated skins transparent and bright orange in the sun sticking out stiffly over their shoulders. On the fringe men were examining the teeth of camels with critical eyes and haggling raucously over the price. A pair of stalwart young Bedouin plucked up courage to ask for their picture to be taken and stood smothering delighted grins in a pose worthy of our Victorian grandfathers. And when the camera clicked they immediately rushed at me and demanded to see the result, pointing eagerly at the back of the camera. It was a homely, almost familiar scene despite its strangeness. So often all over the world you have this feeling, that it surprises you to remember how strange you had thought the people were.

On the way back to Sai'un we passed a couple of women trailing along on foot behind their husband who rode a camel with his son. They were seriously inspecting their faces in the bowl of a chromium spoon from the market.

From Sai'un we made daily excursions to the attendant wadis of the
Hadhramaut, breakfasting once in a grove of date-palms where perpetual
water lay like a benison under the moving air, lunching in villages with
headmen and *Seiyids* (that numerous tribe of descendants of the Prophet),
talking of past and present—of the dramatic change that has come over the
Hadhramaut in the last years. For it is not so long since each village and
certainly each town in the Wadi was to all intents a separate petty state
constantly at war with its neighbours; and the terror of starvation from
untended and destroyed crops, the inevitable accompaniment, was ever
present. The imposition of peace by superior force backed with treaties of
protection made with the local sultans and sheikhs has done much to ease
the horrible conditions of the Hadhramaut, and all honour and tribute should
be paid to men like Philby and Ingrams in the 1930's from whose work and
travels it all began.

One evening we were invited to eat with the Commander of the Kathiri
State Army, Mulazim Saleh el Jabri, at his house near Sai'un, and there on the
roof we dined excellently with this young man and a company of local
notables. As the meal was ending and we were washing our hands in the
water poured from a pot by one of the servants, someone switched on a
portable radio. The voice of Colonel Nasser sent an immediate thrill through
the company and everyone was silent to hear what he said. It was the speech
in which he announced his intention to nationalize the Suez Canal. The effect
was curious, for the cloak-and-dagger Political Officer from Aden was with
us, and so was Ralph and a colonel of the British Army. At the end of the
broadcast our host recovered his presence of mind and plied us with more
coffee, and the talk was carefully switched to avoid the subject uppermost in
all our minds. But there was no concealing the ripple of excitement in the
Arab mind. Islam is a very potent magnet and still draws together people
who have nothing else in common. It was from that moment, as Nasser's
words reached the slumbers of the Hadhramaut, that everything began to
change. And now, if I were to go back, I know it would be totally different
there. The seed does not suddenly become the plant and burst into flower,
but beneath its wrinkled dry skin the potential new thing is germinating.

The decision of Sultan Ali of Lahej (the wealthiest State in the West
Aden Protectorate) to make a goodwill tour of his brother sultans in the
Eastern Protectorate at this time was perhaps an accident, but his timing
could hardly have been more perfect had he known Nasser's mind in advance.
I had already met Ali when he entertained me with lemonade and cigarettes
in a flowering arbour in the gardens of his palace at Lahej. Whatever Ramon
Navarro did for the sheikh in the naïve days of the desert romance on films,
Ali could undoubtedly do better. Son of an Arab father and a negro
mother, he was placed in power by the British after they had intervened in a
welter of palace bloodshed, and, handsome showman that he is, he was not

backward in seizing the opportunity of his unexpected glory. His education in Alexandria had given him almost perfect English and a flair for looking the part of a prince, not to mention ideas far beyond the confines of Hadhrami thought.

He arrived one day with Colonel Boustead in Sai'un on the first lap of his royal tour. Stepping down from the plane in impeccable clothes—white Indian-style coat with leopard skin cummerbund and the most astonishing of all the *jambiyas* in the land, with a gauze cloak floating from his shoulders and a Rajput silk turban—he made a profound impression on everyone present. The assurance of him, the way he took the obeisances of the company with easy graciousness, epitomized all the dormant aspirations of the average Hadhrami.

At the outskirts of the town he stopped for lunch with a local sage. And in the later afternoon he made his entry attended by the Kathiri Sultan, his host, on foot into the town, accompanied by his suite, a band, dancing men, *feu de joie* and a royal salute fired from an ancient cannon perched on the crag above. Nothing I have seen outside India and its princes could be more regal, nothing could be more breathtaking than his speech in literary Arabic which the local intelligentsia had thought a mere half-slave boy with a Westernised education would certainly not manage. His impact was almost magical.

And his mission? There hung the question mark of the hour. The Europeans, accurately, said: Federation of the Hadhramaut Sultanates. And they looked at each other with the expression that means trouble brewing. In the event Ali did not succeed. His inexperience eventually led him too far forward and he was deposed by the British and packed off—to Cairo, it seems.

His visit, however, gave me the opportunity to meet the Kathiri Sultan—a totally undistinguished little man—and to attend State banquets with all the big men of the area. And not least to indulge in gargantuan meals of the delicious food set before us on such occasions. Meals in Arabia are not without their special hazards for the unsuspecting foreigner. Eating with the fingers of the right hand—with decorum and speed—is a technique less easy than it looks. The Arabs eat fast and it is rude to go on eating after others have done; so I often ended with a stomach still eager for more and reluctantly withdrew to wash my hands with the rest when I would dearly have loved to linger.

Colonel Boustead took the opportunity to make one of his periodic tours of inspection of the Eastern Protectorate, and I went with him at his special request. Back again briefly to Al Abr in the R.A.F. plane; and then to Thamud, a place more than a hundred miles to the north-east of Sai'un, another fort on the edge of the sand desert. Here there is a very old well, and indeed the name Thamud is that of one of the ancient Himyaritic tribes.

Van der Meulen, the Dutchman who travelled extensively in the Hadhramaut before the Second World War, recounts the local story of the place.

No European had set his foot there. The name sounded enticing to our ears. Stories of antiquity tell of the people of 'Ad and Thamud. They were giants to whom the Bedouin of today attribute the buildings and monuments of which they see the ruins that consist of huge blocks of stone. Only giants, people much taller and stronger than living mankind, could have put such colossal stones on top of each other. But the Bani 'Ad and the Bani Thamud must have been great sinners, unbelievers from pre-Islamic times, for Allah had wiped them off the face of the earth by means of tremendous catastrophes of nature. Here we touch on either reminiscences of a flood-story which seem to be common human property or a vague recollection of happenings which caused the downfall of the old, civilized kingdoms in Arabia, a tale that has been handed down from generation to generation.

Van der Meulen never reached Thamud—to his regret, for he wanted to look, as I did, for the Himyaritic remains. I got there, easily, in the plane. At Thamud, and at the other places we visited with Colonel Boustead, numbers of men had come from a distance, from their own tribal areas, to talk to him about their problems, to ask improbable favours, or merely to prepare the ground for a favour to be demanded later. There was a variety of costume, and, more surprisingly, several different ways of shaking hands. The men who had seen service in one army or another tended to smack their hand sideways into yours in a hearty way, disconcerting until you knew what was happening. Others used what I called the Hadhrami handshake (doubtless mistakenly, though I have never seen it elsewhere). This consists of a good pumping of hands followed by shaking the thumb separately, and the recipient is then supposed to shake the thumb of the other man. This is a complicated proceeding and requires practice. But the most charming variant I found was given mostly by older dignified tribesmen. They would take only the tips of your fingers lightly in theirs, making three faint kissing sounds by drawing in breath through the front teeth. Since I was with the Colonel I got the maximum three kisses of respect, which was much more than my due.

But the Colonel's schedule did not permit me to see what remains there may be at Thamud. It was disappointing. We hurried on—all too fast for that interminable interior process which in me hardly ever has time to catch up with the present—to Qatn, a town of great age lying west from Shibam in the Wadi.

Qatn is a small town surrounded by a wall which, in the peaceful state of the Wadi these days, is crumbling. That is a pity from the picturesque point of view—the nightly closing of the gates, the watch-towers manned always with soldiers to sound the alarum, the feeling of community within the protection of walls, are as ancient as Troy, though, from the aspect of safety, illusory. Those monumental walls of Peking which I saw much later in my journey never suffered a siege because they were breached by money given to traitors within.

We drove to a house just far enough outside the walls of Qatn to give a splendid view of the town in its setting against the cliffs of the Wadi, a house set aside for such official visits and equipped with the most sumptuous *jabia* in the whole of the Hadhramaut. The pool, half the size of a European swimming bath, lay in the garden with the dry fields stretching away up and down the Wadi on either hand. Not long after we had reached the house when the guard were in a flurry of settling us in, and a crescendo of clatter rose from the kitchen to the verandah, the Colonel appeared in the garden wearing as usual his bush hat and otherwise clad in a floppy pair of swimming trunks. He was attended by a statuesque Bedouin carrying a small towel. Ceremoniously, but with a touch of English schoolboy gusto, he took to the water and swam, calling out to me to join him. The bodyguard grouped round the edge of the pool expectantly, and when we had finished and were cool, the Colonel with a blasphemous shout waved them into the water. He marched off, replacing his bush hat and draping the towel round his middle, while the Bedouin shoved each other into the pool and threshed about with their long oily hair streaming in the water. I noticed that none of them could swim.

Sometimes, as you wander, you are suddenly conscious of treading on embalmed soil, of breathing curiously enchanted air. The fingers of antiquity reach out, and the spirit is subtly sweetened by an aura of past men and forgotten deeds crystallized in a carved stone, or glimpsed in the immemorial eyes of a child.

Etruscan landscapes, the amphitheatres of Greece, the jungle-tumbled ruins of Angkor Vat, Luxor by the artery of the Nile—in these places the feeling is natural. The exhalation of the ages, the crowding shades of human endeavour are condensed in stone and somehow arouse the sense of your own belonging.

But there are other places where no great civilization ever flourished, where tilling and reaping and dying never blossomed into the orchid of great culture. Yet here too the bridge sometimes flings itself across time, and ancient life, vividly contemporary, invades the mind. Such a place is the Wadi Hadhramaut. A bold land of cubes and planes, a wide flat valley incised by long-vanished torrents, it winds zig-zag for a hundred miles like a roofless corridor between sheer walls rising several hundred feet on either hand.

In the eastern reach lies Tarim, the most up-to-date and the least interesting of the three large towns. The wealth gathered by those Hadhrami sons

who emigrated to the East Indies has filtered back here to the great families
and merchants as it did to England and the noble families in the era of Far
East commercial expansion, and to Holland and to Portugal. In Tarim the
telephones, the glazed windows, the lordly houses—even one with a ramp
which enables the owner to drive a Cadillac up to the first storey—slightly
sneer at the rest of the Wadi. The Arabs of Tarim, to a much greater extent
than those of the Hadhramaut in general, have taken the irrelevances of
Western life and are blind to its meaning. They have taken the tin cans and
the squalling radio; yet in the immense stark pride that delineates their
minds and their features they automatically know that their own poetry is
the only poetry in the world, their own Prophet the only path to God. There
is no real place for you—only passionate hospitality and the acquisition of
your clever gadgets. Finally, they seem to say, the sand is defiled by your
soft feet, the blessing of water wasted on your too-tender throat, the sun too
impartial that he doesn't shrivel you up: but you have broken bread with
us and by custom we must not harm you. . . .

In Tarim, where boys throw stones at you as they do nowhere else in
the Hadhramaut, it is like that.

Then there is Sai'un: and to the west by eighteen miles of excruciating
track you reach Shibam. Suddenly, past a bluff, the town materializes,
floating like a mirage on its mound in the centre of the Wadi, its six-storey
houses and castles raising their delicately sloping walls into the shimmering
air. Against the cliff landscape it asserts its perfect vertical complement in
the flattened cubes of the scene. It is undoubtedly fabulous. You catch a
breath at the revelation. You doubt before admitting its reality. For the
traveller it was the immediate material of poetry; such it remains in the years
after.

Shibam is an entity, with only one suburb which is separate and green,
adherent to the cliff wall of the Wadi. There is none of that trickle of
buildings which clot into a town. Shibam rises isolated as a lighthouse in its
sea of sand, as though you had dreamed it.

Cross the sand in your car. Pass the two wells. Thread your way with a
wake of dust among the camel-trains and the donkeys. Grind up the slope
to the gates. And, still dazed, you enter the town, the square. And stop.
There is no car road in Shibam. The mirage now intimately surrounds you—
soldiers lounging on rifles at the prison, prisoners leaning out of the upper
windows, the *Husn* or Fort—a dazzling façade with batter walls and a
hundred blind eyes that are windows; on every side the vertical lift into the
sky of tall dwellings with people dwarfed at their feet. Those walls of camel-
yellow, of rich orange-brown, of white, draw themselves into white teeth
at each corner against the sky, a relic of pre-Islamic times. Even now you
may occasionally see ibex horns curling out of a wall at its peak, and the
whitened apices may be the stylized skull of the beast. The rows of unglazed

windows alternate, small above larger in rows, so that twelve and not six seems to be the number of storeys; and sometimes they are decorated with 'rays' of white paint, one from each corner to break the empty surface of the wall. In older buildings an intricate lace of wood screens the windows. The old doors are heavy, deeply geometric with carving and bossed with iron studs.

All this is mud—five, six, or even seven storeys of it. Not that there is anything intrinsically surprising about mud buildings. But except in southern Arabia, so far as I have seen, mud never reached this exquisite height. And oddly (yet not odd when you consider the severe form of life in the Hadhramaut) it was not fancy which inspired the builders of Shibam, but survival, the necessity for vision over a hostile plain. The practical served, an unconscious genius which had nothing to do with utility made the fortress fit and pleasing; made it for me startling as a sudden close-up of the moon. After an hour or two in Shibam you feel richly stored with it.

We came to see the *Naib* or Governor of the place, and found him in his *Husn* on the square. In fact he called down to us from the upper windows and waved to us to come up and sent his sons scurrying down the long stairs to welcome us so that we met them breathless a third of the way up. The cordial *Naib*, in his mid-thirties, not very Arab in face, with a white head-cloth bordered with *broderie anglaise*, sat us down in the airy room which was audience hall, pillared with carved wood, carpeted and dotted with pillows against the walls by the windows so that we sat between the lights of the windows and between their airs and could casually look down on the square as we talked, and observe what passed there beyond the lattices. Above, near the ceiling, were smaller windows which let in light and air at that level. It was cool and soft-glowing in the room. In the far corner were the boys who made tea in an urn on the floor, grinning at us and jiggling with the handled glasses and the cut-glass pink bowls of sugar and with the spoons which were too short when you stirred the tea; and they were running out and in now and then relaying water, and also information to the mothers and sisters and aunts in the female rooms where they could not see us and where they were curious with the intense curiosity of those who are always shut out. Against the portals where we had entered the room were the banners of the State of Qu'aiti to which Shibam belongs, tall as two men and tournament-plantagenet-heraldic. A fat relation in a *futah* which dipped below the excrescence of his brown belly went and held them for me, one in each hand, mock-heroic, while the *Naib* explained their colours and significance.

And so we talked. The *Naib* was not sure whether he had been slighted and the Qu'aiti State slighted too by the refusal of Ali to come to see him in Shibam when he was so near and staying with the neighbouring Kathiri Sultan; or whether Ali refused the invitation because the mourning for

the late Qu'aiti Sultan was so shortly over and it was not perhaps fitting
to pay such a State visit at the time. The *Naib* was not very pleased. Then
the question of the prison—from which a man with no hands had escaped
the other day. His hands had been cut off in the Yemen for thieving, as is
the custom there, or was. But, handless, he had been imprisoned in Shibam
for thieving and had escaped through the hole which is the lavatory,
and through the ordure below it, into the Wadi somewhere. And
now they were going to pull down the prison and rebuild it on another
plan.

We lunched with the *Naib*, from a prized plastic cloth laid on the floor.
A tin of fruit was opened for my benefit. And the fat relation who was a
roisterer at heart and a man of the senses, unlike the withdrawn *Naib*, took
up a bowl of soup at the end of the meal and quaffed it loudly and gave out
a louder and equal volume of stomach air to allow space for the liquid in his
rotundity. In European terms he belonged with Chaucer, pious and sensuous
withal, the grossness of his pock-marked face softened with little warm
brown eyes. And eventually I realized that he was the Governor of the
prison, and cheerful despite the escape.

The *Naib* went with us to the town square after eating, and we encountered the German woman doctor whom we had wished to see.

Eva Hoeck was crossing the square from the battered ambulance to her
'hospital'. She was the tallest person, the only blonde one, the sole unveiled
woman, the one European woman in several thousand square miles. Behind
her walked an emaciated old man with a Gladstone bag shouldered and an
air of consequence. I was a little in awe of her—of a woman dedicated to
helping Arabs in this pocket of sand and disease, the lone European doctor,
a missionary of the antibiotic god in jungles bacterial: and I was a little
afraid of her too—for she was said to hate the press and journalists.

But in a word or two she cut through all that nonsense and we were at
ease and going into the hospital and waiting while she talked to patients,
and while she went to the women's side of the building where we could not
go. I was standing there pondering on the life she must lead, looking at the
tap—the only one in Shibam—which slightly dripped into a mud hand-
basin and was fed from a hand-filled tank on the roof, when a veiled Arab
girl came into the room from the street and advanced on me and shook my
hand, looking me full in the face. When you come within yards of Arab
women they scatter—but this one shook my hand. In the astonishment of
that moment I forgot to ask Dr. Hoeck how it was, before we became
involved in discussion of her work in Shibam.

On the following morning we came to the Doctor's house in the suburb
of Shibam at dawn as we had arranged, and took breakfast with her in the
cool yellow light. And then the ambulance, an old bashed vehicle, came to
collect us and take us lurching over the wadi to the town and the hospital.

We spent the morning on a round of visits to Dr. Hoeck's patients, walking through the white streets, diving into the impenetrable dark of passage-ways and mounting the narrow stairs to upper storeys where the patients and male relations sat drinking interminable cups of tea and exchanging endless gossip through the hours of heat. Through the openwork of a door I saw sometimes the liquid eyes of a woman and heard breathing like the breathing of night animals intruded on in daylight hours.

   . Then out into the clefts of the streets again, followed by the old man who was Dr. Hoeck's dresser carrying his Gladstone bag. The people of Shibam were coming and going, women sailing along in their trailing sky-blue gowns with black or sometimes red face-veils. The shops tucked into the corridors of the ground floor—all the space that is left when the walls have been made thick enough on the traditional pattern to support the weight of six upper storeys—held clusters of women who, trapped there as we stood at the entrance, fluttered and squealed with apprehension. From the walls of houses spits of wood projected outwards two or three feet, casting their hair-fine shadows on the texture of white and dropping occasionally a spatter of waste water into the central runnels in the streets. A shopkeeper stopped us to ask how to use the medicine the Doctor had prescribed for his wife. Little girls waved to her affectionately, their faces and hands often patterned with henna, their dark curls and silver amulets jumping as they played and their dirty dresses revealing knees at the front and flipping the dust at their heels. In the eyes of little girls in the Hadhramaut you can see the beginnings of that seduction which my Arab friends were always recounting in their expansive moments.

   Then back to the *Husn* where Eva Hoeck had taken a few rooms for the tubercular women who needed to live quietly. Surprisingly, when she asked them if I might enter, the mother of one who was sitting there said I must come in. And I saw that the repute of the Doctor was great, for they did not hide their faces when I looked at them in the little light striking through cracks in closed shutters. The heavy scent of some perfume—perhaps of frankincense—thickened the air and the women reclined in it unveiled, with their hair flowing like black water over their shoulders framing faces of an unearthly pale beauty. But the dim perfumed hand of purdah made them speechless odalisques.

   Then out into the sun again, and a boy ran up all agitated pointing with thin arm and talking fast to the Doctor. The old man who had carried the Gladstone bag of syringes and medicaments round after us listened a moment and then trotted off busily. The passers-by joined in a chorus of alarm.

   'We go back to the hospital,' said Dr. Hoeck. She had a tremendous calm about her. 'A girl has fallen down a well. The boy is her brother. He says she was helping their mother to get the water. They were both in loops on the well-rope and the mother's loop broke. So the girl was pulled up over the top and down into the well.'

'And she is still alive?' I asked.

'They say she is. They are very excited.'

A few minutes after we had reached the hospital a man running with sweat carried in a bundle wrapped in dirty rags and sat with it on his knees on the waiting-room floor. The Doctor talked quickly to her dresser and he went away importantly.

'I am telling him to get the operating-room ready.' She began the running commentary which for my benefit she kept up during the ensuing hours.

'Let's see the child, now.' She lifted the corner of the rags.

A little girl of seven or eight was underneath, her head smashed like a nut. A dent more than half an inch deep extended from the hair-line to the brow on the left side, oozing blood, the hair sticking into the bruised skin. She was breathing very slowly and irregularly. As we looked, her eyes opened. She moved them a little from side to side before they floated up and the lids closed again.

'Semi-conscious,' said the Doctor.

'I shouldn't have thought it possible.'

'They're tough kids,' she replied.

The eyes opened again as if the girl heard. The man holding her, who was an uncle, groaned and looked away as if he might be sick.

The Doctor reassured him, telling him we were going to try to make the girl better. He looked at her uncomprehendingly and took a corner of the rag and began to wipe the blood trickling on the girl's ear.

'Leave it,' said Dr. Hoeck. 'Don't touch it. Hand me a swab from that box,' she said to me. And she covered the wound with sterile gauze.

We went into the operating-room.

'I won't call it a theatre,' Dr. Hoeck said with a hint of a laugh. 'This is the best we can do here.'

It was a small room, white like all the others in Shibam. Three large windows—perhaps enlarged for the purpose—were covered with wire gauze. A deal table stood in the middle and there were other smaller ones round the walls on which various sterilizers were already boiling above spirit lamps, and clean linen-covered instruments. The old dresser was in his element, prancing round after some stray flies which had so far escaped his vigilance—dowsing them with a flit-gun. While we were scrubbing up, an Arab girl came in—I realized who it was that had shaken hands with me— veiled in white instead of black, a white surgical mask over which her marvellous eyes faintly mocked me as though she had understood my consternation of the previous day.

The hurt girl was carried in by her uncle, and another man, also a relation, came too on the Doctor's instructions. They laid her on the deal table.

'Local anaesthesia,' Dr. Hoeck said to me. 'They'll hold her in case she moves.'

The uncles knelt down one on either side of the table and held her legs and arms. The Doctor swabbed the area of the fracture and shaved away the hair, injected anaesthetic round the wound. I began to hand her instruments as she reflected the scalp tissues; the nurse swabbed; the dresser with one eye on possible flies busied himself with the sterilizers. We removed a small fragment of skull-bone which was completely separated from the rest, and gently elevated the largest of the remaining three segments of the oval depression.

'I don't know what I may find here,' the Doctor mused.

'No strong pulsation anyway,' I replied.

'Sagittal sinus, you mean?'

'Well, yes. Could be.'

'In one moment we shall see.' She lifted slowly the fragment into its correct level, held a swab until the area was dry.

'No pulsation, not much bleeding—good. Probably no major damage.'

The uncles had turned their faces to the ground, their bodies streaming with sweat, their faces grey, an occasional shiver running over the back muscles of one.

So it went on for an hour and a half; until I was cutting the spare ends of the sutures in the wound and the Doctor was straightening her tall back and rubbing away the sweat which formed drops on the end of her nose.

It was over. The child had not again opened her eyes. We washed and got out of our white coats, and the dresser carried the child in his arms outside where her father was waiting. All at once she became fully conscious and whimpered and then stared solemnly round. The Doctor gave her some water which she drank, and then she was put to bed. We went for lunch in the Doctor's house.

The sun was shouting midday. The Wadi was floating and shifting in its contained heat, its people stilled and crushed as if by a great burning foot that spanned the chasm between cliff and cliff. Utter quiet, the creak of well-pulleys silenced, not a child's voice or a footfall in the slits of streets below the house, the white wall surrounding the window black with the outside glare, the detail of the window-frets blurred by the pouring in of the light. The cone of a small mosque tower stood unbearably real against the sky.

The whole world of Shibam, of the Wadi, of the Arab land beyond, had lain down in shade between window and door, skin acutely sensitized for the touch of an air—for the merest movement of air—to ease the torpor. Unthinkable to visualize the sun-scoured square of the town, the dizzying faces of the sun-drunk houses with their square black eyes suffering and the wood of doors warping a little more . . . rest the eyes on the moist goat-skin, whose interior has been rubbed with the juice of the 'ishr tree to make it

sweet, suspended oozing slowly in the window opposite, containing long
gallons of water which is so cool when you drink . . . and streams directly
into unsuspected channels in your heart and limbs, and circuits the secret
convolutions of the inner ear with its merciful, but momentary, cold: water
which starts at once from the surface of your skin as though you were
porous like a pot.

At this time there are no consecutive thoughts. A languor comes as
though the vital spring of you had softened into lead and all your bones
were jelly.

Even the tireless Doctor had retired into her room and the erratic young
man who served her in the house had gone away to his own. Ralph was cast
away in a chair with one arm falling to the floor. Not a lizard moved. Two
flies zoomed fitfully, underlining the hour.

Thus it was in Shibam in the daily eternity of the afternoon.

As time passed and the most outrageous heat diminished you began to
think of the dusk. We moved gradually about four with the slight crescendo
of movement outside, and ate a little and drank a lot of water. Conversation
slowly wound itself up and life resumed as though it were somehow new-
born with the cooling air.

We drove out from the house and across the Wadi, skirting the golden
face of Shibam which was now slashed with dusk shadow, and came to the
open sand in the direction of distant Shabwa where the frankincense was
once piled in fragrant heaps. And the pale disc of a moon came up over the
towers of Shibam as though the setting sun pulled it on a string. As we sat
talking on the sand it rose cold yellow and majestic like the white queen in
an African folktale and hung over Shibam in the thickening blue of a swoon-
ing sky. The jeep-driver approached and sat near us and we were all silent,
mesmerized by the sight. The city darkened, the sky seemed to blanch until
the moon dominated everything, casting her brightest light like silver on
the toothed edges of roofs, and her darkest shadows at the feet of the
houses. The stars came out super-real as in a planetarium and shone through
holes in the sky.

The desert is one of the beautiful places of the world.

The Doctor gave us supper. I liked and admired her. I did not know the
reason why she had placed herself in this remote environment where men
rule, men talk, men laugh, men adorn themselves in silk and fine-woven
cloths—in colours that point the tiny natural range of hue in the Wadi.
Why had she chosen to live in the city of white monoliths in the desperate
solitude of a land where women could hardly be companions? I did not ask
her.

A man came with his child in his arms.

'She is very tired,' he said quietly; which is to say, 'she is dying'.

I was somehow shocked that a child should die on such a night.

'But the father doesn't really mind a lot,' said Dr. Hoeck when she had dealt with them. 'It is a girl child and his wife is expecting a baby, and he is a poor man. They will hope for a boy.'

Sound of drums came through the window, but very distant.

'The women,' said Ralph.

'They dance sometimes, all of them together in the closed rooms,' the Doctor said. 'In the house they discard their veils and live in their own quarters in thin garments that are almost transparent. But only other women see them like that. You see how important it is to get a woman doctor for Shibam. A man is useless, for he could not get near the women. A woman is quite welcome with both sexes.'

I was only half listening, my thoughts on the women dancing wild and sad in their filmy gowns, their dark bodies glowing through silk, the sparkling black of their eyes ringed with *kohl* like soot, their chins green with dye and their hands painted in skeletal patterns. I had never seen them. Only half a face with its proud enquiring eye soon frightened away behind the veil had excited me now and then, its un-sunned skin the consistency of fine olive silk.

From the rhythm of the drums and the unearthly trilling the women make with their tongues I constructed a vision of them circling and swaying with thin arms raised, the ghostly pallor of female bodies undulating beneath drifts of sherbet-coloured silk, feet dusty from the whitewash of the floor; and the children sitting by the walls all eyes like young animals, twisting the ends of their *futahs* and wiggling their dirty toes.

But it was unfortunately all mere conjecture.

We were quiet, listening to the sound as it filtered in. It was perhaps nine o'clock and the rest of the city was going to bed, the traffic of voices dying in the streets. An occasional splash sounded as slops fell from the ends of the runnels fifty, sixty feet to the gutters of the alley below. Those women who were not dancing had already cleaned the cooking things and had waited for their men to tire of talk and think of sleep. And they had been called and had pleasured their men. Soon they would be lying separate in waking dreams in the tide of night with a new day gathering its incalculable force somewhere beyond the Wadi.


'It would be good,' said the traveller as we flew away from the Wadi, 'if all this could go on for ever . . . those marvellous towers of Shibam and the *siqayas* endowed with daily refills of water by the bequest of holy men . . . and those blue women floating in the white white streets. It is so long since it began to be like that . . . ever since the Prophet, probably. There's a value in it, in the life, in a hard beautiful place with little to live on but the tenacity of life itself.'

The traveller looked very sad, looked nostalgically out of our plane's window on the ageless sand and the bitter rock, his eyes roving over the smooth tops of the escarpments.

'I would like to live there for a while. For much longer,' he mused.

I felt very gentle towards him and all my tight little replies that sprung up like gnats seemed insignificant in the face of what we had both seen—the dignity of an old life shouldered high above the slick paltriness of the new which was coming on in petrol engines and tin cans and sunglasses.

I said, 'But it is a sort of death as well as a life, what they have now.' Yet at the moment I hardly believed that; for the strength of the people and the wild spareness of the Bedouin mind had taken hold of me in the Hadhramaut. I had fallen in love with them and their cities.

'It is too much to be in love and to be forced to say they must change,' I said to the traveller. 'We must leave discussion till later when——'

'When you will forget a little and say the beauty is only superficial——'

'As it partly is——'

'And that the rise of sanitation and the fall of sultans will not damage it.'

'They will perhaps end the misery, the 65 per cent infant mortality rate——'

'I say they will change it *all*,' said the traveller vehemently. 'And the towers of Shibam will fall down and the goatskins will change into plastic bladders. The old men and women will live too long and the people will not be able to feed themselves. The Hadhramaut will be more bankrupt than it is now.' He paused. Then, dramatically:

'Or they will all have gone away to some softer place and it will be empty and dead; and we will have killed it.'

He shocked me. 'In fact it is none of our business, you mean? All bounty comes from God through intercession with the Prophet? You don't really believe that. Anyhow, the Arabs are the last to resist what lightens their life. They *like* the irrigation pumps when they get them, and only the camel-drivers hate the lorries. Whether you like it or not all this life we have seen will disappear in another generation.'

The traveller didn't reply.

'Which is better,' I said, going on unfairly. 'To guide the change as best you can or to let it come in violence and misunderstanding?'

'Do you think old Pax Britannica can manage to "guide the change", as you put it?' He laughed at me.

'No. It can't. It has nothing to offer but the tin cans,' I admitted.

'So where is the practicality in your argument?'

I was going on—to Arab nationalism, Arabs ruling Arabs for preference and for good—but somehow at the moment I didn't.

'Anyway,' said the traveller, reproaching me with his baleful look, 'is that *all* you feel?'

I had to admit it was not—that deeply I could not but agree with him in his ache over the crumbling of Shibam and the repugnant tractors that will soon be ploughing the bed of the Wadi. But, even within the traveller's romantic framework, there is another thought to be added which holds the possibility of softening his distaste. There is nothing in the Hadhramaut today save some old stones, ruins, and a few inscriptions, which betokens the flourish of the Himyaritic civilization of former days. I wondered, had he and I seen that older world at its end in the Wadi, would we have regretted also its passing in favour of Islam? Perhaps the present Muslim way of life which we had respected in the Wadi would at its inception have seemed as banal, even as ugly, as what threatened now to engulf Islam in its turn. Do not all ways of life as they evolve on people, even those which come from the revolution of people, take on in time things characteristic of the place and the human society there? In the soft sables of the evening sky I would not have sworn that I believed this utterly.

> If thou commit me to the grave, say not 'Farewell, farewell!'
> For the grave is a curtain hiding the communion of Paradise.
> After beholding descent, consider resurrection;
> Why should setting be injurious to the sun and moon?
> To thee it seems a setting, but 'tis a rising;
> Tho' the vault seems a prison, 'tis the release of the soul.

The words of Jalalu 'Ddin Rumi come to mind pertinently across the seven centuries since they were written. He was talking about personal death. But perhaps not entirely.

D

# II. Kashmir

THERE is probably nothing more boring in the world than the prolonged contemplation of mountains. Especially those which are snow-capped.

And as for scaling them—only the English could have been sporting enough to invent the 'climb Everest' nonsense. Only the twentieth-century passion for establishing records could have made the French emulate them. And it served them all damn' well right that Tensing got there first.

Mountains, however, are the inescapable context of Kashmir. Were it not for that circle of silent tyrants closely guarding the paradise at their feet, neither the climate nor the history of Kashmir would be worthy of comment. One must not, then, ignore them. An irascible parent is no less the progenitor of the sweet child for being unapproachable.

The Moghul Emperor Jehangir dying on a journey to Lahore in the Punjab said something more lyrical than most great men say on their death-bed. Surrounded by the panoply of his court, attended by his favoured courtiers who asked him for his last wish, he sighed:

'Only Kashmir. . . .'

It was the wish of a tired man, but also of a realist. For, in the embroil-ment of power, intrigue, and stultifying heat of the northern Indian summer, the thoughts of the living, no less than of the dying, may well turn to the calm that goes with the coolness of Kashmir. It is sometimes too much to ask that you should go on in the heat, in the exacerbation of temper reflect-ing the life of the Indian plains, when the thermometer reaches 120 in the shade. There is no shade there from overwrought emotions. Only in Kashmir where the snow barrier filters the heat from the sun can you relax. There is nowhere else similarly prepared to accept you in the Indian peninsula, nowhere either as cool or as calm.

'The trouble is,' I remarked with assumed casualness to the traveller as we swept several thousand feet up over the Punjab, 'the trouble is—to be frank,' I hesitated as one does when about to make a shattering pronounce-ment, 'that I am not much interested in mountains and I'm passionately

50

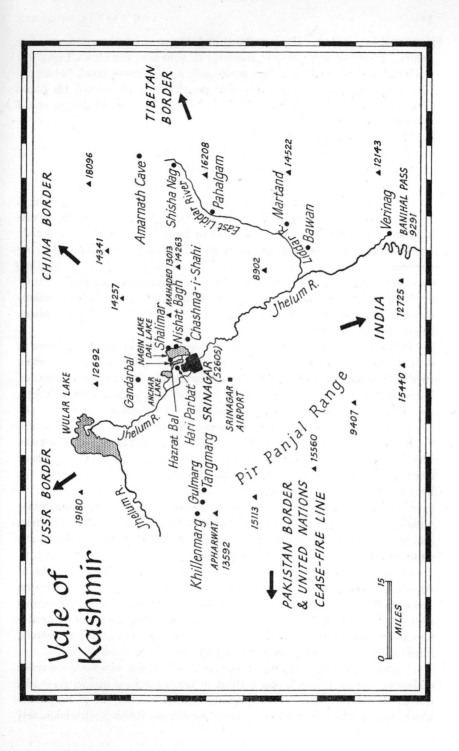

Vale of Kashmir

USSR BORDER
CHINA BORDER
TIBETAN BORDER

▲ 18096

Amarnath Cave ●

14341 ▲

14257 ▲

▲ 16208

Shisha Nag ●

Pahalgam ●

East Liddar River

R. Martand

▲ 14522

Bawan ●

Liddar

8902 ▲

▲ 12692

WULAR LAKE

Gandarbal ●

NAGIN LAKE
DAL LAKE
ANCHAR LAKE

Shalimar ●
Nishat Bagh ●
MAHADEO 13013 ▲
▲ 14263
Chashma-i-Shahi ●

Jhelum R.

Veninag ●
BANIHAL PASS
9291

▲ 12143

Jhelum R.

Hazrat Bal ●
Hari Parbat ●

SRINAGAR
(5260S)

SRINAGAR
AIRPORT ■

INDIA

▲ 12725

19180 ▲

Jhelum R.

Khillenmarg ● Gulmarg ●
Tangmarg ●
APHARWAT ▲
13592

Pir Panjal Range

15513 ▲

▲ 15560

9407 ▲

15440 ▲

PAKISTAN BORDER
& UNITED NATIONS
CEASE-FIRE LINE

0          15
MILES

interested in people—and when the land gets very high there are very few people.' I finished at a gallop in the hope of softening the blow. 'Ergo.'

'But,' said he, making a face as though to say 'come now', 'when the land gets very dry there are very few people also.' He turned his bland disarming smile of 'don't be a hypocrite' on me. 'In the Hadhramaut for example.'

'That's different . . . it's——'

'Broadly it's a flat land, I suppose? That's what you mean?'

Put baldly that didn't seem to me to suffice as explanation.

'Probably. Something like that,' I said defensively.

'How difficult you make things. Such a worry!' He sighed like Jehangir.

'It could be something to do with cold,' I suggested, reasonable as one is in an argument where one is likely to be bested.

'Unnatural passion! Heat and more deflating heat! You will die of liking the heat!'

'I'll die happy, then. I hate cold. And the mountains bore me.'

'So I understand,' he replied, cold as Nanga Parbat, which, had it been a day of Himalayan clarity, he might have seen somewhere on the left through the perspex ecstatically.

Probably it's not as simple as that. Opinions seldom are. A tendency to pass through Switzerland *à vitesse*, and to ignore igloos, comes according to the Freudians from some bizarre circumstances in extreme childhood. Perhaps they are right, at least on the level of fantasy. And surrounded by the snow curtain in Kashmir I managed to be happy and interested, even to climb like a fly on an icicle to fourteen thousand feet.

But we were not there yet. Over the flat exhausted plains we flew from Delhi. It was midsummer and not a gleam of water showed in the beds of streams. The fields were baked reddish-brown, parched, dying under the brazen sky. Only a faint smudge of darker colour on the horizon seemed to give hope of an end to the scene below, a smudge of amorphous substance which gradually formed itself into a range of hills. We climbed slowly from Amritsar and the hills grew clearer, and you could begin to distinguish drifts of thin snow in the highest ravines.

Suddenly it was cooler and we were passing over the only road to Kashmir where it snakes through the Banihal Pass at nine thousand feet. But even the dropping temperature and the sight of snow are small preparation for the Vale of Kashmir. It is a marvellous sight, astonishing because it is green and what you have just left was brown. It cries water, millions of liquid gallons of purest water in a continent of dust flayed by despotic sun. The mountains part, revealing a valley which is not extensive—a mere eighty-five miles in length and a third of that broad—posed in their lap, five or six thousand feet above the interminable level of the plains to the south. It is a valley shaped like an irregular ellipse, flashing with lakes and webbed with canals, a verdant place between worlds of heat and worlds of snow.

There are people to whom you instantly take a liking, and others who, for a variety of reasons, do not immediately arouse that recognition. Ahmed Wangnoo was one of the latter. He strode towards us as we walked from the plane at the airstrip near Srinagar, a curious tall figure of a man, very thin and wearing a tweed jacket which, as to cut, lay somewhere between the formal Indian tunic and the English hacking jacket, drooping to mid-thigh in sad folds of coarse material. Below flapped his Kashmiri white cotton trousers, a garment of Persian origin whose inner leg seams are much shorter than those on the lateral aspect, and which fall in deep festoons around the legs. On his feet were a heavy pair of brogues, and he wore jauntily a black Persian-lamb fore-and-aft hat sometimes called a Jinnah cap. There was a little of the wiry fanaticism of a Paganini in his cadaverous face and his spidery legs: but the eyes belied it with their warm brown sparkle. We went with him in an antique car, bouncing on the seats which, for height and discomfort, resembled the pews in a childhood church; and we came through the capital to a small lake where several houseboats were moored in the shade of trees, their awnings flapping in a slight breeze.

Nagin, a pocket-sized lake where we were to live for several weeks, had put on its best sparkle for our arrival, inciting the photographer Brake, who was my companion in Kashmir, to get going at once with his camera. We reached our destination with a complete lack of fuss, with a metropolitan smoothness. My opinion of Ahmed Wangnoo went up at once.

On the verandah of the houseboat whose name was *Triumph* sat an old gentleman of great dignity. His white turban was crisp and fine in its bellying folds. His shirt of white cotton fell composedly about his knees and his white trousers cascaded to well-kept toes and rich leather sandals. He rose as we approached in the boat across the few yards of water, and bowed to us gravely. He shook hands as we came up the steps to the verandah and addressed us in courtly English with the nineteenth-century accents of my grandparents; and he sent for orangeade. If ever there was an English gentleman of the turn of the century who outdid him in cultivated restraint and well-bred manner, I should be happy to hear of him. This old man was Ahmed's father, the head of the family, a pious Muslim of considerable substance and a kindliness unequalled.

It was not long before a few inquisitive heads peeped round the yellow curtains of the verandah, and their owners, Ahmed's children, edged in and stood shyly, ready to smile or vanish, whichever might prove judicious. I've forgotten the names of most of them, but Ramzana was my favourite and followed me round as often as he could, though he never became talkative and remained a picture of smiling boyhood with almond eyes and curly chestnut hair and small exploring hands on whose sensations he seemed to reflect very seriously.

After an exchange of most civilized courtesies the old man left us with the hope that we would enjoy lunch which was ready, and we went inside the boat.

The houseboat of Kashmir is a remarkable institution. Its origins reach back a hundred years at least into the British ownership of India, and it is an amalgam of the two divergent traditions. Fundamentally it is a flat-bottomed boat made of deodar wood much like the local transport *ba'ats* which carry the heavy loads on the canals, a barge square at both ends and low in the water. On top of this there is a structure built of wood like a large railway carriage and arranged in the same manner with the rooms placed one abaft the other and a corridor running down the whole length of them at one side. The bows are a verandah, shaded according to fancy by curtains of assorted hues, and from it leads a short flight of steps to the water. Behind the verandah is the living-room, furnished in European style but with a ceiling made of hundreds of pieces of wood in patterns—a device at which the Kashmiris are expert. Beyond is the dining-room with immaculate polished table, often carved in the local style, and beyond again the bedrooms—three or four of them—and at least one bathroom.

*Triumph*, which was Ahmed's boat—and perhaps his own triumph in a certain way—was typical of its kind. Its advantages over a hotel were obvious and many. If you tired of the view it was an easy matter to move elsewhere on the lake: and there was a retinue of servants to which you were likely to be unaccustomed these days, to attend your every word. Apart from Ahmed who was our guide, and became a friend, there were others. Nebra his eldest son, adopted during the short span of a childless first marriage, who acted as stand-in for his father, a saturnine youth whose tendency to alimentary stasis worried us all and which the combined remedies of the local *hakim* and myself never did anything to alleviate—Nebra served table and did a lot of talking whenever he could. Lalla the handyman, who helped him and made ready the baths by stoking a dangerous boiler at the rear of *Triumph*, and washed dishes and generally fussed as only an old man who is a bit of an old woman can—Lalla was slightly blind and something of a character. The sweeper whose name I never learned and who performed the meaner tasks was always silent in contrast to the others and smiled whenever he thought you might be looking at him. Finally we had a fat cook whose province was in the cookboat moored astern where he presided amongst the women who always seemed to be there to help. These were the basic providers and cosseters. But we hired, on Ahmed's advice, a decorative *shikara*, a curtained palanquin that glided over the water, the sybarites delight, which was owned and paddled by two unmarried brothers. It may have had something to do with their unmarried state, or not—but Ickballa and Salama were two of the most obliging men I ever had to deal with. They moored alongside *Triumph* and slept and worked and prayed in their *shikara*, ready to spring to our aid at all times as soon as they heard us move in their direction.

It would have been hard to remain at arm's-length—at the other end of a command—from these kindly people, as used to be the manner in some circles of British India. I did not think they were angels but also I did not consider them thieves or idiots, an attitude which used to be equally common. In next to no time I became fond in varying degrees of all of them and couldn't help getting to know a little of their woes and happinesses. Initially they seemed to find this a little baffling, but they managed to overcome their surprise very quickly. Lalla used to discuss his cataract with me and ask my advice about his wife's stiff joints; Nebra learned the rudiments of photography from Brake, and Ickballa talked about religion and girls when there was nothing to occupy his tough hands otherwise. All these men were very ordinary Kashmiris, and through their conversation I supplemented and explored what I learned of the country in other ways.

In the afternoon the *shikara* lay ready by the steps in the dazzle of water, its curtains gently moving their yellow folds in the air, the slender length of it sitting lightly like a racing shell in the shade of its awning, the admirably sprung mattress upholstered in gaudy cloth. The multitude of soft cushions invited, and Ickballa stood at the stern grinning over the verandah, his moth-eaten fur cap rakishly set on a fine thick head. Very soon we were gliding lazily over Nagin with the slow plunging of the paddles measuring the watery silence, and the giant *chenar* trees passing by. Reclining in the *shikara* shaded from the direct rays of the sun, shoes off, with Ahmed sitting opposite talking of this and that, we spent the hours until sunset meandering in the canals, under humped Moghul bridges, past the small fields. The easy verdant beauty of the place is almost too much and too perfect. In a first few hours you can only lie there passively and let it all imprint itself in that bottomless part of the brain that remembers. You take it all in like a bird takes seed to its crop for later digestion. Ripped untimely from the desiccation of the Hadhramaut, and plunged into the jade coolness and abundant water of Kashmir, there must be time to adjust.

Fortunately life seems not so urgent in Kashmir and the climate is easy, a lenient sun pouring radiance into the green basin of the Vale and the courteous sky holding its benign canopy over the coronets of the mountains. All nature conduces to your relaxation; almost to your anaesthetization, were it not punctuated with tall spires of poplars shivering in the water, gaudy palanquins of *shikaras* sneaking through their own reflections, and the lumbering of laden barges poled by whole families straining with lilliputian force to move a real dead-weight through the fantasy of air and water and god-like peaks. The anaesthetic is never quite complete. Now there is a man sitting on the bow of his boat with his *hookah* for which he has no fire, and he calls to you for a light and you see his rags and his contorted hands and the dumbness of his eyes as they look at you through the cataract of their suffering which is not acute but continual: now there is a woman in a flat skiff piled high with lotus leaves, bent like a human paperclip over the bows, her hands skimming amongst the leaves floating on the water, plucking the tender ones to feed her cow that is tethered in the shade of that tottering cowshed of a house where there is no land for a cow to graze: now there is a very old man paddling in a tiny leaky boat, white beard and face of Moses, robed like an unwashed god in stately dignity; he clutches up a few lotus flowers and holds them gently and insistently to you and whines his poverty which is true enough as well as irritating, and you take them for a few pence, knowing that the lotus, picked, falls to pieces in an hour, that whole lakes are carpeted with their pink and that the blessings of Allah he calls upon your somewhat righteous head are both perfunctory and real—and in the end irrelevant. And over all this the lofty immaculation of mountains smiles or solemns down as though nothing at all had happened beneath their very noses in all the centuries: and the tourist loves them for it.

This complication of feelings needs to be ordered in you. A thousand birds warble and flash across the air and the tomato-red flower of the pomegranate is just appearing. A woman in a vibrant red cloak walks like an animated Venus on the feet of her own reflection along the bank of the canal. The fort of Hari Parbat on its mound, which grew from a pebble dropped by the goddess Parvati to crush a demon in the middle of the Vale, surveys the intricate pattern of canals like a woman seated who admires the lace of her own skirt. There is that quality of pastoral beauty, which is peculiarly Indian even in the perpetual water of Kashmir; the singing sadness of sun and sharp colour, of dusky skin and poverty, the bad dream of spiritual malignancy which is sometimes religion and sometimes landlords and sometimes both, the small warm homeliness, crapulous and dear, of the village with its aromas of curry and urine, and its long empty days of boyhood and its niggling eroticism of pale purdah women. In Kashmir where most people are Muslims and few are Hindu you still feel this particular thing which is India: for India is village still with little scratches in the dust which are farms: and those Kashmiri Muslims are Indians as well as followers of the Arab Prophet.

On Dal Lake at the feet of the great cone of Mahadeo in the setting of the sun that afternoon, the fishermen were out in a circle of boats. Their families too sat in the boats, women cooking the evening meal on charcoal stoves and the children scrambling or helping with the nets. The men stood in the bows and, the circle of boats manœuvred into position, they cast together with a chorus of shouts. Pulling in the nets they tossed the meagre catch behind them into the blackened boats and the children gathered up the fish and stowed them away. Suddenly the gold air turned red. The hundred-foot mushrooms of the *chenars* became silhouettes and the poplars gothic spires; a confused orchestra of birds sang out and flew in streaming forma-tions across the water; the faces of the high Pir Panjals to the south flushed pink, and the breathing land seemed to pause after the day and before the commencement of night. Only the birds and the fishermen violated the universal musing—and Ickballa, who had made Kashmiri tea in the samovar which he always brought with him, now began to rattle cups and spoons.

The cinnamon flavour and the accents of something like menthol, which come from seeds dropped into the boiling brew, immediately clarify the internal air lurking like another dusk beneath your brain and countermand the slight bemusement and also the slight chill that falls with the sun. Ahmed takes the *hookah* which serves for all occupants of the boat and sits quietly opposite us puffing a little smoke as we turn for home.

'Everything depends on the God,' he says in the silence, as though summing up some reflections of his own. 'Ours is a poor country.' He seems to be aware of the paradox—of this terrestrial paradise which Jehangir called his private garden and for which out of all his domains he sighed; and the poverty of the private gardeners in it; and perhaps too of the flag-rant beauty that looks over the head of human torture and says only: 'Look! I am beautiful. Worship me!'

'Tomorrow we will go to the mosque of Hazrat Bal,' says Ahmed. 'It will be a great day. Plenty wonderful pictures,' Ahmed smiles to Brake whose Leicas are strewn on the cushions. 'And much to write about,' he says to me. 'I will tell you all that you ask of our religion.' Ahmed can neither read nor write but is aware of the power of words and respectful of them.

'Read me what it says in your book of Hazrat Bal,' he says later after we have bathed and changed and had dinner and we are sitting in the living-room with him. He is crosslegged on the floor before us and attentive, pour-ing coffee for us. 'Read it to me and I will tell you what is true and what is wrong.'

I read him the passage which says that Hazrat Bal is the shrine of the Hair of the Prophet, a holy mosque where the Faithful come most especially on one day of the year to the showing of the Hair; and that on that day it is particularly important to pray there and gives more grace than at other times.

'All that is correct,' says Ahmed in his courtly English. 'But there is no word of the miracle! The Hair is a wonderful thing. It was said that it would not be destroyed by fire, and some people did not believe this. And they threw the Hair on the fire. And at once it crackled loudly and sprang out of the fire! They found it on the turban of a holy man. It was not burned by the fire. They have not written that?'

By the time I finished with it my guide-book was found out in all its heinous inaccuracies and regarded by Ahmed with deprecatory humour. A serious mind, he never quite understood how someone with the fabulous skill of reading and writing could be so slovenly. And several times, as though to ensure that I would not do likewise in what I wrote for my 'rich magazine', as he styled the *National Geographic of America* for whom I came to Kashmir to write an article, he coaxed me to recite to him what I had learned of this or that point, and corrected my errors solemnly. I was both amused and grateful, and now take full responsibility for what mistakes may remain.

On the following morning we reached Hazrat Bal hours before the ceremony was due to begin. We went in the *shikara*, although we could have walked across the neck of land which separates Nagin from Dal Lake. Ahmed, rising at four or five in the morning winter and summer, walked there daily and said his morning prayers with that simple and thoughtful devotion which I came to respect in him. Early as we were the crowds were beginning to gather, to buy at the market set up for the day, to haggle over vegetables on the boats sandwiched along the waterfront, and to wash prior to the religious event. Nebra, Ramzana, and of course Salama and Ickballa the paddlers, came with us, all carrying their towels, and later reappearing with shining faces and slicked hair. I strolled away along the lakeside road and sat on the grass in the aromatic coolness that falls from the boughs of a *chenar* tree, watching the procession of the Faithful as they walked into the village. The fishermen had beached their boats here and were squatted amongst the cooking pots and debris of drying nets and worn out parts of boats. The *dood-wallahs* carrying their pots of milk and cream one on top of the other, sometimes three in all perched on their heads, trotted along to market; and the women passed in twos and threes completely extinguished beneath their *burqas*—the Kashmiri equivalent of the flowing cloaks of Shibam, but frilled and tucked like old-fashioned nightgowns, with gauze or lace visors let in at eye level. (But the wearing of the *burqa* is not nearly so universal as the wearing of the cloak in the Hadhramaut and you quite often see the peasant women and the poorer townspeople unveiled, their heavy bunches of bangle-like earrings tearing at the lobes and chinking as they move.) A dozen thin cows were grazing beside me, herded by some small boys and girls in rags, the girls collecting fresh dung in their hands and mixing it with leaves in baskets which they carried, to take home and dry for fuel in the winter; violent children beating the animals with sticks to move them on. Ramzana, who was gently brought up like all Ahmed's children, watched the young herdsmen and did not dare to join them in case they would not play with him. For these were working children.

At the Mosque the people were flocking into the square. The lake in the morning sun was fan-patterned with *shikaras* crammed with whole families converging on the village. I sat for some time in my own *shikara* moored amongst the others to try and understand what all this flux of people was like. I tried to eliminate pleasure in the mere colour and unfamiliarity of the scene, and to feel what they felt on the day of the Hair of the Prophet; which was also the day when you could buy cheaper vegetables and when you had the opportunity of seeing cousins and other family who came from a distance, to hate them a little more or love them a little more; the day when you could get a brightly patterned scarf in the market and also the new pot for cooking the rice from the man who made such good ones and always brought them to this market; the day when, as I saw, a young man might be almost anonymous in the crowd if he let his relatives slip on a bit in front, and make a furtive date with a local prostitute who sold a few not very convincing vegetables as cloak for her real trade.

We joined the crowd seated crosslegged in the forecourt of the Mosque, the reflected blue of the sky adding bite to the colours of their clothes under the shade of the *chenar* trees. The women kept to one side with their babies, the men and boys to the other. The market alongside becalmed as the ceremony started. The *mullah* came out under a canopy and began his sermon, pausing for the cries of the congregation. Soft 'Allah! Allah!' now and then, but felt, like the words of a man who whispers 'Love! Love!' to his mistress in the height of summer when he feels new-born because of her. Then the old *mullah* dives a hand into the folds of his robe and holds on high a rather greasy test-tube.

'Allah! Allah!' comes a great cry from the deep throats of men, and a sort of squeal from the women. For this is the Hair.

Another prayer. Suddenly the crowd stumbles up like people just before the final curtain. The orderly rows dissolve.

It is over, anticlimactic as the ceremonies of the East often are. No sense of showmanship, nothing in the nature of dramatic structure, no dénouement, no lysis with which the West fittingly terminates such an affair. That is not the Muslim way of things. They end on a shout and the scene physically dissolves. Presumably the echoes of that ultimate cry ring on in Muslim minds to their inner satisfaction.

It is unknown in the lands of Islam—as in Buddhist and in Hindu places —to experience anything whatever other than in terms of religion. Unknown, that is, for the populace. In medieval Europe it must have been like that: it is not so in Europe today. There is a unity—even if a tenuous one—in the East, in this and that country, which we lack in our own place. You must never forget this unity that the Oriental feels, this touchstone of faith which to a greater or lesser extent guides his actions and their mental motivations and their reverberations in his soul. It is useless to observe and to feel wholly as a European. You must be partisan wherever you go—a little—in order to understand. Even in horror and in sadness at the spectacle of religion's fanatical dogmatism in the face of our century in the East. I slowly understood in experience what it must mean to exist in the bestiality of life in this place and that.

'Everything comes from the God,' Ahmed said and truly believed; for nothing much comes of one's own efforts. It is a doctrine of despair, but not difficult to understand in the context of misery and poverty. I had often to quell my anger with the cruelty of one man to another; their cruelty was senseless and bred more which returned to smite the smiter. And after all this journey was over and I had lived a little longer I read, wondering all the time why I had not read it before, Gorky's autobiographical trilogy. Every page of the despair which he describes sounded like the voice of a great gong in my soul. A gong whose sound I had heard before.

It is not long in Kashmir before word spreads of new arrivals in the colony of houseboats. We were sitting on the verandah in the afternoon. It was remarkably peaceful. Suddenly the sharp prow of a *shikara* edged along at our feet. A head in a skull-cap bobbed up smiling.

'*Salaam, Sahib!* I general merchant. Toothpaste, razor blades, orange squash, hair cream, aspirin, process cheese. . . . You need cigarettes today?'

And then there was a whole flotilla of similar boats surrounding us, each with its expectant owner in the bows. A chorus of '*Salaam, Sahib!*' sounded on all sides. Word of us had got round and all the tradespeople turned up, eager for our favour.

There is nothing much you can do, except resign yourself to spending money, when ten different merchants try to sell you a hundred different articles at one and the same time. We called for Ahmed, and the vendors were quickly sorted out. As we sat in something approaching state they came and spread their wares on the floor at our feet.

There must be few places as small as Kashmir where craftsmanship is so varied. Much of it is skilled, and some of the products are beautiful. Weaving, embroidery, wood-carving, leatherwork, carpet-making, silverwork, papier-mâché, are all common crafts. But skill and application unhappily produce not only fine things but sometimes atrocities which have to be seen to be believed. The wood-carving in general is highly skilled, but the tables and chairs and even the small boxes they sell are carved often to a depth of an inch all over the surface, and as a result would be only for looking at were they not so hideous that the eye is immediately blunted on their mechanical flower and bird and foliage patterns. All this frequently comes in walnut, the commonest wood in Kashmir and one which, on account of the complexity of its structure, requires the severest handling. But in a land of industrious craftsmen there is unfortunately a blithe disregard for aesthetics. The old innate knowledge of what is right for this metal and that wood has gone almost completely and the craftsmen today are mechanical reproducers of unfelt designs—human carving and painting machines.

It is disappointing. But there is in fact some small quantity of fine work done. I found some papier-mâché with the most lively battle scenes from Moghul times executed very finely; and there is still embroidery which can almost match the traditional Kashmir shawl.

Buying confers no immunity from commerce. Not even the purchase of quantities of improbable articles buys you out. After breakfast as you sit drinking the second cup of coffee and planning the day, a head will pop up at your elbow.

'Good morning, *Sahib*, I show you some things. *Sahib* just look. Tibetan rice bowls. You see. Set with real turquoise. Just look. *Sahib* not buy now.'

'*Sahib!* You take look my flowers. My name Marvellous. Gladioli, carnations, lilac. All fresh.' The *shikara* of Marvellous is always stacked with flowers, some of them fresh. He edges up to the houseboat, his son, about four, standing in the boat with a marigold in his hand, offering it to you.

'He give you present,' says Marvellous, inspecting over your shoulder the dozen vases in the living-room. 'All flowers,' he calculates, with the little piece of emotional blackmail standing with that marigold still in his hand, 'all flowers three rupees.'

And towards dusk: '*Sahib!*' A tubby little man in a big white turban pokes his head through the window. '*Sahib* like massage? Vairy nice for *Sahib*. Make *Sahib* feel good. . . . My name Satara. I show you many good letter from English gentleman.' It is a bad move from my point of view, the letters from the English gentlemen; but Satara couldn't know that. He hops aboard from his *shikara* like a plump bird, a small attaché case in hand containing the bottles of almond oil, the barber's kit, and the book of condescending and sometimes effusive letters from ambassadors and Indian Civil Servants recommending his honesty, trustworthiness with the women, and general skill in pummelling. He is exceedingly proud of this collection, and we enthuse over the letters, not to let him down; for he is a companionable little man.

Satara got to be a habit. We jokingly suggested one day that he come with us on an extended trip of several days to the Wular Lake, teasing him about getting a breather from his wife and many children. He agreed. But in the dawn, as we edged through the grey canals at the beginning of the trip, we were surprised to find him waiting in his boat for us. He hopped aboard with many smiles and protestations of delight and we had him with us for the four or five days of the journey.

On such a voyage by water through the Vale a *shikara* of twice normal size is used. The retinue included Ahmed and his boy Ramzana, Ickballa and Salama with two extra paddlers, the cook, and Satara. We also took some live chickens in a coop, to be killed as necessary, many boxes of other provisions, the stove for cooking, and a mountain of miscellaneous paraphernalia.

The sun was coming up as we swept effortlessly down the muddy Jehlum River through the city of Srinagar and out into the country. Unseasonable snows earlier in the year were causing the river and the lakes to rise far above their normal level, and disaster had overtaken many villages and many hundreds of farmers whose houses and fields were flooded. In hundreds of years the banks of the river have been built up into bunds so that the level of the surrounding fields is lower than that of the normal water. The slightest breach in the bund and the water pours into the lands. As we went down river there were many such gaps, and flocks of sheep and herds of sad cows stood isolated on islands of higher ground from which they had long cropped all the vegetation. Farmers were ferrying loads of leaves to them. Whole villages stood isolated, only the children enjoying the water lapping at their doorsteps.

It was twilight when we reached Wular Lake, the largest stretch of water in Kashmir, and hard to define its contours; for all the surrounding fields were flooded. Before supper in the *shikara* Satara laid us prone and massaged us, pouring libations of almond oil on our skins and waking up flaccid muscles with his small hard hands. By the light of a hurricane lamp we ate an excellent duck bought alive earlier in the day from a passing farmer on the banks of the river. As we prepared to bed down for the night Ickballa went and tied another rope to a tree so that we should not be in danger of drifting away in the night. A light wind whistled in the straw canopy over our heads and we seemed a very tiny object in the imagined lake and under the dark gaze of the mountains. By the time I woke in the morning we were paddling half across the lake in early sunlight and everyone had a good laugh at my death-like sleeping which admitted no sensation of others' activity. The 13,000-foot peak of Apharwat looked even higher above the inundated world. The surface of the lake was covered with the square leaves of water-chestnuts. Ahmed, examining this, said:

'It is good. The farmers will get some harvest from these.'

Certainly from their lands they would get none.

Salama began to tell me a story of this part of the lake, which he called the Gulf of Corpses.

'All things drift towards here,' he said. 'They cannot help it. And it is said by old men that if you dive into the water at this place you will never come up again.' And truly there was perhaps some sense in his words for the lake was dotted with carcasses of dogs and other animals, each with its guardian kite tearing at the rotting flesh and flapping its ragged wings menacingly as we passed. It seemed likely that there was a subterranean outlet, just as, in other Kashmir lakes, there is without doubt an inlet for water which arrives at the bed of the lake from some hidden river.

We spent the days very pleasantly meandering along canals, getting out to wander in villages where women pounded grain in huge wooden mortars while the children and chickens played in the dirt. Coming back upstream in the Jehlum the paddlers got down and hauled the *shikara* by rope, trudging bent along the towpath, one lad, very thin and creamy-skinned, stripping to his pink underpants for the job. The Jehlum is congested with transport boats pulled or poled by the families who own or operate them. It is a scene of interminable labour, picturesque and also excruciatingly terrible in terms of human struggle for a living.

Turning off the river we paddled our way to Gandarbal, where not so very long ago a maharajah used to keep his hundreds of dogs in special grounds, and where men still fish for wood up to their necks in water which flows directly from the glaciers. The river here is dotted with boats, some with fires burning in them and all with a woman collecting the wood which her husband dredges up in his net from the bed of the stream. This water-logged wood is dried out in heaps in the sun along the banks, and sold to the town for cooking and heating fires in the hard Kashmir winter. But the manner of getting it is gruesome. The men stand immersed to their necks in the shallows dredging with their nets on long poles. Sometimes when the current is strong they perch one of their sons on their shoulders as anchor. Periodically when they can stand the cold no longer they come out stiffly, helped into the boats by their wives, and stand in their loin-cloths over the fires, thrusting their dead-blue hands into the flames or sitting almost on the fire until they are unfrozen. The comfortable houses of the merchants who buy the wood and resell it to the towns nestle trimly on the banks within sight.

Srinagar the capital, to which we went again and again by *shikara* from the houseboat moored a few miles of canal away, is a curious muddled place. The Jehlum, which is the main artery, source of water, sewer and bathing place for the town, winds through it, piled high on either hand with tottering houses of wood and mud. The great mosque of Shah-i-Hamadan, all wood and not a nail in its whole fabric, reposes stately and calm on one bank, its gold-tipped spire flaming in the sun, its feet in the river cluttered with ablution rafts, and its Islamic nature curiously tempered by the existence of a rock sacred to the Hindus and marked with red paint. Climbing the spire through a maze of wood-piles which support the complex of roofs, there is a view of the town unrivalled in intimacy from any other vantage point. Driving through streets of medieval narrowness in a trap called a tonga, pulled often by a sorry nag, you see the influence of the British who made Kashmir their holiday camp and refuge from the torpor of the Indian summer. The signs are mostly written in English, often comically in the effort to abase the self so as to command esteem. Cheap John, Suffering Moses, Subhana the Worst, proclaim three of the most respectable traders in Srinagar. The wood-carvers call themselves Ganymede for no apparent reason, and in the shop of Mahomed Shah you can find cloth called *shahtoosh*

made from the breast feathers of the eider duck collected in Ladakh to the
north and woven in Srinagar. It is hard to realize that this extraordinary
material originated in feather, except that it has almost no weight though it
resembles wool.

The river is main street to the town. Along it pass the ceremonial
processions, and once a year come the *shikara* races. Stripped of their
awnings and curtains, of their Full Sepring Cushions (as some advertise
themselves), they are manned by ten or twelve paddlers equally stripped.
Great crowds go to the Mosque to pray and the weight of the Faithful on
the ablution rafts partially submerges those jerry-built structures. Every
window in the long tiers of houses flanking the river is packed with people
like the circles on the first night at the opera; but the women have their
own windows and the men have theirs.

The stimulus of the *shikara* races is not wholly sporting. Each crew
surveys the assembled multitude for a likely patron and, willing or unwilling,
if you look as though you might have a few rupees to spare, you are dragged
into one or other boat and sat firmly amidships. A foreigner is automatically
known to have money (and truthfully by the Kashmiri standards, he has). So,
urged on by Ahmed and manhandled by a tough crew of paddlers, I was dumped into one boat, not entirely unwilling. As the ten blades of the paddles
dig into the water you have to hold on fast to the boat to avoid being cata-
pulted out of it. And careering down the river you go, in the afternoon sun
and the spray and the glare of the crowds, with the paddlers making crude
jokes about each other's prowess in various fields to urge themselves on.
Naturally my crew won and I parted with a certain sum of money—and
was promptly restrained from disembarking so that they could have another
profitable race at my expense. It was an enjoyable afternoon and I repaired
to the house of an unctuous silver merchant for cinnamon tea while watching
the remainder of the races from his window. The sun fell, slowly drawing
the shades of *chenar* trees and houses over the disturbed blue of the river,
gilding the brown wood of the Shah-i-Hamadan Mosque and making a
blue gauze of the air above the town, through which the Pir Panjal
mountains distantly glimmered, all virgin and aloof.

In these cool evenings returning to Nagin after the strenuous day, the
strange history of Kashmir somehow seemed appropriate matter for reflection. The scent of Ahmed's *hookah* and the low-pitched crooning of a sad
song that sometimes came from Ickballa as he paddled gently behind my head,
the faint smell of cinnamon from the remains of the tea in the samovar, were
all slightly sad, slightly tinged with Orient and the passage of so much time
and the forgetfulness of death after a weary life and the aromatic love poetry
of India and the philosophical fatalism of Islam.

You wondered about this private garden of Kashmir. 'This whole
*soobah*,' Ayin Akbari remarks, 'represents a garden in eternal spring.'

And Abu al Fazl ibn Mubarak in the sixteenth century remarks on 'the fortifications with which nature has furnished it [being] of an astonishing height'. And Marco Polo, gathering travellers' tales about the place, says that 'There are also woods, desert tracks and difficult passes in the mountains which give security to the inhabitants against invasion.' In these three opinions lie the heart and the long anguish of Kashmir. It is a garden—if not in eternal spring, certainly full of attraction for the rulers of neighbouring states. It is surrounded by a mountain wall almost but not perfectly impassable, which has never prevented invasion, though had the Kashmiris been a warlike race, it could have kept them safe from the desires of centuries of rapacious emperors.

In fact from the earliest times its history is one of repeated occupation, massacres, wholesale conversions to Buddhism, Hindu, and Islamic faiths by a succession of emperors—Asoka who brought his Buddhist faith, Tartars, Indo-Scythian Kings, Muslims, Moghuls such as Akbar and Jehangir, Sikhs, Dogras, and finally the British. Each and every one of those—with the possible exception of the British who ruled through the Maharajah, a Dogra, and could be considered only indirectly responsible for the status of the people in Kashmir—maintained the inhabitants in a condition of near slavery, of misery in the terrestrial paradise which emperors so coveted. Such they remain today, in effect, though technically as part of the secular state of India they are free. For the heritage of slavery is its abjection, and that is an attitude of mind which it is hard to overcome. Despite the improvements which were made in the living standards under the British, there remains fundamental disorganization and apathy. It has only begun to change a little since Indian independence. Even today Kashmir is torn in two, between India and Pakistan, torn haphazard without reference to territorial sense or to economic reasonableness. A political deadlock kept quiet by a demarcation line cutting through the heart of the area and policed by the United Nations threatens every day to explode and bring catastrophe to the country once again.

The Kashmiri himself is not the stuff of soldiers. His fierceness is the desperation of poverty, and sometimes the passion of his religion. I have seen men quarrelling over a load of hay on a canal bank and biting each other's ears off and tearing at each other's flesh like animals. The bundle of hay was worth almost nothing in money, but it represented something so hard-earned and so intrinsically precious that they fought in this bestial way for it. I have seen the Shia sect of Moslems on their Mourning Day for the martyred Hussein, their saint, beating themselves with bunched knives on chains as they chanted dirges and the blood covered their bodies and ran on the ground. And I heard how in the previous year an unsuspecting cyclist rode into this procession and was torn apart by the Shias for desecrating their martyr Hussein, whose hand in silver replica rides under a gold

E

umbrella on the saddle of a milk-white mare kept unridden for this holy purpose.

'You must not smile or look happy,' one Shia cautioned me as I stood by the wayside to watch the procession of black-clothed men beating their breasts in unison and singing a mad anguished dirge. 'It is our day of mourning and we cannot bear laughter.' He was a kindly man and I thought, as the knifemen massed scourging their bare flesh, and the women on balconies beat their heads on pillars until they were insensible, and the children goggled at the blood, that he was wise to tell me. There was a primeval violence in the air to which the flowing of blood contributed its special arousing lust. The stomach turned over to see men whom I knew as traders in the town shredding their breasts and rubbing the blood into their cropped hair.

Ahmed, a Sunni Muslim and tolerant, said:

'Only one died this year from the knives. Last year six passed away on the road to the Mosque.'

It is about four miles that they walk beating themselves, and it takes six hours to cover the distance in the heat of the day. At the end, the men's eyes are starting out of their sockets, and they collapse sobbing in a hysteria of exhaustion and grief. 'Only the poor men beat with knives,' Ahmed said.

Amongst the merchants who regularly called on us was a tailor, a scruffy man of maybe forty-five whose beard was always a three-day growth—which, when you come to think of it, is a remarkable achievement. He was a kindly man and, once you got used to his whining voice, friendly.

'I'll come for the fitting to your house,' I said to him several times, since I was to be in Srinagar on the appointed day.

'Oh, no, Sahib. I come here. It is better,' he always replied. 'Mine is a poor place. I am ashamed for Sahib to be there.' And I never pressed the point.

But one day he remarked that he could not manage to finish what he was making me by a certain day, because his eldest son was being married. When I expressed interest he suddenly overcame his scruples and invited us to come to the wedding.

We stumbled through the back streets of the town on the appointed night and found the house with little difficulty. The noise and the unusual number of lights would have told us where it was even if there had been no inquisitive neighbours at their doors to point the way. In the courtyard the tailor welcomed us, distractedly waving a broken fan at his damp face. A jumble of men scampered about in the light of pressure lamps, and a dozen hired cooks were sweating freely over open wood fires on which sat huge pots of food. The smell of cooking and woodsmoke filled the place, and some of the hundred wedding guests were beginning to arrive. The tailor looked very worried, seeing his substance dwindling before his eyes, doubtless mentally counting the costs of the cooks and the food—the whole terrible expense; but he took us upstairs to a room swarming with people and we sat down to a meal, attended by the bridegroom's brother who had successfully persuaded his father to make him a new suit on European lines in pearl-grey serge. After that we all repaired to another house where the bridegroom reclined dressed in white on white cushions at the end of a big room. Paying one's respects to this young man, surrounded by his male friends and brothers who talked to him in the manner of relatives talking to a man on the threshold of the operating theatre, we went and sat down on the floor with the other guests while boys came and poured cinnamon tea for us. Not the slightest further notice was taken of the bridegroom; once you had greeted him and given your present of money which was recorded in a book, you sat down and ignored him.

In half an hour there was a general move towards the door and we came out into the street where a white-painted jeep was garlanded and surrounded by guests who completely blocked the narrow road. Some carried flares and others pressure lamps, and the women concealed themselves in the shadow of doorways and keened a little. There was a band, dressed in a shoddy imitation of Scottish kilts and doublets playing recognizable Scottish music on bagpipes.

The bridegroom emerged, now dressed in a new coat of Indian style, with a white turban and many tinsel necklaces. He looked very pale as he drove off in the jeep with his brothers and friends, accompanied by flares and Scottish music; and the women raised their bereft wail as he went, reminding me of the Hadhramaut.

The house of the bride was not far away, and here an immense concourse of guests sat down to another meal—mountains of rice saffroned and garnished with gravies, pastes of pounded poultry wrapped in edible foil of pure silver (which, I was informed, aided the digestion—I profoundly hoped it did), and the inevitable tumblers of strong water which no spell of mine would change into good red wine. The bridegroom hung his head throughout the meal and acted shyly, as is the custom, and very little notice was taken of him as the guests discussed their own affairs. Eventually in ones and twos they drifted away and the bridegroom was left to collect his bride who, naturally, had not appeared at all, and to take her to his house.

And so they were married. The little tailor, scruffier than ever and still unshaven, looked as though a good stiff drink would help to pull him together. But, a good Muslim, that was what he could not have.

'He has nothing to worry,' said Ahmed when I marvelled at the expenditure on the wedding. 'He is a clever man. He has chosen a girl with a big dowry. The wedding. . . . Phhhhh!' Ahmed blew a deprecatory breath through his muscular lips. '*Tritt!*' he said. (*Tritt* is 'nothing' in Kashmiri, 'chicken-feed'.)

'Tell me about weddings,' I asked Ahmed. By this time he knew what I meant when I asked to be told about this or that.

'You mean the man does not see his girl until they are married?'

'Yes. How strict is that?'

'Oh, vairy!' said Ahmed, rolling his eyes and wobbling his head side to side. 'Vairy . . . but maybe he remembers her from when they were little children. And he has a mother and aunts and sisters and they can all give their opinion on the girl. So he gets a good idea of how beautiful she is.'

But it wasn't the question of the bride's beauty so much as her character that interested me. Of that the bridegroom can probably get only a garbled version.

'For my own children,' Ahmed surprised me by saying, 'I will let them marry who they love. Nebra is old enough for marriage, and I will not arrange it for him. He will choose the girl from families we know who do not sell their daughters in this way.'

My respect for Ahmed increased from day to day. Illiterate, he was none the less wise, and, more surprising, progressive in outlook. He forbade his wife to wear the veil in the strict manner, and she was the only Kashmir woman of her class whom I saw closely without the extinguishing *burqa*. 'The women, though dark, are very comely,' says Marco Polo. They are no darker than Italian women of the south, and to judge by Ahmed's wife and glimpses of others, comely is not the word to use. Patrician, nubile, like the women of Grecian urns—that is nearer to truth. But some, of course, are merely plump and pretty.

Kashmir is a land of outdoors: you can climb a mountain—a difficult or an easy one—or spend the time fishing, botanize among the foothills on a carpet of wildflowers, swim in the cool lakes, sail for ever in the network of canals which pattern the Vale; or you can just sit in the glorious air and ruminate on the *angst* of existence elsewhere, ignoring, of course, the reality of life in Kashmir. If your temperament is Gothic, as so many northern European temperaments are, you can contemplate the empty mountains.

You can hire a horse and ride through forests of silver firs that leap up two hundred feet above you into the sky, and climb to a *marg* or mountain meadow where green grass like the grass of England spreads its sweet-smelling cloak on the lap of the Himalayan giants. Gulmarg is the most famous of those greenswards, beloved of the English with their passion to escape from the passion of heat and to air their northern heads in a fresh breeze and sleep under blankets in a slight draught. The passion is not shared, unfortunately for the fortunes of Gulmarg, by too many other people; and since the English have diminished in number in the ten years of Indian Independence, Gulmarg is now nearly deserted. The two hotels look forlorn, the row or two of shops are empty and their shutters bang in that slight draught. The paint has peeled and stray dogs wander in and out of flapping doors. Parts of Gulmarg are reminiscent of a boom town after the boom. The hooves of your horse echo in the silence. Even the golf-course is a little shabby, the greens rough, and the clubhouse, newly built in an effort to attract tourists, has a parvenu air in the haughty poverty of the rest.

Gulmarg is about nine thousand feet up. Another two thousand take you to Khillenmarg—from the Meadow of Flowers to the Meadow of Goats. There were many flowers in Gulmarg but no goats in Khillenmarg, if the proprietors of two tent restaurants, who fought over which was to have our custom, be excepted. While they lunged at each other, and their henchmen tried to lead us to one or the other tent, we sat down on the brow of a hill nearby and the bearers brought the saddle-bags and unpacked our excellent lunch.

The view over the whole Vale of Kashmir is bewildering in its beauty. 'If there be a paradise on earth, this is it, this is it, this is it. An emerald set in pearls. . . .' The description of a Moghul Emperor is in no way exaggerated. Even Ickballa, sensitive to people and their feelings but not, I had thought, to natural splendour, sat long with his tough head between his thick hands looking out over the enchanted chasm of the view, before he lay back and fell asleep. The horses wandered about nosing in the sappy grass, and cloud streamed from the iced peaks above.

Kashmir is a land of outdoors: but an Oriental outdoors. The trim villages, neat fields, clean pubs, post-offices which always charge you the same for sending a letter, the visible order of the country to which in Europe (and especially in England) we are accustomed—are here replaced by confusion, squalor, cloacal villages crumbling under the sun, post-offices where the bureaucracy of petty power rules, irritating and arbitrary. The sickness of the Orient—exploitation upon exploitation—is terrible to see, when you are thinking about it, but at least it is not banal or politely dissimulated. The springs of people and their life are easier to discern in poverty and dirt than under the seemly blanket of English order. And the outdoors which is partly people is thereby different.

Never in Scotland have I found myself with a religious pilgrimage going through the Grampian Mountains to a holy cave where the ice lingam—or phallus—of the Holy Ghost, tumesces with the seasons and the moon. Our deity is firmly caged in comfortable churches. In Kashmir, in the country, it is a very ordinary trip. Or it seems ordinary enough, for this is East.

For weeks before the start of the pilgrimage the Hindu *sadhus* had been gathering by ones and twos in Srinagar. They camped in the gardens, fed from the houses of those who wished to make a pious gesture, and they slept in the yards of temples and bathed in the river; at local markets they told fortunes, and the unworldly ones, the real zealots, just sat crosslegged, sometimes doing their *asanas* in the *yogi* manner, their senses withdrawn from external things. Almost all were naked except for a loin-cloth or a *dhoti*.

Amarnath was the word on everybody's lips for weeks, because not only the *sadhus* but many hundreds of pilgrims from all over India flock to Srinagar to join the pilgrimage, and trade takes a steep upward curve. Weeks ahead you must book your conveyance and arrange for your food supply if you intend to go.

In the afternoon of a rainy day we went to a temple in the heart of Srinagar from which the devout party was to start out on the march. The ground was deep mud. Awnings had been put up on one side of the court-yard, and under them a crowd stood shivering and talking. Round the central shrine, where people continually thronged praying and having red thumbmarks applied to their foreheads by the priests, the *sadhus* sat on bits of old planking, their flesh twitching with cold like the flanks of horses with flies. Their beards were ragged and their long hair, bleached to an un-pleasant brassy shade with cow's urine, hung in matted tails on their shoulders. All of them were grey, ash-covered, cyanotic, like men in a deep faint. Some had built a small fire of old wood and boxes and sat round it naked and spectral and chanting. One was completely naked, beautifully propor-tioned, sitting as though he were a statue carved from lava into which two huge animal eyes had been set. And there was a standing *sadhu*—a curious bloated man who had been on his feet for thirteen years, and silent also for that time. He had placed himself under shelter with a sling suspended from a beam in which he rested his elbows. He stood apparently oblivious of the admiring onlookers around him.

Some thoughtful person brought a roll of transparent polythene and handed out long yards of it to the *sadhus*, some of whom began to play with it and to cavort in the mud; while others wrapped it round them or tied bows with it and wore the diaphanous folds of the stuff cascading from their heads, at once ludicrous and pathetic.

Rain began to fall again, thinly and with insistence. The stragglers amongst the crowd went about under umbrellas or bits of sopped card-board with 'Mars Bars' or 'Colgates' written on them. A young *sadhu* in a saffron *dhoti* came up to me, a ritual red and white grid painted on his noble forehead.

'I hear you are a writer,' he said in perfect English. 'You must be sure to tell all about the glorious example of the Hindu *sadhus*.'

He held me by the biceps of one arm between his thin fingers and smiled with his grave liquid eyes. Momentarily he was human under the god-paint and beneath his ghost of ashes.

'Be sure to write about us,' he reiterated. I assured him I would. 'That is good,' he murmured. And he went away, releasing my arm, to join some other *sadhus* who stood smoking and chatting like a group at a cocktail party.

The rain insisted and thickened. We stood there waiting for something to happen. A *sadhu* came and asked me when they would be likely to start. I did not know. An unhappy young *sadhu* begged my last cigarette; he held it in his ashen fingers and blew smoke the colour of his skin from blue lips. The naked one sat on, oblivious, with his alms-bowl of shining brass beside him, his toes pressed into his groin. Looking long at him I began to wonder if either of us was really present or if we were separately in our own fantasies.

The rain now beat down steadily and some dignitaries and a soldier or two in khaki-and-pink turban entered the shrine, and the priest climbed on a box to replace the electric light bulb which had blown some fifteen minutes before. Some women *sadhus* sat on a broken wall under a verandah, warmly clad and less ethereal either in fact or in pretension than the men. Some of them looked positively motherly.

I wandered outside and sat in the tonga with the driver who was huddled in his blanket, and also out of cigarettes. Interminable delay: rain on the thin crowd waiting for the procession to start; the horse rearing a little and its mangy coat smelling; some worldly *sadhus* sitting in a shop waiting to join the pilgrimage in comfort.

The first wheezes from the bagpipe band; crowd pressing forward a little, children being shouldered; then the band defiantly striking up and marching out in cheap cloth doublets all wet and bedraggled; the officials wet and pompous and the priests from the Bawan temple carrying the sacred emblem. And finally the *sadhus* in streaked ash carrying their little bundles and begging-bowls.

It was an odd dispirited straggle, not at all like the start of a great pilgrimage, that wound its way through the streets and away, fluttering damply with shreds of crushed polythene, padding along on its thin and sometimes varicose legs on the first lap to Amarnath.

These were the zealots and the exhibitionists and the crazed. We met the sober and the well-endowed and the sick and the halt and the blind and the camp followers at Pahalgam a few days later when we drove there to join the march.

At Pahalgam in the East Liddar valley, where the river rips down from the eternal and inescapable snows of the Himalayas, the small town was swamped in a great encampment of pilgrims. Warm mountain sun burned in shelter but hardly tempered the keen wind. The head of the procession had already moved off with the sacred *chedi* at its head and here were the stragglers trickling away up the path. For at Pahalgam the road ends and you must take to horse or foot. Our broken steeds were saddled and the ruffianly owners smiling with their mongoloid features, draped in blankets and wearing gnomish woollen caps.

I had misgivings when the track began to zig-zag on the face of an almost perpendicular cliff and thought of dismounting to walk up the three hundred feet. But Ahmed said:

'Leave it to the horse, *Sahib*. She is an old one but she is experienced.'

And apart from a minor stumble or two the horse laboured successfully up that dizzy cliff, and I dismounted at the top to give her a rest, and to enjoy that expansion which somehow echoes inside you in the midst of mountains. Perhaps it is this feeling of tremendous physical freedom that draws men to the mountains. But for me it is a passing thing and no continuing justification for the sterility of heights.

Pilgrims strung out along the track, mostly *sadhus* trudging along all naked and exposed with their staffs and inconsequential piety. We met an old man with rather more clothes than most, a voluminous orange turban and a white walrus moustache and a blanket roped over his shoulders, coming in the opposite direction.

'Thirteen times, I have been to Amarnath,' he said. 'This was the fourteenth year. But I am old. The mountains have made me ill. I could not reach it.' He was downcast like a child who has failed his exams.

He was a charming old man from somewhere near Bombay. He had walked most of the way, begging his food as they do, and I felt sad for him that within two days of his goal he had had to give in. I liked his clean saffron shift and the stoic under it, but he remains vividly in my memory because of the incongruity of his footgear, a pair of white tennis shoes.

On the brow of a *marg* with the snow peaks all round and the grass greener than green underfoot we came on a party of *sadhus* resting. The ashen faces, the pinks and yellows of their scanty clothing, the brass gleam of begging-bowls were unforgettable in the setting—with the shock of a rose in a desert.

By evening we came to Shisha Nag at twelve thousand feet where there was snow and a small lake and a racing brook of green glacial water diving under a snow-bridge. On the far side of the meadow some Gujer shepherds were encamped with their sheep, having not long moved up here as the snow ebbed after winter. We went to talk to them, over the crevassed snow-bridge. They looked puzzled when I came up, and I asked Ahmed what they said.

'They thought you must be a Persian with your light skin and astrakhan fur cap and they wondered if you would understand Kashmiri or Gujeri.'

People expect what is partly in their minds. In China later, I was wearing a padded jacket and a worker's cap. Perfectly sensible inhabitants used to come and ask the way or the time, dissolving in fits of laughter when they realized their mistake.

Turning the horses loose we pitched camp there at Shisha Nag and tied the live chickens to the tent pegs until such time as they were needed for eating. The wind came up and it rained before dark and it was very cold indeed. We were grateful for the *kangris* and the Kashmir blankets, and sat in proper Kashmiri fashion with those earthenware pots filled with live charcoal under the tent of the blanket with only our heads exposed. Once you have learned how to place it, the *kangri* is better than any hot-water bottle in bed, and in winter the Kashmiris regularly sleep with them.

But this was a journey which reached no culmination; for Brake was taken with a fever in the night and was too shaky to go on to the winds and heights and assorted ardours of the rest of the march. So next day we started back rather sheepishly after a brief reconnaissance in the immediate district of Shisha Nag; and I never saw the miraculous *lingam* in the snow cave.

Nor did we manage to get to Ladakh where the people are all Buddhist in the Tibetan manner, nor to Gilgit which now lies within the borders of 'Azad Kashmir', as Pakistan calls the portion of the country on its side of the demarcation line.

But within the Vale there is much to see. Chunks of the history of Kashmir materialize here and there, their ruins standing about the country, warm in the sunlight, remembering greater days. They are lost things in a country of peasantry, surviving like knots in mnemonic strings of pre-Columbian times in Peru which are nearly all we have to warn us that a language and a former dream flourished here; which have now disappeared. The Buddhism which Asoka imposed in Kashmir while Hannibal was leading his army against Rome survives only in a few stupas of Ladakh. Even in the early seventh century when the Chinese pilgrim Huien Tsiang visited Kashmir 'this kingdom is not much given to the faith, and the temples of the heretics are their sole thought'. But perhaps it lingered on in nodes, for about a hundred years later another Chinese (Kashmir, under Lalitaditya, at the time, had embassies in China) remarks that despite the general chaos Buddhism was nevertheless in a flourishing state at Pandrethan. Today there is only one relic of the great capital which used to exist at Pandrethan a few miles outside contemporary Srinagar, a small stone building whose roof is a single stone carved interiorly in the form of a lotus, the flower of Buddhism.

There is no architecture to indicate any peculiarly Kashmiri form of building through the ages. The roots of earlier times are in India, and, strangely enough, in Greece, thanks to the influence of Alexander's kingdoms in the Punjab. At the Temple of Martand now in evocative ruin, posed in the huge space between mountain and Vale, the spirit of Greece married to the East strikes you like a voice from home in an alien country. Hard to say what it is that is Greek in those surviving walls and columns whose bases are surrounded by earthenware jars half buried and big enough for Ali Baba to hide his forty thieves: but there is a cool classicism about the place. The old bearded Muslim who shows you round is altogether out of place; perhaps that is the measure of its Hellenic quality.

Yet at Verinag a mere twenty miles away are the remains of a building which is purely Moghul in inspiration. Essentially an octagon built to enshrine one of the sources of the Jehlum River, it encloses a tank of sparkling green water alive with striped fish among which the spring rises perpetually, and flows out through a garden. The pool and its surrounding walls—broken by a series of camel-hump arches, roofless, with the sun glowing on brick and scintillating on water, and the slivers of fish darting—is one of the supreme examples in Kashmir of the marrying of space and mass into a delightful whole. It was this feeling for landscape that the Moghul princes had as they built, that constitutes their genius. Nowhere is it more perfect than in the famous gardens, Shalimar, Nishat Bagh, Chashma-i-shahi.

Shalimar has suffered from the sob-stuff of generations of British holiday-makers in India and is lodged in that unholy shrine of 'Pale hands I loved, beside the Shalimar', with all its grisly sentiment. Nothing less suitable could have been written about the elegance of the garden, nothing could be further from the formal delicacy of its turf and pavilions and fountains and central watercourse rippling down the terraces between self-conscious beds of flowers to the spread magnificence of Dal Lake. Behind all rises the monarch Mahadeo with his head in the sky, and a gardener is placing lotus blooms in the stone niches behind an artificial waterfall so that their pinks and yellows blur through the curtain of water as it falls. Yet Shalimar is a little spoiled by its approach through an artificial canal a mile long which is choked with decaying boats, and stinking. The grand design, the avenue of mighty trees that reached their magnificence long after the Jehangir planted them and now sentinel the canal leading to the gates of Shalimar and to the pavilion of black marble under whose floor the cooling water runs—the grand design is matchless indeed.

'There are three things in life which ease the heart from sorrow—water; green grass; and the beauty of women.'

We were picnicking at Nishat Bagh, the collectors' piece among the gardens of Kashmir, a mile or two east of Shalimar, in the shade of an umbrella tree, when Ahmed repeated the Kashmir proverb to me. With his accuracy of mood and response to everyone and everything around him he capped the genius of the moment with this saying.

'Is it not correct?' he asked, surveying the grass and the flowering women —Hindu and Muslim sitting near us with their families—the Lake, across which an old road runs on a bund with an exquisite Moghul bridge. He spread his hands, slightly raising his thin shoulders. 'But ours is a poor country.' The defect of proverbs is that they are almost true.

Truly Nishat Bagh would ease all but the most hardened heart. As we lolled on the grass in the afternoon sunlight, Ickballa, Nebra, Salama, Ahmed and myself, and Brake, we lacked little but the beauty of women to complete the time. And even that was at hand. Nishat flows in terraces down the gentle slope right to the edge of the lake. Its central stream gushes down, paddled in by small boys and naked infants, reflecting the strong colour of saris and the monastral blue of sky. Calm trees watch over its flowers and birds and verdant acres and cast their shade on the weekend Srinagar crowd as they listen to fortune-tellers or gossip away the singing afternoon with the children screaming and holding their hands out to catch water from fountains. Nishat is the collectors' piece: in it are condensed in right harmony all the paradise of the other gardens, ordered as the petals of flowers and the veins of a leaf.

Fortunate indeed to have Ahmed with us in Kashmir. A true Kashmiri, he understood everything and knew everything; and he was generous with his knowledge. No question was too trivial for him, no mad-cap idea of mine about what I might do or see here or there was too stupid. About some projects he exercised his teasing humour at my expense, and at other times when I had probed all afternoon in the importunate manner of one who wishes to know all in double quick time, Ahmed would begin to question me in the evening as he sat pouring coffee for us after dinner.

'Now. Tell me, *Sahib*,' he would say with a twinkle in his eye, 'what was the name of that purple hedge we saw in the gardens?'

'Wistaria,' I would reply, or something equally improbable, for I had forgotten to write it down.

He would look at me with regret. 'No, *Sahib*. You have not taken my words seriously. It is Persian Lilac, famous for its scent.'

And I would write it down.

'And what did I call the fishing we saw on the way home?'

'*Tshippe-gaad*,' I reply promptly. 'Which means hiding-fishing because the fisherman leans over the edge of his boat with his head in a sort of bird's nest of leaves and watches for the fish under the water.'

'I think I got a nice shot of that,' Brake chips in. 'Just at the moment when he was going to drive his long fork down and spear the fish. Very tricky.'

'Ah,' said Ahmed, mollified. 'I see you have understood this little thing!' And he would call for Nebra who was dozing somewhere in the kitchen to get another pot of coffee. 'Soon I will show you the way of floating gardens.'

But in fact before Ahmed could show us the 'way' of the floating gardens, there was concrete evidence of them one morning bobbing round the houseboat. During the night a high wind had sprung up and the gardens had come adrift and sailed across Nagin Lake until they stuck against the boat with their tomatoes and marrows flourishing round the verandah. There is a shortage of good cultivable land in Kashmir and a shortage of money to buy the fertilizers that would make the land more fruitful. For the small peasant holder living often insulated on a little bit of low land in the wilderness of canals and lakes there is only this ingenious means of enlarging his territory. Choosing his time and place with care he cuts off a long strip of the bank of a canal or lake, a matted conglomeration of earth and roots tangled with many years' growth, and tows this 'garden' to a suitable spot where he anchors it by stakes to the shallow bed of the waters. He manures it assiduously with weed which he tears up from the lake-bed on long poles —weed which rots in the sun and makes a nutritious compost—and on the floating garden plants his fruit and vegetables. In the late afternoon any day you can see the peasants leaning perilously from skiffs tending the gardens, sometimes quarrelling about the ownership of this or that strip, or sometimes towing a fully bearing garden to a better anchorage while the tomatoes ripen on its substance. Endless quarrels bicker amongst these people over gardens which have been stealthily unhitched in the night and towed silently away to some remote backwater, never to be found again by the rightful owner. The fierceness of their defence of ownership is some index of the value that a little row of beans on a band of old roots can have in the struggle for food. On the borders of lakes carpeted with lotus blossoms beauty is the only abundant thing. That paradox is part of the flavour of Kashmir.

Another is the fervent Muslim air that penetrates even the smallest event.

'I go to pray now,' Ahmed would say suddenly as we were in a shop or in the museum amid the rotting Kashmir shawls and the church-bazaar jumble of the exhibits in their greasy glass cases. And with a sober smile he would be off to the nearest mosque to lay his face towards Mecca and touch his brow in the dust the ritual number of times. Sitting in the *shikara* while I waited for Brake to get some picture he wanted, I would be talking to Ickballa, and, after a lapse in the conversation I would turn round towards him and find him upturned in prayer beside the samovar and the *hookah*, lips moving as he recited the formula. There was no self-consciousness about it. They prayed as simply as I wash my hands and when it was done they felt cleaner and happier in themselves. You had only to look at Ahmed's face after his prayers on a holy day to see the clear newness in his eyes which had come from his God. It is curiously disturbing to be with people whom prayer washes clean and lifts out of their terrestrial trap.

When prayer bursts its ordinary confines it produces the alarming fanatics of various creeds who sit by the mosques and in the environs of the places of pilgrimage on holy days. I watched reluctantly, rather as Baudelaire wrote in a sort of fascination *La Charogne*, a youth with a madness in his eyes sit beating his head on the ground rhythmically, shouting crazed prayers to the world as it went by unheeding; only some children stood round and watched him, wondering what he was doing: and by him were the leper women and the beggars with no legs, faces eaten away by syphilis and lupus, the women among them clutching contagionable children and yelling for pity for the love of Allah.

> Rappelez-vous l'objet que nous vîmes, mon âme,
> Ce beau matin d'été si doux:
> Au detour d'un sentier une charogne infame
> Sur un lit semé de cailloux. . . .

> Les mouches bourdonnaient sur ce ventre putride,
> D'où sortaient de noirs bataillons
> De larves, qui coulaient comme un épais liquide
> Le long de ces vivants haillons. . . .

It was a sight which tore the heart out of the breast, and the easy lotuses bloomed serenely in the canal.

But there is joy, too. Ahmed's uncle Sobra, a venerable old man with a white beard, returned to the Vale from a six months' trip to Mecca on the Haj. He and his wife were met by an excited crowd of relatives and friends as they came towards Srinagar in a car, and taken garlanded with flowers to another conveyance which was almost smothered with blossom. They drove in state to Dal Lake where old Sobra was installed in a special floating pavilion newly draped in white cloth and massed with flowers, equipped with electric fans and heaps of cushions. Here he sat every day for many days and received the congratulations of thousands of the Faithful who came to touch him and to hear a word from the man who had breathed in Mecca by the holy Black Stone. It was a moving sight. The grandchildren massaged his old legs and Ahmed gave him a new turban which he ceremoniously bound on the old man's head. And the old man's happiness that he had achieved his Haj was like quiet jewels in his watery eyes.

In Europe these days the faith of a people can be ignored when you make an assessment of their political tendencies and aspirations. In Kashmir to ignore Islam, in which 90 per cent of the population believe, is to falsify the picture of their hopes out of all truth. All the wordy arguments that have spattered the international press since the débâcle in Kashmir at the time of Indian Independence are utterly meaningless until you realize that the people of the country would like—almost to a man—to join with Pakistan; for the simple reason, none other entering their minds, that Pakistan is a Muslim State. The history of what actually happened at that time—the invasion of Kashmir by armed bands of men from Pakistan supported by the Pakistan Government and Army, the Hindu Maharajah's vacillation and final decision to opt for India at the moment when the raiders were hammering at his palace doors, the Indian airlifted troops which entered and pushed back the incursion to the present cease-fire line—all that is disregarded by the average

man, except that he bewails the loss of relatives and friends in the fighting.
Whatever the rights and wrongs, he cares little and wants simply to join
the believers of Pakistan. His reasons are purely pious, naïvely otherworldly.
Considerations of the Pakistan position, invidious as a member of the
Western bloc in a continent mostly neutral or leaning towards the opposing
side, considerations of the oppressive Government of Pakistan, considerations of the mostly innocuous actions of India in Kashmir, do not enter into
the argument. For it is no argument but an obsession.

Despite all that there is almost no friction between Muslim and Hindu.
Many Muslims told me stories of how Hindus had helped them and their
wives to escape the rapine of the raiders as they swept through the country;
and Hindus—amongst them the merchant who came every morning with
his general store in the *shikara*—countered with stories of their survival
at the time, hidden in Muslim houses. With those other blessings which ease
the heart from sorrow I think one must include racial and religious tolerance
in Kashmir.

Ahmed once summed it up for me:

'We are not angry with the Hindus because they are not many. And
they are not angry with us Muslims because we are *too* many.'

There is one scene above all that epitomizes Kashmir. It occurs before
dawn most mornings, but especially on Tuesday which is the day when it
is most propitious to pray at the mosque on Hari Parbat. On several mornings we went over the grey lakes and through the silent canals to a village
at the foot of the hill, and from there walked the mile or so to its base.
Through the quietude of the Moghul arch we went, not talking for it was
too early and the night was still clinging to everything; and we slowly
ascended the hill. A few people were usually going up this way, but most
came from the other side which is nearer the town. Past the ruins of older
and more solid buildings the mosque sits on the brow of the hill fronted with
a tank for bathing, and crowded inside with men and women praying in the
square courtyard and chanting low in the hush of the air. A few peddlars
generally stood in alcoves with their baskets of bread rolls. By the doors
were many men who did not enter the shrine, standing in their thin white
clothes, hands raised above the level of their upturned faces in prayer, lips
moving, the beards of the old men trembling a little as they murmured.

A few were trickling away from the mosque after their duty; single
men, pairs of men who were friends, threes and fours of women swishing
through the dirt of the track in their frilled *burqas*. They went towards a
level place high on the hill where a huge *chenar* tree stood silent. Here, at
the edge of the cliff which falls a hundred feet and more to the Vale, they
took their positions facing towards Hazrat Bal, which is over the valley at
the feet of Mahadeo.

All the Vale is blue wraiths of fine mist at this time. The sheets of paler blue are the lakes with here and there a row of darker poplars. The sky gets imperceptibly lighter as the minutes pass. The men join hands and begin their chant. An old thin man with a bare bird-like face moves a pace forward and holds his hands out, palms upwards to the lemon glow that is coming behind Mahadeo, and he sings with his high thin voice the few repetitive notes of his melody. The shapeless heap a few yards away is a shepherd still asleep under his brown blanket. The falling rags of washed-out purple are an old woman. Her skinny hand just appears amongst them.

The yellow behind Mahadeo increases and its incandescence lights the world and wakens birds. It is unbearable to wait.

Misty sky turns faintly blue, and the cone of the mountain blackens to silhouette, its edges sharpening against the radiant yellow.

Then, at one moment, the old man stretches forward his hands as if to receive the heavens, the old woman hides her eyes with her hand and cries in anguish to God: and the blinding Cyclopean eye of the day swims over the peak of Mahadeo. The figures are suddenly golden, suddenly real. The stones at their feet take weight and texture. The *chenar* tree rustles like a sleeper waking and a choir of birds shouts for morning joy.

In a few moments sun floods the whole valley and it is flashing with lakes and webbed with canals and greening with green. It is day: the sun is born from the unconsciousness of night and the grey ache of dawn; his energy flows down and galvanizes all living things. The devout go away down the many steps to the rousing town with the blessings of Allah somewhere in their hearts.

This scene you can never forget.


'I smell your breakfast,' says Ahmed as we near the houseboat on the way back.

'Good morning, *Sahib*!' shouts Nebra over the water, his head still tousled with sleep. The shout brings the rest of Ahmed's seven children running along the catwalk at the side of the *Triumph*, yelling with glee at their father's return.

We go aboard and the children surround him.

'You have a good photo this morning, *Sahib*?' asks Nebra, surreptitiously buttoning the sleeves of his shirt.

'Such a trouble, they are!' Ahmed murmurs, smiling affectionately at the faces of his children. 'Such a trouble. . . .'

And the day begins.

# III. Ceylon

W<small>E HAD</small> been to Ceylon several times before, the traveller and I. We had had a first taste of the East there, years ago; and dysentery, and all other random experiences.

First of all towards the end of the war I went there and stayed for many months; and later I came again once or twice for shorter visits. So to arrive once more was like coming to the house of friends. Ceylon is a friendly place. That was my memory of it.

But the traveller with his touchiness and his permanently heightened sensitivity to the present, and to the present as it meets the past, was a little dubious about the island.

'Someone on the plane said they had had a strike recently in the hotel,' he remarked. 'A strike! In the Galle Face Hotel! Just imagine that!'

'And they had riots too, not so very long ago,' I reminded him.

He had forgotten that. A riot or a strike was outside his picture of Ceylon. In the hotel, now out of strike, he sighed a little, looking from the window on Galle Face Green as one looks back on the past which is gilded by a sun, much as the Green was yellowing at this moment in the late rays. It seemed to be very much as it was on his last visit. But to him the prospect of another view, an exploration that might go deeper like a return to scenes of childhood, was a little daunting.

'It's natural to cling to first impressions,' he said apologetically. 'Especially when they are good ones.'

'Like one's grandmother clinging to the memory of broad Victorian acres of prosperity?'

'Which have contracted to rather beastly allotments with a hard-won cabbage or two. I know what you mean. But there's a sort of glory in the moments of time past. Like good historical novels. Like the first months of being in love. You needn't throw it all away because the present has moved on.' He had fallen in love on his first visit to Ceylon.

'Or because you haven't moved on with *it*? That's the other aspect, isn't it? The baby shouldn't go out with the bath-water because you ought to have removed it before.'

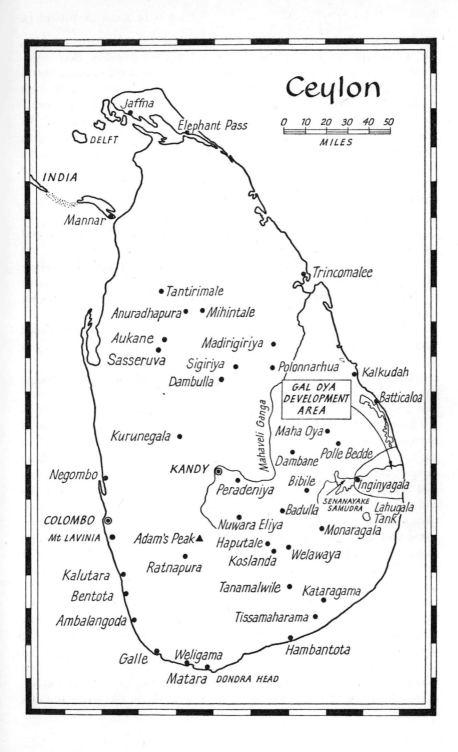

It was irresistible to tease him a little, to take a gentle rise out of him, for at this stage we were not in sight of solving our problem. Both arguments had flaws—the traveller's sentimentality was perhaps no more unreal and partial a view than my own hard distrust of romanticism. We were both reluctant to modify our outlook; fundamental views of the world are painful to alter. The comforting charms of the traveller's point of view with its poeticism were seductive to me, and at times I succumbed. But those sights, terrible in human terms, on which we had had our feelings lacerated in the Hadhramaut and in Kashmir, were beginning to nibble at the edges of the traveller's romantic domain: and the variousness, unexpected as it was bewildering, of human beings, was beginning to make me modify my own too rigid and systematized opinions.

We talked on while the Galle Face Green darkened under a flamboyant sky and disappeared, recalling episodes and adventures in Ceylon on previous trips when we were still bright-faced with more youthful ideas—ideas pivoted on ourselves.

'How easy,' he exclaimed as we bestirred ourselves into the clothes for dinner, 'to know the world revolves around oneself!'

'And not to notice the fingers of birth, money, opportunity, which keep it spinning that away! It's part of the romantic essence. Let's go and eat.'

'Riots . . .' he murmured, shaking his mental head. 'Doesn't sound in the least like Ceylon.' He was in the mood to continue, but we went down that passably noble stair to dinner. You have to start with the next thing.

You dine late in the tropics, a habit which suits because enjoyment of the day increases as the evening goes on. As you sit in the pillared lounge of the hotel the sounds of music come out from the dining-room and it is so carefree and pleasant that you are tempted to eat. Through the archway past the venerable old man who prevents guests who are not wearing ties and jackets from entering (and supplies you with a tie if you happen not to have one) the vast dining-room is all lit in candle yellow. The polished wood floor reflects a hundred ceiling fans which depend on their single legs twenty feet or more from the roof and twirl their blades like the wings of dragonflies at least forty feet above your head. The small white-clothed tables stand in rows under them with skirts fluttering. The orchestra plays from a dais, very natty in a palm-court way. And if you are early for dinner the boys, fifty or sixty of them in white sarongs reaching to their bare feet, white jackets tight over their slim shoulders, stand around outnumbering the guests.

It is the kind of room you can sail into, specially made for elegant women who have a mind for such entrances. Alas that few European women in the tropics have the figure, poise, and wit in addition to the wish. But the orchestra plays gaily on—Strauss waltzes, 'Pale hands I loved, beside the

Shalimar', polkas, Chopin mazurkas—with a nostalgic sweetness that beguiles the critical faculties and floats you away into the bright mists of the 'twenties and 'thirties when Empire was still Empire and those diners were the ruling class. Momentarily you are in a little tropical Vienna, the Vienna of pre-1914 when that peculiar brand of sentiment and luxury reached its cloying but somehow exciting apogee. In Ceylon nowadays the scene is a little flawed, for almost no one travels with evening dress, and those evening toilette tunes soar with bitter-sweetness over heads for the most part lacking even the remembrance of their temporal origins.

But I should not deny that there is pleasure in sitting there admirably served by the silent boys gliding about on bare feet, with the Gothic decadence of middle European music on the ear. No one loves it more than the middle-class Sinhalese, for whom it represents the height of European culture. It is a pity that by and large it is the lowest common denominator of our civilization that has been strong enough to impress the inhabitants of the Empire. They are as wrong about us as travellers sometimes are about them.

We started off next day in the joy of an Eastern morning, down the road to the south, in an old car with an old driver. I chose him for his excellent English, the serious comedy in his eye, and the probability that at his age the speed of his driving would suit my taste for slowness. Having discovered what I did in Ceylon, the driver took me rather seriously, and this was helpful—because he repeated all the information he knew on all subjects; and amusing—because I am less sedulous about the way I take myself.

Hard to describe the Orient. There is always something missing from the layer above the details you may put down. Especially in mornings when something like the wonder of an awakening child's eyes laughs over the coming day; and in the evening when the fulfilled life of an old woman's smile lingers in the dusk. In both, the tooting and ardour of Colombo's traffic follow you down the road through the suburbs past the rows of villas and shops for many miles until these give way to more purely pastoral sounds and scenes. This quadrant and this coastal region of the island are densely populated. It is practically one long village from Colombo to Galle, and that is seventy-two miles; but a village endless in its variety, never boring, yet coherent and all of a piece.

Not very far from Colombo you begin to notice that the groves of toddy or *kitul* palms rearing sixty feet above the houses have their heads tied together with ropes, and the air grows heavy with alcoholic fumes. We stopped where some men were pouring the milky toddy into a big barrel by the wayside.

From a species of tree resembling the date-bearing palm they procure an excellent beverage in the following manner. They cut off a branch, and put over the place a vessel to receive the juice as it distils from the wound, which is filled in the course of a day and a night. . . .

Thus Marco Polo on 'tree wine', as he calls it.

The men had just gathered the cups of toddy from the trees and after they had filled the barrels would roll them along the road to the store. One of them, a fat man whose paunch ballooned over his sarong, offered to send one of his boys up a tree to show me how they collected the juice. The boy hitched up his sarong and started upwards. The climb is made easy in Ceylon by steps made of slivers of the coconut husk tied on to the trunk so that if you start with the right foot it is as easy as walking up stairs. Once up among the sprouting leaves the cup of juice is emptied into a container and the boy walks from one tree to the others on the ropes joining the heads, holding on to another rope placed parallel at breast-height; and so down again to the ground with his fresh toddy. In the morning before the juice has had time to ferment it is an opaque soapy colour and refreshing in a pungent way, full of bits of leaf and impurities.

The tree-climbers, as they are opprobriously known, are one of the lowest castes in the island, and they bear the marks of their social inferiority —a slightly hang-dog look and a tremendous enthusiasm when you show interest in their occupation and life. If I had wanted to get drunk on toddy I could have done so for nothing at the roadside that morning and earned the friendship of the tree-climbers and the disapproval of my starchy driver.

'Three palms give about a gallon a day on average,' the fat man told me. 'If only we had the right kind of factory,' he lamented, 'we could make whisky out of toddy.'

I asked him whether he was interested in the whisky or the profits, and he said 'Both,' with engaging frankness. In fact they distil a spirit called arrack which is not unpleasant though it lacks the character of whisky.

The tappers were mostly a little boozed; not much, just an aura of alcohol hung about them as it does about those who continually tope. But an old man marching along the road as I got back into the car was frankly drunk. Carrying his umbrella like a rifle across the shoulder he strode along addressing the world in general in Sinhalese, and, when he saw me, in English too. A few heavy spots of rain began to fall and he plucked a big leaf and placed it on his head, singing, and went off with his umbrella still over his shoulder.

There are a thousand scenes along the road to Galle, each competing with the next for place in your affection and interest. The whole area of the south-west is watered by the regular monsoon from that quarter and is lush to the point of confusion. The bounty of nature flaunts all around, filling gardens with flowers and plants that threaten to obliterate the dwellings, a profusion of trees and shrubs equalled in very few places in the world. The coconut, *kitul*, palmyra, talipot, and other palms grow wild, each bearing its fruit or nut or leaf or bark that is used for a multitude of common purposes in daily life. The gardens are crammed with fruitbearing trees— mango, jack, breadfruit, banana, custard-apple, mangosteen. Pineapples are common and the slender stalks of papayas weighted with fruit hanging nude on thin stems spring from crops of chilli and other spices on the ground. Trees of heady temple flowers and hedges of pagoda flowers startle the eye amongst this riot of greens, as do the occasional flamboyance of sarong colours that are like the wilder natural shades, and the pale exoticism of faces with outsize eyes that are like the waxen elegance of the temple flowers themselves. The road slips through all this, taking its course not far from the sea whose glances pierce the vegetation now and then, naïvely sparkling. The road is running with traffic—bullock carts like covered wagons with swaying roofs made of plaited palm leaves, old rusty cars and a few spanking new ones, buses jammed with chattering people, children on bicycles too big for them, children toddling home from school with slates under their arms, naked infants with fat fingers on their domed bellies and mouths open and amulets round their necks. All the lorries are marked on the tailboards 'Fully Insured'—a thoroughly sensible investment, since accidents are frequent and followed by loud altercations in which all the local inhabitants join with a passionate involvement which tells you how alive they are and how little they have to do. Periodically you come to a total block on the road where some cart has cracked under its load of coconuts and spilled them rolling all over the highway. The distracted driver scrambles about retrieving them from the wheels of cars and the feet of water buffalo and from the surreptitious hands of small thieving boys, while everything comes to a standstill and the horns make the air hurtful and the shopkeepers stand smiling with cynicism at the doors of their establishments. My driver felt he must apologize for those divertissements, and was amazed when I described to him the hopeless mess of central London traffic.

'The English gentlemen have told me before that all is well done in England,' he said, wondering and profoundly shaken. . . . I was not sure whom I had let down more.

There are many places along the coast where to linger a month or two would be both interesting and delightful. With all the urban man's nostalgia for a past he personally never knew, and in my case a longing to be by the sea, which is a direct product of childhood, you stand about in the south-coast villages by the sands, and the traveller says:

'Why do we hurry? What the hell do we hope to find that we can't find here?'

He is irrefutably right and I know it. But . . .

'We have only a couple of months for the whole island, you know.'

'And you suppose that is enough? To find anything, I mean?' he counters.

And I laugh. Because I don't think I will ever find what I'm looking for. And nor will he. 'We can go on looking at things,' I say vaguely. For that is what one does: sometimes learning in an instant, as the sky learns of the lightning when it jabs through the air, some small thing that seems to bear on the question of people.

At Bentota at lunchtime the outriggers were driving in on the wind past the white foam of the reef, through the gap and over the lagoon to the shore, laden with fish. They come like strange birds on snow-white or rust or patch-work wings, charged with the winds of the Indian Ocean; like birds and like argosies from a magical land that lies, maybe, under those piled powdered coiffures of clouds on the horizon. They come to shore among the surf, delicately made of hollowed log and supple branches and rope of coconut fibre. Ingeniously made, the slit of standing room in the main hull deepened by a board sewn on at either side of the concavity and pitched and painted; the mast sprung simply and the slim banana of the outrigger whipped to the hull with only two curved stems of wood. Families wait for the boats and the children help to haul them up on the beach, and the men bring out the fish, the scarlet and the black, and the yellow-finned varieties.

More and more boats come in all the time, sweeping unerringly through the gap in the reef's jaws, crowding ashore. It is a fine sight and there is very little to tell you this is Ceylon and not a Pacific island whence those boats somehow derive.

The coastal scene does not change, nor the vegetation appreciably alter as you go on south to Ambalangoda: the spiritual climate does. For at Ambalangoda the heart of the devil-dancing country throbs mystically, even in the middle of the twentieth century and hired buses to take the dancers to their various destinations at Festival times. But the pulse is not very evident at once; you have to feel very carefully to sense it.

There is a Rest House there built (or rather tumbling down) on the crest of sand dunes by a dip where a village snugs amongst its palms, and boats are being refurbished and an old man is twining two strands of string to make a stronger one. There is a solitary electric-light bulb in the rust of what was once a sort of lantern, on the promontory.

'The outriggers' lighthouse,' said one of the fishermen when he saw me looking at it. He was serious, unaware of anything comical.

Here at Ambalangoda I learned a little of how they make the out-riggers and mend them, and a man who ran the local dancing school showed me the masks for the dance. He was a mild little man with perhaps a trace of Dutch in his blood for he had very little the appearance of a Sinhalese. His father and grandfather before him had been in charge of the dance in this region. The 'school' seemed to consist of a collection of huts near the beach. But what fascinated me were the dozens of masks inside. There are two distinct types of dancing; the *bali* or devil-dance administered to the sick rather as one might in the West give a course of treatment for some malady; and *kolam* which is also a masked performance, but is really danced drama and has no magical intent.

Nowadays the old forms of *kolam* have been altered to something more mundane. But as I gazed at the masks, surrounded by a group of young dancers and their tutor, I remembered the description of a scene from one of the old plays of this district, and remembered too that these people were the direct descendants (spiritually and emotionally, not least) of the performers of the iridescent piece called 'A Woman Consisting of Five Women'.

Five women link themselves together, and bear a pot on the top of their head. Their bodies shine like gold and precious stones. In this form the woman consisting of five women comes quickly.

Their paps are like goslings; their persons are dressed in all sorts of habiliments; and without fail they will attract the heart of every man. Come forward, you group of women. . . .

They are adorned with golden chains and splendid garments. Their paps, like golden dishes or goslings, are trembling. Whoever beholds the handsomeness of this woman resembling a golden image, their hearts will be agitated, and they will be subject to great evil.

These five women dance perfectly in a flowerpot. They shine in beauty surpassing an image of gold. Their hearts are not backward in animal affection; and the gazing gallant is affected and distracted.

Behold these women so formed that their bodies shine beyond the beautiful island of Ceylon. How could the gallants turn away without surveying the nipples which project from their breasts? . . .

Their faces shine like a full moon—their bodies tremble—their paps are like golden cups; and those gallants that see them will desire them. If they have golden coin, they will be disposed to give heaps of it.

Despite its complexity as stage direction, description of action, and statement of idea—this old scene rings with an exact Sinhalese note—there is nothing improbable about it when you stand fingering the masks at Ambalangoda, some of which are at least as old as Callaway's translation of 1829. There are girls in any village here who would be excellent in the parts, and had there been a sudden performance that night in this village of the woman consisting of five women, I shouldn't have been surprised. But there was no *kolam* about.

By chance we stumbled on the preparations for devil-dancing as we drove towards Galle. Outside a house some altars of young palm leaf and bamboo were being constructed. Asking what their purpose was, I discovered that there was a woman sick whose relatives had paid for a *bali*.

The family were making the necessary structures and getting all ready for the dancers, and the session was timed for 8 p.m. I promised to return. It was great good fortune, and I was tremendously excited.

That evening we retraced the eighteen miles to the village along the Galle road to see the devil-dancing. All the hamlets were dark on the way. I was apprehensive in case I shouldn't know which to stop at. But it was a groundless fear. The village was full of its villagers when we came there late in the evening, all standing in the road in a big circle round the house of the sick woman. Several pressure lamps illumined the scene, hanging shiny and new from the porch of the house where the relatives sat on hard chairs and on the ground with the village elders and a priest.

Our arrival made a temporary diversion and stole some of the audience from the dancing; and when they recognized me they seemed very happy that I had come, and pushed me through the crowd to the front ranks where small boys were admonished for getting in the way of my camera and other people tried hard to sit me in a chair. The altars I had seen in the making were set like yellow curly screens at either end of the area in front of the house, hung with coconut-oil lamps and various edible offerings, so that they and the house enclosed three sides of a long rectangle. The remaining side was filled with the crowd who pressed round me, commenting freely on my clothes and hair and features and age with a forthright village interest. Three dancers, two men and a boy who was learning, were gyrating in the space. Stripped to the waist, their white pleated skirts swirling, the bronze skin of their chests shining with sweat in the interstices of gold chain-harness adorned with mirrors, and wearing crowns of curly young palm leaf, they flourished torches and vied with one another in the dance. Two drummers beat complex rhythms, and the feet of the dancers thudded with hard heels on the beaten ground, their ankle-bells jingling, occasional cries coming from the thongs of their throats. The various stanzas of the ritual succeeded one another at the change of drum rhythm—a cyclic movement suddenly arrested and forced into the shape of a different one. Debased as a form of dancing it may be, lacking the sinuous and yet angular grace of Kandyan dance which in its turn is only a hint of Bharata Natya from India—yet I found it infectious. I felt like a small boy, less inhibited than me, who was trying to imitate the steps of the dancers and puzzled that he couldn't manage it, but tremendously thrilled as well.

As midnight passed the dancers began to swig arrack and to dip their torches into it and to breathe in the flames and exhale spurts of alcoholic smoke. Then they spread the flames on the running sweat of their chests as you singe a chicken, and the dance became more frenzied. Each man in turn took his place in the middle of the arena and executed a complicated solo to the cries of the crowd, and retired temporarily exhausted to the wings. After a lull, when the lamps were pumped up, the dancers reappeared wearing masks, grotesque and, in the little circle of light in the thickness of the surrounding night, impressive and weird. They danced again, fascinating and hideous under the curling snakes and gaudy faces of the masks, their human bodies appearing incongruously soft and tender. There were moments now when their movement had a trance quality, when one or other man leapt and seemed suspended in the air longer than was physically possible, or when he spun in the air in the manner of the Cossacks; and the air was stifling with the smell of burnt torches and arrack, and the children were falling asleep in arms. The dancers, now washed in their own sweat, gleamed in an access of male flesh, muscles warmed up and pulsing, and eyes in the openings of the masks like sharp knives stabbing the air. The drums beat maddeningly their basal interrupted rhythm forcing a pace which steadily grew more hectic. Somehow you had the feeling of the essence of movement being liberated through them and the dancers, of a difficult essence forcing itself out into the air from its hidden place inside them; and the dancers were drugged progressively by their own movement, excitement stimulating more excitation.

Waking up in Galle in a tall cool white room with black beams on the ceiling, it is hard to imagine the Ceylon outside. This is Dutch. Its relation to the other seems only historical, and not actual. To understand Galle and other ports of Ceylon, and to understand the island as a whole, you need a little history—even a mere sketch is better than none. You require to know that in the first years of the sixteenth century a Portuguese merchant fleet was driven by a gale to the shores of Ceylon and anchored off Colombo. The King of the region at that time had his capital at Kotte near the town. 'Parangi Kotte giya Wagey' is a cautionary saying even today in Ceylon. 'How the Portuguese came to Kotte,' you say of someone who in some manner deceives you. For the King, wishing to impress the Portuguese with the extent of his lands, and also to confuse them about the location of his capital, had them led by a most devious route to his palace. But his simple cunning failed to put them off and, first for commercial reasons, they returned and gradually subjected the coastal strip of the island. The Portuguese occupation is a story of massacre and insane destruction. Even one of their own Jesuit priests lamented the terrible history of their rule.

'We have no reason,' he said, 'to be surprised at the heavy punishment which God there inflicted on the Portuguese nation ... till finally the whole island was lost and God gave over to unbelievers and heretics what Catholic Christians did not deserve to keep.'

The ruthless Christian zeal of the King of Portugal specifically commanded the destruction of the temples and shrines and the wiping out of heretical inhabitants. It was not so much for trade, for the spices which

Europe craved, but in the name of the God of Portugal that those villagers were tortured and their defenceless places sacked and pillaged.

The eclipse of the Portuguese was achieved not by any local force but by the arrival of the Dutch, that nation of slogging traders in the seventeenth-century Orient. They must to begin with have seemed like a blessing to the people, for they governed with much less severity, closed their eye to local heathen custom, while usurping the whole of the island's external trade. While the Portuguese had brought their brand of the Catholic faith and built churches to house its idols (the idols of other people's faith being always anathema to the idolatrous sects of Christianity), the Dutch brought their own bleak religion and built their barren churches which so often have exterior charm but are hollow and bare within. Solid business men, they also built forts and harbours with strong walls of local stone and rows of bourgeois little tight white houses, and they cleaned the place up and made it so dull that they felt at home.

Galle was one of their fortress-harbours; its ramparts still stand against the sea, clean and durable, prosaic; its churches too are there, white and cold; its rows of respectable houses are still there, ready for the painter of merchants' domestic scenes in the manner of Pieter de Hoogh. A walk round those ramparts leaves the impression that the Dutch departed not very long ago; the greensward which tops them is deserted, the emplacements for cannon with their semi-circular iron runners making rusty arcs on stone flags, the Dutch roofs and an air of Europe about the scene belie the East. I met a fisherman with his rod coming home for breakfast, a boy who was watching a handful of thin cows grazing; no one else in an hour's walk round the circumference. But turning the eye inwards to the town it could not be anywhere but Ceylon. The mixture of Dutch churches, Buddhist temples— even a small dagoba—the imposing white mosque with its crescents on pinnacles, and men in the narrow streets wearing coloured sarongs and the ubiquitous *banion*, as the singlet is called—those together are undoubtedly Ceylon. And there is one other scene in the heart of the town which reveals its geographical location—the central square where the law courts flank a green lawn. A notice on the road reminds all cars not to honk their horns while the courts are in session. The square is filled with people standing in groups talking animatedly, with stalls selling lurid drinks, with bicycles parked under the lovely trees. Outside each of the two courts which were in session a crowd had gathered leaning slightly towards the open windows whence the sounds of the proceedings filtered out on the warm air. Everyone was intent, alive with interest. There is no more revealing witness to the litigious nature of the Ceylon people than this. I have never known a people so inclined to go to law and to stay there for years, quibbling in a fog of details: there are a host of stories, all of them comical and tragic too, about this passion for litigation. Whole inheritances and patrimonies are regularly spent on legal fees for the satisfaction of getting the better of someone else. But when you read the laws relating to property and inheritance and other legal rights in Ceylon (most of them codifications of a muddled and haphazard tradition) it is not altogether surprising. As far as land is concerned I heard more of this later, and saw its tragic results.

The importance to which Galle grew under the Dutch (ibn Batuta in the fourteenth century calls it a small town) has waned with the British championship of Colombo and the building of the great harbour there. Its name is from Sinhalese *gala*, rock, but the Dutch preferred to derive it from the Latin *gallus*, a cock, and a chanticleer stands over the monogram V.O.C. (Vereenigde Oost-Indische Compagnie) on the inner side of the old gate. Galle is nowadays a small port again. Its charm is its recommendation. Here a retired mariner of the old school might well pass the remainder of his days in quiet and interesting contentment—indeed some do.

From Galle the coast leads away south-east. A succession of small bays rivalling those of the South Seas adds charm and variety. In one of them I found the stilt-fishermen. In such a bay where they worked and lived you are far from the world and, because you are a fisherman, very near to its fundamentals. Stilt-fishing is probably the next most primitive method of catching fish to spear-fishing. The stilts are driven into the sand ten or twelve yards from the beach, and three men wade out to each. One perches on a crossbar near the top of the stake and sights the shoals of small fish as they move about in the shallows; the next man climbs to a crossbar lower down on the stake and perches there with a bundle of seaweed, ready to throw it when his higher companion tells him a shoal is approaching. The third stands thigh-deep in the water with a circular net over his shoulder ready to cast it when the fish have followed the seaweed as it drifts past a few yards away.

I spent a morning with the stilt-fishers clinging naked to their wobbly stake. They taught me how to cast the net, happy in the lowliness of their station to be taken notice of, and to show off a little of their peculiar skills. Neither I nor they caught a fish, but I think we all enjoyed it; and I ate some food with them on the rich yellow sand of the beach with the breakers rolling in from the tail of the monsoon. They are charming generous people and, to a stranger who fell in with them, unprejudiced and clear in their simple thoughts, which is often the way of very poor people.

On past Welligama where the rock-hewn statue of a king who was a leper and came here to be healed served as the shady spot for a couple of black and white kittens as I passed, on to Dondra, the most southerly point in Ceylon where there is nothing but water between you and the South Pole.

A curious thing happens at Dondra. The lush vegetation abruptly ceases. The coast turns sharply north-west and the influence of the south-east monsoon is lost. From here onwards the ground is progressively more arid and the whole picture of Ceylon which you might have built up till that moment is in dire need of revision. Before Hambantota the country is desolate, thin scrub, and monkeys. But before the vegetation quite disappears there is Dikwella where, a mile from the road, a temple is hidden. It is possibly, and in some respects fortunately, the only one of its kind in Ceylon; a sort of Buddhist Madame Tussaud's. Ignoring the hideous lions emblazoning the façade you enter and in the half-light come on the great reclining Buddha surrounded by his disciples. The light from the doorway shows them dimly but the effect is of reality, every feature delineated with truth and not with art, so that you start back feeling that you have interrupted a meeting of the real Gautama and his followers. It is disconcerting and nauseating like all waxworks. But in the courtyard of this monstrosity stands a curious shrine of two storeys, the upper one of which, octagonal and small, has its interior walls painted with a delightful series of 'primitives' showing the visits of the Buddha to Ceylon and the conversion of the kings and much else besides. Here, all unconscious, is something that can be called art, though not very skilled. But the local people like the waxworks very well—as well as any greater art—and were coming with their offerings of temple flowers in their hands to lay them at those all too real feet of the Buddha.

Past Hambantota where a semi-lunar beach serried with ranks of outriggers, where the depressing damp salinity of the salt pans corrodes a flat landscape, and a Shell pump, familiar and vulgar, stands disastrously contemporary on an archaic shore, and where on the headland there is a decaying monument to one Henry John St. John, Esquire, who died here in 1821 'of a bilious FEVER', whatever that might be, 'much regretted by his Friends and Acquaintances' of the Ceylon Civil Service—past Hambantota (which itself means the harbour of the Arab *hambans* or sampans) the choking smell of wood-smoke fills the hot air. *Chena* cultivation is the name given to the method of burning the bush and planting crops on the cleared patches, and this is the common means adopted here as elsewhere in similar country in Ceylon. It is a poor thing, this *chena*, yielding a steeply diminishing crop for about four years; and then the ground is exhausted. The poverty and desolation of the south-west sector of Ceylon are perhaps no more dreadful than in many other places, but the contiguity of barren land with the exuberant lushness of that a mere fifty miles away, and the difference in the life of the people, strikes disproportionate pity into the heart. The poor little farms burnt out of the scrub, the wattle huts and half-starved children with long black hair falling greasily to their shoulders, the apathetic women overcome with the impossibility of their lot, make you weep for them, make you wonder why they don't walk the fifty miles to the land of water and abundance. To see that they do not is to understand how little the appearance of things tells the fundamental truth of economics. For here in the dry zone at least there is plenty of land—for what it is worth; and there in the apparent plenty of the wet zone of the south-west is a dense population and acute land-hunger. So it is no use walking that fifty miles; there is no place to put a hut on the ground, no place to plant another chilli.

Outside the huts by the road as you travel northwards there is an occasional earthenware pot with a cloth covering it, suspended on a stake. Sometimes even a scrawled, ill-lettered inscription mentions the contents, which are buffalo curd for sale. This is the road by which the pilgrims to Kataragama, near the coast which we had just forsaken, make their way from the hill country and the north of the island. The seven toothed hills of Kataragama dominate the land all the way to the centre of Ceylon, much more evocative than the rebuilt dagobas which the zeal of pilgrims has made into a sort of religious equivalent of suburban grandeur. It is this passing trade the inhabitants hope to catch with buffalo curd.

I went into several of those huts, and in one bought some of the curd made from the milk of the water buffalo. It was not new to me, but in this place the curd is reputed to be the best in Ceylon. It has a melting shortness and astringency which, with lumps of *jaggery*—the brown sugar crystallized from palm juice—is refreshing and makes an interlude for the gourmet which he would hardly have expected to enjoy in the pitiable land. The family were astonished when I liked it so much that I ate a whole bowl and used up all the *jaggery* they had. I remarked that they must find it useful to give to the children—some of whom were suffering from malnutrition. The woman of the house laughed at me.

'But you don't give curd to children,' she cried, amazed at my ignorance. 'They get worms from it.'

I tried to explain to her what it was that gave children worms, that they could get worms from all sorts of food which was not pure. She listened with a puzzled drawing together of the brows, holding her youngest to her breast.

'Oh, yes,' she said courteously. 'But they always get the worms from the curd.' And her husband and a neighbour nodded their agreement.

I bought another bowl of curd and we went on our way. It was sad. The half-starved kids waved and screamed to us as we went in our lordly car with our costly cameras and our careless superiority. I wanted to stop and go back and try again to tell the wife about nourishing her kids, but . . . You are often too far away in life, and your good intentions just hang in the backward air like the smoke from the *chena*. They mean nothing. They cannot mean anything to the other people until you have stayed for months and lived like the people live, until they know you are the same as they are; the same flesh and desires and laughter. And your children perhaps subject to worms.

'It is no use,' said the traveller. 'We are only onlookers. Perhaps we shall find, but can we ever partake?'

At that moment I had no reply. I consoled myself with the thought of the stilt-fishermen and how we had known each other briefly but well. You succeed and then you fail.

The long road from Kataragama rises into the central hills of Ceylon but if you turn at Wellawaya you can skirt them, driving east, and the panorama of the dry zone hundreds of feet below stretches away to the sea. The foothills are forested and ringing with birds, patched with rubber trees grown too high for rubber and with tea rather too low for the best tea. Under the rubber grows coco in its fat reddish pods. There is a bend in the road near Koslanda where all travellers stop. Away over the dry plains to the south the seven hills of sacred Kataragama appear blue in the heat. There is a flat stone on the wayside, on which burns a small oil flame, and above it a sharp stone. You get out of the car or lorry or bus and stand facing to Kataragama with a young coconut raised in front of your face, making your vow. And in token of your decision you smash the nut on the sharp stone. Just below on the hillside, where the fragments fly, three young boys are waiting like three-quarters for the ball out of a Rugby scrum. They have a sack and collect the pieces to take home, to sell or use in their houses for the curry. Hardly a driver will pass this spot without making his vow, so there is a rich harvest of coconut.

Gradually the road descends towards Ratnapura and thoughts fly back to the Hadhramaut and the Sabaean Queen whose gems, it is always said, came from Ceylon. Ratnapura means 'City of Gems' and it was from here if anywhere in the East that Sheba drew her diadem. In many such myths there is a solid basis of trade-route history.

The town is an undistinguished little place with a few men sitting at the doors of their shops cutting inferior jewels with crude saws, grinding facets at clumsy stones revolved by means of a primitive bow worked back and forth over the spindle as though they were playing an instrument only they could hear. But there is something harsh about the place, for the souls of the people are owned by speculators who have bought the mineral rights in the alluvial gravel where gems are found. The workers are mostly Sinhalese and the speculators chiefly Moors—as the Muslims are called in Ceylon. In theory the Government gets a cut on all gems found. In theory the specu-lator owns the gems found. In theory the worker who finds the gems simply hands them over to the speculator, his boss. So every pit from which the gravel is brought to the surface has its quota of inspectors in the pay of the Government and others in the pay of the speculators; and everyone concerned in the process is put on the mettle of his cunning to cheat the other.

The mining is an interesting sight, primitive and probably unchanged during all the centuries since the Arabian Nights when Sinbad told Haroun al Raschid of the precious stones of Serendib (as the Arabs called Ceylon). Some few stones are found by panning in streams, but the method of choice is to dig a pit in the ground and bring up the muddy gravel in small baskets. Nowadays the pits are lined fairly efficiently with pit props and the worker is moderately safe at a depth of twenty or thirty feet as he gropes up handfuls of the mud with his bare fingers in the water at the bottom of the shaft. A few men stand at the head of the shaft to raise the laden baskets on a pulley. All of them are naked except for a bit of cloth on a string, and daubed with grey-yellow mud. Near the shaft others, similarly naked, are cutting props from trees and shaping them. Everywhere there are heaps of discarded washings from the gravel, and a couple of the toughest men carry between them a bigger basket of tailings and dump it on one of the heaps, walking and tipping and returning with a unison of movement, waiting for a refill in the attitudes of statuary, their wide chests and swelling calves tautening as they take the new load.

Little boys who had followed me to the pits tried to sell me bits of coloured quartz, and the workers, equally opportunist, offered more probable but worthless fragments of amethyst and beryl.

The place is running in mud, the dilapidated kadjan roofs sheltering the mouths of pits sagging and askew; the miners scramble about, climb in and out of the holes like water-rats, the overseers stand with crafty eyes and everyone is on some sort of cut-throat make. And it is from this mess that the world's most fabulous sapphire came, a jewel half the size of my palm as I held it in the shop of a Colombo merchant, bewitching, liquid, crystalline: and worth about £60,000. In my other hand I held a cat's-eye of the same size, the biggest flawless specimen to come out of the pits. It mesmerized me with its feline slit of an eye as though there were invisibly surrounding it a head with a cat's brain.

'It is the mascot of our firm,' the merchant said. 'We have kept it for many years since my grandfather who founded our business. It is not for sale.'

My eyes were riveted on the eye of the cat. I waited for it to blink, for the iris to contract round the pupil, for the invisible paw to shoot out and scratch my face. Doubtless it was such a cat's-eye that the Queen of Sheba brought on her visit to Solomon, which, combined with the charms of her glamorous person, so inflamed him.

The week I had taken on this round trip seemed, when I got back to Colombo to the hotel's combination of barrack-room and luxury, to be bursting out of my head. The drama in Ceylon is purely one of people; it is not played out against any fundamental austerity of natural surroundings as it is in the Hadhramaut. The country has great charm, but it is never fiercely beautiful; it never acts on the people with the quality of a knife-thrust—the avoidance of which is the main activity of life—as it is in southern Arabia. On the whole it is a gentle land breeding a people whose qualities normally match it. Theirs is a soft yielding beauty without the hawk-like eye and the spareness of bone and flesh of Arab peoples: theirs is a mellowness tempered with laughter and passing tears, innocent of high tragedy as of the wilder forms of fanaticism.

There is a word used in Sanscrit poetics—*rasa*—which denotes the quality inherent in art, the thing which we loosely call beauty. *Rasa* is a better word because it includes ugliness and all conditions of the quality of art. You might call it the flavour, rather as you talk of food having flavour. Viewing a meal as art (for the sake of illustration) its flavour would be its *rasa*, the sum of sweet and astringent, bitter that kicks the palate in combination with variety of texture between the teeth and on the sensitive surface of the tongue. In Ceylon the *rasa* of life is as complicated and as perpetually exciting an experience as a lifetime of Chinese meals cooked in China. A lyricism runs through the island, turning sometimes like the inward eye to mysticism, turning again to passion, to simplicity, to nostalgia; and only occasionally, with a shock which it feels itself, to violence.

In the great cities of the world life is thundering round you and you are part of it. There is no escaping, only sporadically the desire to escape. But in the old-fashionedness of the countryside in the villages in the Kandyan hills the thunder is remote—a storm battering far beyond the horizon. A sort of security hangs in the air. You feel that everything is safe, that the small houses will go on dreaming in their flowering gardens, that this rice at your feet in the ripe field will go on growing season by season for ever as it has always done, that this tree will push forth its pink blossom always, and the water buffallo will take its daily rest as it is doing now in the shallows of the river with only its nose and eyes above the muddy water.

And then one day as you are waiting for someone to come and take you through the fields to a village where they are reaping and threshing you pick up a scrap of old newspaper that has been wrapped round some small parcel. It is shoddy and dead in a world of very alive things and people; but it is part of you, part of the remote thunder of your native cities in the great throbbing struggle of the metropolitan world; and you cannot resist reading it. 'In a discussion on the radiation hazard Professor Blank gave his opinion that we were on the brink of a concentration so near to the danger mark that our children would run the risk of serious radioactive contamination. . . .'

The thunder suddenly comes in like a herd of enraged elephants charging from all sides at once. Peace is shattered. The flowering tree is now infinitely futile and infinitely precious because you see its blossom wither and shrivel; and the imagined children in the wombs of those girls reaping are secretly deforming in their genes, while their mothers laugh for the joy of them.

You cannot escape. You can't do anything, even in panic, to tear down the walls of the prison nor to quiet the echo of a blast which releases its slow corrosion of death. It is the twentieth-century jungle fear.

And standing there in the sweet countryside in the Kandyan hills I sometimes knew I was the only one in the landscape who realized this. I felt great sorrow. I, knowing the threat, was almost powerless, and they, unknowing. . . . Only a tiny fraction of one per cent of the world knows that for the first time in history the future of *all* the rest is about as certain as the toss of a coin.

The fact that we may destroy ourselves, and that if we do it will be a very tiny tragedy in the vast cosmos, makes life around you a bit more poignant and if anything more absorbingly interesting. Kandy and its district are the repository of medieval Ceylon, so rich in its ways and its art and in the special beauty of its people that many years could pass you by as you wandered from village to village amongst the people and the temples, and in the almost inexhaustible store of myth and folklore which even today are an important part of life there. This richness, this patrimony, is passing. It must pass just as the context of ancient Greece passed when logic developed from analogy. But I should like to have been in Kandy fifty years ago when the worst medieval abuses had been taken away but while the fecund mythology was still wedded to the people. For in the same way that the pantheon of Greece was the product of Minoan and Mycenaean beliefs married to the entirely different forms of the original Achaeans from the north, so that of Ceylon before the Western logic of the twentieth century deflated it was a compound of Hindu religion admixed with aboriginal animism, with a deep penetration of Buddhism worked through it. That Ceylon was (and is still) regarded as one of the great centres of world Buddhism need not blind you to the fact that the practice has exceedingly little to do with the original doctrines of the Buddha as far as they have been handed down. What matters is the moulding of history by the beliefs as they evolved in the country.

To carry the analogy a fraction further is tempting—to recall the epics of Homer as repositories of the garbled history of a race and equate them (not of course on the poetic level but on the plane of documentation) with the Mahavamsa of Ceylon, the substance of which takes you back five centuries B.C. and does for Ceylon prehistory what the possibly mythical Homer did for the prehistory of the Eastern Mediterranean. But perhaps it would be fairer to compare the earlier parts of the Mahavamsa to the Shu Ching of the Chou Dynasty in China with which its beginning is almost contemporary; neither is literature in the strict sense, but both are anthropologically and historically of immense value.

G

The Mahavamsa is a chronicle of the high politics and religion of Ceylon from mythological times down to the mid-eighteenth century. Its existence was known to a mere handful of priests in the early nineteenth century, but it was an English Civil Servant, George Turnour, who found the key to its mystical verse—a *tika* or prose explanation as valuable as the Rosetta stone in the translation of Egyptian hieroglyphics. With this he set about the task of learning Pali in which the chronicle is written, and of which there were no grammars at that time, and translating the million words of the documents. George Turnour has never publicly been given his due. Without his intellectual courage and his patient sparetime labour in the Kachcheri at Ratnapura where he was stationed in 1826 we should be tremendously ignorant of what happened in Ceylon and southern India during much of the time covered by the manuscripts. Archaeological discovery continues to prove the accuracy in general terms, and often in particulars, too, of the Mahavamsa—and therefore, too, of the translation of George Turnour, much in the way that digging in the rubbish heaps of the Middle East has confirmed the existence of a series of Trojan cities and other Homeric details.

Kandy is a quiet place, the Ceylon equivalent of Canterbury. In its midst is the Temple of the Tooth rising sedately by the artificial lake. In the morning, as you breakfast in the hotel nearby, the sound of drums and the reedy *horanova* for the morning offering, and the incense, float out from the temple adding a medieval spice to prosaic ham and eggs with which you are automatically served. Set in its wooded hills the town sleeps for most of the year, gathered to itself in a loop of the biggest river in Ceylon, the slow Mahavelli Ganga, full of myth and temples, of Hindu *devales* and old kingly buildings of the last Sinhalese dynasty. All the country for fifty miles around is low hills terraced with small paddy-fields, studded with gem-like villages—some not yet on any road and tucked away in the gentle folds of the country. It is Ceylon at its softest and sweetest and most characteristic, with flowering trees in many a garden and avenue, with work-elephants plodding along the roads at midday to have their bath in the river, with the ancient crafts of lacquer-work and weaving and brasswork continuing in the villages at the unhurried pace of the past. There is even a small village industry in one place which consists of grinding a special quartz into lenses for spectacles; and you can still find men to carve wood with the facility of the medieval craftsmen, though the stone-masons have vanished and the rebuilding of the Temple of the Tooth had to be accomplished in its finer points by imported Indian masons.

There are villages out of the past so near to Kandy that you could walk to them in a day, villages which in their Oriental way are as untouched by the twentieth century as English villages of the time of Goldsmith. And it is this flavour of the seventeenth century or the eighteenth that percolates into your feelings when you walk for miles through wood and paddy with a man whom you found mending the road and who offered to take you to the place you mentioned. He just put down his tools and came; and now as he leads the way he is suddenly struck with the feeling that he ought not to be appearing in this village, which is not his own, in his old working clothes. But we persuade him that it will be all right and that he will be able to say that he had to bring us otherwise how should we have found the place? And he is satisfied.

Maybe there are twenty houses in Hapuwile, and it was still as noon amongst them. Everyone was out in the fields. Only an old man sat alone on his porch, benign and absorbed, with a soft fleece of beard that fell over his naked chest. His face was remarkably unlined, the eyes, when he looked up, small for a Sinhalese and still clear. He welcomed us and sent for chairs which I would rather have done without (and later abandoned) and for a boy to run up a tree and cut some coconuts for a fresh drink for us. I gave him my message of goodwill from some friends of mine in Kandy who had used some of his lacquer-work, and he nodded sagely.

'You come not to see me,' he remarked, unsmiling, 'but to see how I make the lacquer. I will show you.'

And as he worked we conversed. I discovered that he was a wit whose arrows of thought struck accurately into the heart of people, including myself. He was lacquering a bowl all the time, turning it over a pot of hot charcoal like a Kashmir *kangri* to keep the resinous colours soft. One of his fingers had a nail more than an inch long which he used in applying fine strings of *lac* in intricate patterns, making here and there fine absolutely parallel lines with it, freehand. I offered him a cigarette in a lull as he began to look for a colour which his wife had mislaid.

He took two from the packet. 'You see how they stick to my long nail,' he said.

I wondered that he didn't break the nail in the ordinary course of daily life.

'Oh! By now it is as strong as a knife. Tempered with life, it is. I could probably take your head off with it very easily.'

His wife was a querulous old woman with a mouth gory with the stains of betel. She brought out all sorts of scrolls and medals, even a silver turnip watch which had been awarded to her husband for his work at various times since 1882—the date on the earliest certificate I saw.

I asked him if he ever worked in the fields when he was younger.

'Why should I? I have always had this to do. Why should I work in the fields?' It astonished him that I should think such a thing.

'Shame!' he shouted to the children who were beginning to crowd round us. 'Do you want to suffocate our guests? See! You have even frightened away the bird that was sitting on the tree.'

The children drew back in awe of his flashing eyes and his fine angry head. The tree was at least fifty yards away. I congratulated him on his eyesight.

'I do not need spectacles,' he said scornfully. 'I can see to split a hair. If this brother of mine,' who had joined him, 'had one, I would show you.'

I doubted if my own eyesight would last as long.

'Well, you sit up in that electric light all night like a mad one. In any case the young ones aren't made of the same stuff as we were. Even my own brother has lost his hair and wears glasses.'

The brother, a traditionalist, too, showed me his heavy quartz glasses made locally.

When we returned through the ripening paddy I wanted to reward the man who had guided me to the village, but he did not wish to take anything.

In Hapuwile I merely saw the old man and his lacquer, without investigating other conditions, although I suspected several things. But in the following week I spent most of the time in other villages learning about what it is like to live and die there. There is one word above all others which describes the state of Kandyan villages. Land-hunger.

We came to a house clasped in a small valley of the village of Wallala, kissed by the sun, all white and thatched in its compound of hard earth. Back of it was the side of the valley thick with trees and steep, and in front terraces of paddy emerald with rice. A woman came out and, seeing us, went in and brought a chair. A small boy in pitiful clean rags came with her. Her husband was at work somewhere. She dusted the chair for me, and we talked. In this house there lived until a year ago the descendants of a man, her husband's grandfather, who died intestate. His property—the house and the twenty yards of ground on which it stood—was divided by law amongst his five sons. Besides the sons there were three daughters, and two of the sons were married. In all thirteen people lived in the house and not one of them had any land to cultivate. The woman was the wife of one of the sons. The members of the family eked out some sort of existence by doing work on the roads or helping in other peoples' harvests as opportunity offered. But in the depths of the country there is very little casual labour.

This household was not unique in the scattered village of Wallala. Among the 275 families in the village there are 108 who have no land at all. Most of the land is owned by three rich families and of the remainder most is owned in plots of one and a half or two acres.

There was no solution for this family except a drift into the towns and a chance taken in the cut-throat over-crowding of city life which they were individually ill-equipped to cope with. What in fact happened was that all the family, with the exception of the brother who was this woman's husband, went off to the resettlement scheme in Gal Oya where they were given virgin land reclaimed from jungle.

I saw many many people like this around Kandy, living out their lives with courage in a paradise which was only seeming. Living, when you came to investigate the circumstances of their lives, in a small hell to which, like country people elsewhere, they are affectionately attached. They are reluctant to move away even when near to starvation. They move eventually with terrible sorrow and a rending of the family which is more painful to them than we of the West can readily imagine. Even in their poverty there is a courtesy and quiet nobility about them as there was about this woman in her worn-out but clean clothes and in the way she dusted the chair, in her factual statement of their lot. All the dazzling beauty of the country lay around us, but her family even now had scarcely enough to eat.

In Gal Oya later I went to see her relations on their new land.

In revealing contrast that afternoon while I was drinking the contents of a coconut in the house of the young headman of Wallala there came in an agricultural officer who had about him the hopefulness of one who has at least some of the answers to the problems of growing rice in Ceylon. He took me to a village a few miles away where a whole valley was planted with a new type of rice in a scientifically controlled way. Coming to the edge of this village you suddenly see an amphitheatre of paddy fields which belong to the community, where the tall heavy rice is spread as rich and fine as a carpet in the sun. The villagers joined us and eagerly showed me the twenty and thirty strong yellow stalks in every single planting. Each bunch was set at the regulation ten inches apart and the rows were as straight as Chinese rice rows. Here for the first time in Ceylon I saw healthy vigorous paddy like any normal field in China where rice is tended with as much care as babies, and always has been. Here the villagers had been galvanized out of their sweet rural futility which is the charming and disastrous condition of peasant Ceylon when it comes to consecutive effort, and they were suddenly growing a double-weight crop from the identical area of land.

At first thought it would seem that this new rice and this way of growing and tending it would catch on like fire everywhere in the surrounding country. But it does not. The effort of weeding and general daily work entailed is too arduous for the farmers. They prefer individually to grow enough to subsist on while they take their cherished leisure in the shade and talk and argue endlessly about local politics and local gossip. Having their little plots of land they make very little of them as long as they can exist. It is not hard to do that with a couple of acres of paddy in Ceylon, a vegetable patch, a betel creeper in the garden and an areca palm to grow the nut and a penny or two for the lime that goes with both for a good satisfying chew. Sometimes I was tempted myself to give up all this ugly struggle in the world and cultivate a patch of paddy and that sweet futility of the villager. To have felt that is to have begun to understand them. Of course they are lazy! But so are we when we can afford to be. Of course they live in a little unreality of their own, which is peculiarly vital none the less. But don't most of us in the West slip off from work with relief and sink ourselves in some vital little bit of unreality like a detective story, or a row of high-kicking girls, or in alcoholic oblivion? We are merely more economically pressed than the man with a couple of acres of paddy. The man without fields (also his wife) will work as long as he needs, to get the same monetary basic. But he is not bourgeois and has very little craving for the outward show that dazzles the neighbours. So when he can eat he lays off.

There are so many entrancing things in the Kandy country. Nearly all take you with a shock of 'flavour', with the poetry of pastoral living. In a village where I had been looking at a co-operative run, surprisingly, by a priest, I came unnoticed to a square between several houses. Four of the village women were sitting round a big flat drum on the ground, chanting and tapping out with their long fingers a complicated rhythm. When their work is done they amuse themselves with this *rabana*, exchanging in song the local gossip and local rhymes. At night a candle is placed under the drum to keep the skin taut and to give a little soft flattering light. But they were shy and I had to sit down with them and persuade them to continue. And then they stuck to their folksongs and cut out the gossip.

Hidden in such villages are masterpieces of art and architecture. At Embekke we were guided by a boy in a green sarong and a red head-tie. He was loafing by the roadside as we stopped, and when I spoke to him offered to take me to the village.

'Do many people come here after the time of the pilgrimage?'

'Not many,' he replied. 'But the other day some white men came in a big funny car like an aeroplane.'

Further questions made it obvious that they were Americans.

He took us a mile or two through a valley where boys were ploughing thigh-deep in liquid mud with water buffalo yoked to wooden ploughs. And then we found the village. At the end of the street was a temple in the Kandyan style, its wooden pillars carved with dancers and elephants and homely scenes—but superbly carved. Tucked away in a room was a metal peacock used in ceremonies, fierce and so utterly bird of bird that it might take off before your eyes. And in the courtyard is a granary belonging to the temple, a double cube under one red-tiled roof, sitting on wooden beams whose ends cross at the corners and rest on huge smooth boulders the shape of curling stones. In all the architecture of Ceylon after the decay of the classic forms of the remoter past the granary here is perhaps the most unconscious and at the same time the most astonishingly perfect building. In its basic form a Ceylonese Le Corbusier might find a starting point for a

new classicism in local architecture. Alas, we have instead given them the
monstrous concrete box and the suburban semi-detached. The lowest
common denominator. . . .

One could dwell longer on the flavour of rural Kandy, much as you
could live there for a long time absorbed and happy. There is a web of
interests and of problems—local myths and folktales, seldom-performed
dancing, the vampire of rural indebtedness whereby most peasants are in
the hands of the local moneylenders, the whole story of the origins and
growth of Kandyan architecture, the history of temples and the mingling
of Buddha with Siva and Vishnu and Ganesh and other Hindu deities, the
relics of animism and pantheism in the religious thought, the local medicine,
the marriage and death, and other ceremonies connected with New Year and
the festival of lights. One day driving in the country lanes we passed a pair
of white-garbed men beating tambourines outside a house where some
women and children were standing at their door watching. I got down and
walked back to them. They were singing. One was obviously blind. When
I came nearer the second and younger of the two noticed me and sang a
couplet.

'There is a white man with his Sinhalese friend who has come to see
us, there they are standing not far off.'

The blind man who was singing the responses then replied with a
couplet of conventional blessings on us. His companion, turning him in our
direction, went on with another line or two about how we were from the
car down the road and were making pictures of them. And again the blind
man sang his blessings on our heads. So they alternated in lively fashion,
beating the tambourines all the time. There was something very moving
about them, partly the combination of sight and blindness teamed to earn
a living, partly the spontaneity of their descriptions as we all stood in the
middle of that country road with the pink flowering trees fanning their
delicate boughs over our heads.

But the Kandy country is subject for a book in itself, a book that a man
with a warm heart like the villagers, and their fundamental simplicity and
softness of response, might write—if he had, like them, plenty of time.

Sometimes you feel you want to fulminate against the rich temples and
indolent ignorant priests fat with land and cynical with power. But they will
pass with the passing of other things. The whole system is much too complicated to treat in a small space with the justice it deserves. On a mid-morning at the temple of Lankatillaka on top of its great grey rock I chanced on
one of the less iniquitous aspects of priestly ways. The priests were going
out to lunch at the house of a villager who annually offered this feast to
them as a gift to the Buddha in commemoration for a son killed on this day
ten years before. The children of the house came to escort the six or seven
priests and to carry the temple banners. They set off from the shade of the

trees around the temple with the banners ahead. The priests, all saffron in their robes, put up their umbrellas as soon as they left the trees and came into direct sun, and in their midst were the relics from the temple which always accompany them, carried by a couple of lay retainers under a red canopy. Two men played drum and flute and they all wended their way in single file down to the valley of paddy amid the glorious greens of the scenery. I followed them and caught them up as they came to the house, where the banners were laid against the wall and the drummer and flautist played on as the priests had their feet washed by the people of the house before they went in for the feast.

My friends in Kandy who offered a meal to the priests of the temple near their garden gates had the reply in politest terms that the priests had no opportunity to come for about three months as they were fully booked for meals during that time.

There are also hungry people in Kandy.


Kandy is *kande*, a hill, short for *kande uda pass rate*—the five villages of the hilltops. On one of those hills sits, precariously, a house where I have stayed and been reassured that I have not overstayed my welcome. It is a funny rambling decaying house up the end of a precipitous and landsliding drive and at the foot of an earth cliff that threatened to fall in the rains (and later did, burying the bathrooms). The garden is hard to define as to boundaries because it has reverted to sub-jungle in which a flower-show of orchids show their enchantments to the air. The poinsettias are all aflame with vermilion leaf, and mosses and plants with purpled velvet leaves lurk in shady corners amongst flowering shrubs bowered in a multitude of fine trees. The porch has many damp photographs by my friend Henri Cartier-Bresson, and others of lesser renown, of George de Silva, the late husband of my hostess, a one-time cabinet minister before Independence came. George de Silva is something of a legend in Ceylon—a man of low caste who rose to be Minister of Health. But it is his house which is a legend for me.

In the garden you will probably find Ahchay, a wisp of a Tamil woman who used to wear a saffron sari. The circumference of both her ears is pierced many times and filled with chunks of raw gold which are part of her life savings, her capital. The other part, I always suspected, she carries in that screw of cloth hanging from the waist folds of the sari. She will be squatting weeding, in the casual preoccupation of her life. Last time I came she crept into the room wearing a royal blue sari, and peered at me out of the web of wrinkles that is her face. She is one of the indelible people, the people who come complete and eternally vivid to the mind's eye. She is at least seventy-five. I teased her that in her new sari she was looking more

ravishing than ever. And she went off in a spasm of suppressed chuckles.
Between Ahchay and Mrs. de Silva there is a lifetime of acquaintance, affection—and feud. Ahchay is a squabbler by nature and nothing is ever right
for her and she is not shy of showing it in a spate of querulous words. So
they go on with their little wordy feud year to year.

The de Silvas are a remarkable family. They attract some remarkable
people round them. Almost all the famous people who have come to Ceylon
over the past twenty years or so have been to this house. By now it must be
well documented. Beryl de Zoete, the greatest authority on Oriental dance,
has many amusing anecdotes of the house and the family in her evocative
book on Ceylon. She, like myself, used it as a base from time to time, and
despite the intellectual qualities of Mrs. de Silva, and Minette her daughter,
who is the only woman architect in Ceylon, you are not far from Beryl de
Zoete's Dance and Magic Drama in this house. The temple at the bottom of
the garden is seldom still and the many daily observances of the faith come
up through the wild greenery in thrust upon thrust of drums and monody
of chanting.

John, the cook, was very upset one time because he had lost his medal,
or it had, as he averred, been stolen. It upset him so much that he threatened
to leave. But David Lean, who was making the film *The Bridge over the
River Kwai* in Ceylon at the time, bought him another in a shop in Colombo.
And now he is all right again.

Last time I was there Minette told me the sad story of the cow. It was a
venerable animal and, in charge of the gardener, supplied milk for many a
year. But it developed some sort of ulcer on its side, and sickened; and
nothing seemed to help it. Somehow or other they decided to

'. . . give it Nigel's medicine,' Minette told me. 'You remember you had
a bottle of stuff when you had dysentery a few years ago. Well, that has
been sitting on a shelf ever since and we referred to it as Nigel's medicine,
and somehow it never got thrown away. So we gave it to the cow.'

Minette paused. 'The cow died soon after that.'

When I was unable to conceal my amusement at this, Minette saw the
humour of the situation. She had not seen it before.

It is like that in Ceylon. Life is a series of little accidents. You forget,
even sophisticated people forget, to regularize things so that unpremeditated
oddities don't happen. Ahchay has seldom weeded the part of the garden
that needed it most, but instead some other bit that took her strange fancy
when she went out. The gardener sometimes cuts down the wrong tree, and
in expiation chops it up in a frenzy for firewood for the next year or so. A
giant orchid seven feet tall with many stalks sprung from the ground and
suddenly sprouted dozens of leopard-spotted miraculous flowers, and
people came from miles around to inspect it. But it was only by chance that
someone took photographs of this botanical curiosity. And a snake stupidly

died in the waste pipe from the bath. It had never happened to anyone before and caused a major plumbing catastrophe, but it happened in the de Silva house.

There is one other delight in the house. The cooking. Mrs. de Silva must be one of the best cooks in the world. In combination with John she produces banquets of Ceylon food that I have never had the luck to eat anywhere else in the island. In a stay of three weeks I ate almost every meal in the house and never had the same dish twice. Even an invalid diet, from which in Europe the invalid recoils and gets better so as to relinquish the ordeal, in the hands of Mrs. de Silva proved a continual gastronomic excitement.

It was from these meals that we tore ourselves away night after night for a whole week to go into Kandy and see the Perahera.

The Esala Dalada Perahera—the Procession of the Sacred Tooth in the Eight Lunar Month, to give it its full title—happens in that sublime month between the monsoons when the country is radiant with a mature beauty. The *esala* trees are in full bloom and the weather is settled, the earth burgeoning with growth; even the aromatic air seems blissfully laden with the alchemicals of life. It is because of this magic perhaps that *esala* is the month of festivals. There is none that rivals the Perahera in splendour, in its summation of the people's essence. Naturally such a consummate thing cannot happen all of a sudden, it has to be a culmination. And for many nights before the great week the several temples of the city are having their prepartory ceremonies and little Peraheras in their own precincts.

But then one night the processions of the four great *devales* or temples of the Buddhist faith join together, and with them, at their head, is the super-sacred procession of the Dalada Maligawa—the Temple of the Tooth. The origins of the Perahera are purely pious, and at least two thousand years old, but in its present form it dates back no further than 1775 when the king, Kirti Sri, an unusually devout Buddhist who brought Siamese monks to reorganize the rituals and observances in Ceylon, probably put the Perahera in its present order.

Night after night for a whole week the procession forms in the streets of Kandy. Night after night it makes its circuit which gets longer and longer as more and more elephants are brought in and more and more people crowd the velvet shadows of the pavements under the trees by Kandy's lake; until the blazing climax of the ultimate night.

From the Octagon of the Temple of the Tooth the privileged look down on the scene as the kaleidoscope of event and light is made ready. The perforated walls of the Temple are filled with lights, the streets are blazing with torches and sections of the procession are joining up. We wait while the great Tusker—which bears the casket of the Tooth, set 'with 168 beautiful, costly, resplendent, diamonds, 171 topazes . . . 585 blue sapphires and

4,880 rubies; also 788 pearls'—is draped with silver and gold cloth, his tusks cased in gold sheaths, blue lights in his ears and the silver and gold howdah with the Tooth casket placed on his back. Naked stalwarts with whips stand ready, circled in torches; the long file of banner-bearers, the Temple Registrar carrying the *ola* leaf manuscripts of the records, the musicians —drummers with the *tammatamma* and *magul bere* drums, the frightening *kombuwa* horn, the conches and the sad oboe called *nalawa*. Then the Chief of the Royal Elephant Stables on his beast, and rank on rank of elephants caparisoned like sagacious kings.

The great Tusker is ready at last and, shimmering and twinkling, lurching as if he felt the sea of acclamation on his sides, he lumbers down from the court of the Temple and over the moat, and takes his place in the road. The whip-crackers launch a volley and the drums pound and rattle their incitement, the horn bellows and the conches bray above the plaint of the *nalawa*: and in a wild dazzle and fire of exoticism the great Perahera moves off.

It is the last night. More than a hundred elephants are swaying through the streets, hundreds of drummers and hundreds of Kandyan dancers posturing in their white skirts and naked gold-mailed chests with grotesque metal hats and shoulder-caps of gold, bells at their ankles, and hard heels turning on the cobbles. White sheets of cloth are laid on the ground before the great Tusker so that he may not step in the dirt, and handfuls of jasmine are thrown over his head. Behind him walks the lay custodian of the Tooth in his costume of a Kandyan chief, all muslin and vermilion cloth and amethysts and a pincushion hat. All is sound and the flames of torches and the urgent interrupted rhythms of the music, the bulk of elephants tinselled in delicacy, the virility of dancers frothed with skirts; silver lances and banners spring in sheaves from the backs of elephants whose beady eyes look out from holes in their rich coats and whose earthquake backs are huddled with men and boys.

Standing in the Octagon it is an evocative panorama, a train of movement and light and mysticism and grace moving and shattering the night, exotic and barbarous; and highly civilized. The eyes of the crowd shine in the torchlight and children dance with the dancers; the frenzy is perfectly controlled. The naked giants with the whips stride on and the cortège shambles slowly and chromatically into the mystic enjoyment of the people. All this night in the air, and the cicada trees of Kandy, tinkling elephant bells twinkle in your ears like sound stars. And all the little world of this island has been once more shaken to its spiritual foundations with the drama of the natural that is the supernatural.

You linger in Kandy country. You go back to places for sheer love of them, for delight in the villagers, in the medieval frescoes, in the jumble of boutiques (as they call the rows of little open shops). It is hard to leave, for this is like a nursery in which grown people who have not lost their childish wonder live and cry and play and work out their tiny span of life. For all its harshness in detail, it has a flavour of simple honesty. That it is a society outliving its time a little, decaying and distressful, is somehow balanced by its physical beauty. Women, incarnations of dark beauty, move on the roads with pots of water or babies rested on the hip, or wash in water-moulded saris in the rivers; men sit in the dream of the end of days chewing betel at their doors and carmining the road with squirts of the juice; young men soap their naked gold skins at the wells at sundown and pour buckets of water on their heads, their lank black hair streaming over their faces. Nowhere except in Indonesia is physical beauty so subtly joined with abundance of country charm. And nowhere but in these two countries does resilience and genius of vitality in people so spring to the mind as well as to the eye.

But there is a plant, one of the family of camellias, called tea which is grown in the hills of Ceylon, not far from Kandy, and constitutes the island's major source of income. It is a pity about tea. No duller plant could be imagined, and when every hillside is covered with it like a dull green carpet of somewhat open but orderly pile, it becomes for me a blight. The merest weed of the hedgerows takes on the fascination of an orchid by comparison. The sight of tea in those vast areas reminded me of that tide of tea which washes over England in bland and unexciting waves as often as possible every day of life. Both, in their different places, are unavoidable and, statistically, important. Not only tea but planters too produce a yawn in me, and a vague feeling that it was a pity their adolescence never developed into maturity.

These things apart—and setting aside the chill of the nights in the hills, the bleak English suburbia of that spa renowned throughout the English East and called Nuwara Eliya (pronounced, in typical British deformation, 'Newrailya')—the tea country is interesting. It used to be coffee until the fungus disease of the coffee plant which spread disastrously over the whole of the island's one quarter million acres of plantation in 1877 wiped out the industry in a few years. In desperation the planters turned to tea. And in every way except intellectually they have never looked back; neither has the economy of the island since it thereby gained a source of steady income outstripping all the others.

There are now over half a million acres of tea. A vast amount of research and experimentation has been carried out in every aspect of its cultivation, health, optimum environment, processing, packing. And at its best the industry is a thoroughly well-run machine in which the unsuspecting camellia is bred and nurtured and then plucked, not of its flowers, but of its tender leaves, as soon as the long-suffering bush sprouts them.

The pluckers are almost all Tamils—Ceylon Tamils, those who after several generations are native to Ceylon, and Indian Tamils who are not. When you drive through the tea country almost everyone is Tamil, dark with a Hindu look, the women in jangling colours which suit their skin and studded like Ahchay with gold in nose and ear. Perhaps partly because of this inane plucking they have to do all year round they are completely different from the equivalent Ceylonese people. They have about them the feeling of the strife of India which is not the feeling of Ceylon, and they are the only large coherently Hindu community in the island, with the special feeling of Hindu communities—a feeling as special as that of Polish people in their clubs in London. They are living in Ceylon, but they are first Tamils and Hindus and a long way after that Ceylonese. The shrines on the side of the roads are purely Hindu—to Ganesh and Siva. The tea-pluckers live in 'lines' sometimes squalid and sometimes newly built by the owners of the plantations in the effort to quiet the recalcitrance of the Tamil workers. I had the impression that the Tamils on the estates are treated reasonably well now, and that they are a thorn in the estate management's flesh because they are such poor workers. So I suspected that there was a long time when they were slave-driven, and that they remember this time. I may be wrong. Maybe the Tamils in the tea are special and not like other Tamils (in Jaffna, for instance) who work as well as any other people.

The tea in Ceylon, ten years after Independence, is still largely owned by British interests, a state of affairs which the left wing of local thought and government is continually nibbling with tiresome regulations. They are a little stupid in their methods, for those estates which are owned and run by Ceylonese produce rather inferior tea as a whole. The British there, who still have the hangover of imperial confidence—not to say imperial preference—roundly assure you that the death of the industry will rapidly supervene if they are pushed out. This is probably so, but given suitable incentives from the Government of Ceylon they would stay and could over a period be made to teach and train Ceylonese to their own admittedly high standards of production efficiency. The British say this is not possible (which is mere paternalism) and I think it would be quite difficult. But the British feel, as is the British imperial wont in these shabby days, that this is the last ditch. The Roman Governors of the empire in the east Mediterranean at the end of things must have felt rather like this. It is an aspect of historical process, dreary but inevitable. In twenty years there will either be no English planter in Ceylon, or there will be many and all of them will be paid employees of the Ceylon Government. It isn't really so unfair—Britain has made a tidy whack out of Ceylon tea for sixty or seventy years. Doubtless we have spent it by now but that doesn't mean we never had it.

You travel in tea for what seems a long way through hills that must once have been splendid jungle. The home-made green rug is dotted on hilltops here and there (for tea likes to be dry when it is processed) with aseptic factories whose insides smell like a newly opened packet of tea, and where Tamil women sort the finer grades by removing the impurities with small suction pipes. Upstairs in the draught of fans the mangled leaves are losing the desired amount of water-content on canvas tats. Never had a substance so sterile as the final product such exotic names! Flowery Orange Pekoe, Flowery Pekoe, Broken Pekoe. The origin of the words is obscure. Where the Orange comes from is unknown, and the Pekoe is probably Chinese *pak ho* meaning 'white down', which occurs on the buds and some immature leaves. Over half a million people out of Ceylon's total population of about ten millions are directly employed in getting one quarter of the world's total production of tea outside China. Every day they are out in the tea plucking that 'flush', as the 'two leaves and a bud' is called, filling their baskets with it and getting their pay accordingly. The pay is not bad by Oriental standards, but I wouldn't change places with one of them. I would, perhaps, with a paddy-farmer somewhere near Kandy.

In Badulla to the east, when we had shaken the tea-dust from our wheels, we were met by a young man, the son of a Kandyan chief, called Tissa Pilimatalauwe. In Kandy you can see his ancestor's name on the document which surrendered the sovereignty of Ceylon to the English in 1815, not in gold-dust-ink like that of a Kandyan king when he signed a letter to a Portuguese official, but in old faded ink of the ordinary sort. Tissa arrived from Colombo by train (which was six hours late) rather black about the chin, crumpled in clothes and spirit as one is after such a catastrophe. I took him in the jeep lent to me by an amiable Government Agent to the Rest House for a midday breakfast. He brought my accumulated mail from other parts of the world with its content of outlandish doings like taking the usual bus to work, a holiday in Cornwall, and the monsoon summer in England. I read while he bathed and ate and began to release his spirit into the stretches of Ceylon and time that were before us in the next few weeks.

Tissa has the right combination of sensuous seriousness and serious sensuousness, together with an intellect and a frankness which make it profitable to be with him for weeks on end all day and every day. You end up feeling extremely indebted to him in the best sort of way. In other words you have made a good friend. He is moreover perfectly bi-lingual with a command of nuance which make him a remarkable interpreter; and a love of people which make him if possible even better.

My luck in Ceylon was good. Even drivers of cars such as Said the Muslim, who had been with me every day in Kandy and all the way through the hills of tea, seemed to respond to someone who really wanted to find out how it was in Ceylon. Said called up all his accumulated information about the region of Kandy and as we drove along volunteered little bits of it, enquired of his friends for this or that village ceremony or craft so that I should be able to see it. I was sorry to see him go at Badulla and looked at the rangy Sinhalese who was to drive my jeep with distrust. He had that kind of bare face whose skin seems too tight for the bones. His eyes seemed to be pulled open, and the nose in a colder climate would be raw and Scots Highland. He wore a powder-blue sarong, oilmarked, hanging in desolate crushed folds about the stilt-like length of his legs; and he chewed betel which, kept under his tongue, thickened his reluctant speech.

The jeep stocked with supplies for a week, we set off from Badulla in good style and left behind the muddled town and the unpleasant Rest House in its vibrating centre. The rest houses of Ceylon, some owned by the Government and some by local authorities, are generally pleasantly situated, but there are some, like that in Badulla next to the petrol engine which makes the local electricity, which are torture to sleep in. Gradually we left the remains of the tea country and came northwards through Bibile to a dry lightly jungled zone where the land was panting for the north-east monsoon, not due for a few weeks yet. Our objective was a settlement of Veddah people called Dambane, not marked on any map I had been able to find, lying many miles to the west of the road along a track.

At the turn-off point we were to meet a friend of Tissa's, referred to as Vijay, who was the officer in charge of the backward communities in this whole area. But here our well-laid plans broke down. There was no Vijay. The boutique keeper on the corner proffered a crumpled note which asked us to go on our own to Dambane as Vijay was otherwise detained. It was by now very late afternoon but we decided to press on north to Maha Oya where Vijay lived, and talk to him. I wanted to have a word about the Veddahs before I blundered into their midst all gauche and unaware except for what I had read in books. We found him lying in a chair on the rudi- mentary verandah of his house clad in a lurid sarong, with one Michael, a Sinhalese health officer, who shared the accommodation with him. After half an hour's discussion we started off again back down the road we had come and turned off towards Dambane with instructions that the local postmaster would help us to see the settlement on the following day. The fly in Vijay's ointment was a certain German woman doctor of sociology who had been foisted on him at the last minute, and he intended to take her to another Veddah village to please her, having been warned that I did not care to join forces with other unknown travellers when I was working.

By the time we reached the track it was dark and John the driver was muttering about not having enough petrol in the tank—the nearest supply was thirty miles away. But we bumbled into the jungle at a good five miles an hour, the headlights sweeping up and down from treetops to rockhard ruts of mud as we bounced along. John had once been to Dambane before and thought he knew the way, but quite forgivably lost himself at a clearing where the rudiments of track spread out and pointed in no particular direction. We chose at random what proved to be the wrong exit and had to retrace after a half-hour and try again. Luck put us on the right way and we went on, once or twice stopping to remove a fallen tree blocking the road. It became eerie, the air made of a thick impenetrable felt, lit now and then by the ruby eyes of nightjars on the ground.

Suddenly a grey shape of an animal plunged across our bows and there was an impact as its hindquarters hit the mudguard. Its antlers revealed it as a sambur, alarmed probably that we were coming between it and its mate. We stopped and the crashing of the undergrowth told us of its flight head-long through the jungle. Then silence fell again. Like that of a great city at middle night when a figured base of sound underlines the silence.

We drove on and on. There was nothing; only choking trees arching over the track with confusion of stems and trunks and bush all grey in the rearing headlights, and a particulate fog of insect life like plankton of the air, through which we moved clumsily as a whale engulfing them.

Then a clearing, a rough wooden hut, the sweep of the lights revealing a monstrous concrete well; a shout in a language I did not recognize, the laughing faces of two youths, one with an earthenware pot in his arm. Dambane. The house of a surveyor who had gone away, his two servant boys who had stayed. Giggling a little, they inspected me and the tins of meat and packets of biscuits and processed cheese which they unloaded. Both phenomena were equally interesting. It was too dark to wash at the well so they flurried until they set an enamel basin outside the door of the kitchen so they could watch me wash while they made ready a curry. It was hot and the insects thickened around the lamp on the table, singeing their wings and writhing on the bare wood amongst the tins and plastic tumblers of water. An occasional terror of animal attack struck with its sound of tearing foliage and scream of anguish through the squares of night in the window-holes. A calendar on the wall indicated the previous month, and a day was ringed with a girl's name written beside it. It was absurd to feel you were in a lost place, divided from the rest of the organized world, for this was not really so. Analyse the content of the feeling and it is fundamentally compounded of no telephone, no organized services, no channel of easy touch with the things we have built in our civilization to make it easier for us—doctors, shops, trains, lighting, sources of immediate help. Most of the world still lives like this, minus help.

It was too hot and still for even a sheet in bed (had a sheet existed). But at dawn I woke shivering and pulled a coverlet over me. By breakfast it was again hot and airless, and the voices of strange people came from the direction of the well: the well which was almost dry. I watched the women put down their buckets and wait for many minutes until they were full enough to be worth raising. John was lolling in the jeep, accompanied by one of the servants who was catcalling to the women as they walked off with their pots of water swaying on ample hips.

'The way you walk,' he jibed, 'you'll spill the lot anyway before you get home! Put the pot down and come over to me. Come on!'

But they just giggled and slowly went off.

Kaluapu came as we finished breakfast and were sitting in sarongs over Nescafé, the boys fiddling with the old porcelain water-filter in the corner. He is reputed to be the oldest, and also one of the very few pure Veddahs left. He came in and stood in the doorway with his axe carried on his shoulder so that the haft hung down his back. Leonine features and a very long straight nose, hair that is different from the other races of Ceylon, marked him as a Veddah. He had distinction even when he accepted some biscuits and talked with his mouth full. He asked us to come with him one day's journey to a rocky place where he was going to collect wild honey. But when this proved impossible for me he contented himself by saying he would show me how he could find honey in the trees.

The postmaster arrived at this point, a Sinhalese in flappy shorts and a khaki shirt with a kind of beret like a green bun on his head. He married a Veddah girl and spoke the language, this being his qualification for guiding me in the territory, as it was for his appointment to a post office which never received a letter. (But after all in England we have an office of the Lord High Admiral who does not exist.)

Kaluapu took us into the jungle and demonstrated with the efficiency and promptitude of one selling the idea how to find honey cached by very tiny bees within the integument of creepers and other growth that invests all the larger trees. Then he led us to the village of Dambane.

The Veddahs are at heart still a pre-agricultural community. Only within this century have efforts to settle them been partially successful, and they have intermarried with Sinhalese. But even the mingling of Sinhalese agricultural blood has not entirely tamed them, and when settled nicely enough the men tend to disappear for days or weeks on end into the jungle, hunting and gathering honey, on a paleolithic spree of freedom. Thus does a child run wild on a country holiday when the constraint of a house and rooms and clean fingers irks its nature. The cultivation is dry zone *chena* on whose blackened acres pathetic little sprouts of maize are grown between the charcoaled branches of fallen trees. First crops are always bumper but succeeding ones tail off until, after four years of harvest, the rich soil is exhausted, partly by the cultivation and partly by erosion in the wet season. The northern plains of Ceylon get fifty to sixty inches of rain, but it all comes at once and the rest of the year is an agony of parched earth. Two

H

thousand years ago this problem was solved, not by Veddahs but by the great dynasties of the north who built those ancient cities I saw later on.

The staple diet of Veddahs is the multicoloured seed from a small plant, *kurakkan*, which they mix wet with some maize flour and eat in a paste which has no flavour at all unless you put some herbs or spices with it. But by the end of the dry season there is no food left except tapioca. They make no provision for this recurrent calamity and hope that by hunting they can get by. A little fishing goes on in stagnant pools here and there, and there are traps of the most simple kind for jungle fowl. Occasionally they summon energy to make a pit with sharp up-pointing stakes in it to lure the sambur to his death-fall.

Kaluapu and all the older Veddahs had beards, and their bodies, naked except for a strip of dirty cloth, showed a curious skin affection which covered them in pale greyish patches about the size of an old-fashioned threepenny-piece and which irritated so that they scratched perpetually. With the alteration in the balance of natural wild life caused by incursions of other people who have cut jungle and built roads, and by the destroying edges of a sharp and hurtful civilization not their own, the Veddah dependence on hunting is now unreal; but so, largely, is their paltry attempt at agricultural economy. They marry at fourteen or so and most families have four or five surviving children to feed.

I wandered about with Kaluapu amongst their pitiful little huts of stakes and bark thatched any old way with any old leaves or grass that come to hand. There is nothing in the interiors. A raised platform of stakes holds a dirty muddle of pots and clothing such as they have, and perhaps a small bottle of honey. The clothing is a novelty, a result of flood relief gifts, and proudly worn by some until it is in tatters. It is hard to raise a smile in them after the age of childhood, which is not surprising when you see whole families lying listless and semi-starving. The wife will be standing with a baby at her hip—a baby that makes no sound or motion—while the other children are sprawled on the dirt floor gazing at you without interest. Flies swarm over them all and the still heat soaks through them and there is no water for the withering maize in the ashes of the *chena*. They were maybe better in their original condition, for despite the work of conscientious people like Vijay all this is alien and undigested for the Veddahs. The great owl that sits in the trees beside them and the monkeys that swarm in droves through the branches are nearer to their hearts than the maize.

I stayed at Dambane a little to try to understand them. But it is hard to get through the crust of very primitive minds. The women when they menstruate are put in the little kennel structures that are beside each house until the function is over, and the vile scrofulous dogs wander about howling and maddened by flies in their diseased coats. The peerless sky duns you all day and there is absolutely nothing for a Veddah to do.

All this time the postmaster and Tissa were following me and sitting about with me and the Veddahs and translating all their words—the incoherent outpouring of a starved old man and the cries of the children and the answers of listless women when I talked to them. Tissa is a photographer, still an amateur but with a beginning flight of the kind of genius that makes some men with a camera tell the suffering and joy of people on a bit of film. He already knew of men like Cartier-Bresson and was happy when I could tell him something from much conversation with that great photographer. In those few weeks we travelled together there was an unending, and to me most rewarding, dialogue between us on people and living, and, implicitly, the means of recording this knowledge and feeling in the manner of the photo-journalist who is something of poet and something of humanity at the same time. To see the expanding of such a person as Tissa in contact with ideas which he innately understood was for me an exciting experience in itself.

Returning to Maha Oya we stayed with Vijay and Michael. There was no water or sanitation in the house—the lavatory having dissolved in the last rains and returned to earth—but there was food of an excellence that was surprising in a bachelor household, and good talk. We washed at sundown at the well down the road and slept well on truckle beds which they insisted in vacating in our favour. Fortunately it was the dry season and the holes in the roof let in nothing more serious than pencils of sunlight. When it rains they put up a tent in the garden and sleep there. The Government would not repair the house, for some reason or other.

Vijay took me to Pollebedde. Only thirty miles distant from the hopelessness of Dambane, Pollebedde was a more advanced Veddah community and showed the beginnings of hope. Here with government financial aid they have built themselves new houses, planted good maize and pineapples, plantains, saffron, coconuts. Here as in Dambane there is an old tank being restored in its original design as reservoir, the work dawdling to completion. The difference between the two places is amazing. In Pollebedde it is not too difficult to raise a smile, and some of the families are doing well as cultivators—though others have a father who still takes his periodic release in the jungle. The community was rapidly approaching the level of agricultural effort and skill of the rest of Ceylon. Admittedly this community was even more intermixed with Sinhalese than the people at Dambane.

Reluctantly we left Vijay and Michael and their excellent hospitality, and John the driver brought us speedily south to a place called Monaragala, which means 'Peacock Rock'. John's pale blue sarong was now a crumpled oily shadow of its former cerulean self, having been slept in and apparently

used for titivating the more delicate parts of the engine of which he was
very mindful. But he very slightly blossomed out as the days went on and
at Monaragala seemed genuinely sorry to depart back to the familiar chores
of his life. He eyed with some deprecation the jeep sent for me by the Gal
Oya Board, and indeed it was not in the mint condition of his own vehicle.
But having four more or less round wheels it served to carry me through
the land between, along new roads slashed wantonly through jungle in
its millennial dream, past quarries at the wayside whose warning signs
always said: 'Beware! Blasting in Progress!'—and it never was when I
passed, though at times we came on a scatter of fragmented rock over the
road. We came through this torn land to the bund or earth dyke of the
Sennenaike Samudra where the huge new tank which is the heart of Gal Oya
is full but still spiked with the dead tentacles of trees submerged beneath
the water. To Inginyagala where the hydro-electric station sits aluminium
and ugly as a gasworks in a country village, and where there is a rest house
that was once the quarters of Americans who built the dam.

   Gal Oya is the biggest of the land reclamation and colonization schemes
in Ceylon. Comparatively easy to tear down jungle with modern machinery
and to find the land at its feet; but then you must water it, and for this
reason a dam is always necessary in a country of seasonal rain. Gal Oya,
on the east coast, is within the dry zone, and the scheme is a modern equivalent in a small way of the achievements of the ancient civilization. A huge
slice of land has been cleared and irrigated, and altogether 100,000 people
have moved into the area either as farmers parcelled out with plots for
paddy and garden, or employees of the Gal Oya Board who are still at work
on further construction or on maintenance, or those opportunists who
have come here as traders and set up haphazard in the valley.

   It is a bold experiment, none the less bold for being small by comparison with the schemes of irrigation and land development which covered
the whole northern half of Ceylon fifteen hundred years ago. To have re-
settled even 100,000 people is an achievement—although a very expensive
one—and to have irrigated 120,000 acres of land is something. In eight
years this triangular stretch of country has changed from thick and almost
uninhabited jungle to one of the largest slices of agricultural land in Ceylon.
One huge and many smaller dams have been built in the manner of the old
ones whose remains can be seen elsewhere.

   All this in answer to the disease of the East—land hunger.

   The Bilinda family, relatives of the landless household at Wallala near
Kandy where I had been, were eventually tracked down in village 20 in
Gal Oya. They were tremendously surprised to be visited by one who had
lately seen their relatives in Wallala, and half apprehensive that I might
have something to do with tax collection or other horrors which they were
probably avoiding in their tiny penniless way. But after a little, when I

had been sitting with them in their house and talking about crops, they were more or less reassured. Especially when I told them how the children in the old village were growing up and mentioned several of their old friends there.

There were nine mouths to feed and four acres of paddy to do it. Various members of the family had gone off elsewhere leaving the father and mother, two girls at school in the village here, two sons (one of whom was married with one child), and a relative. They had a two-room house of the standard pattern built in the valley and had added a room to it. And they had a garden where they grew plantains for sale and the usual crop of spices and vegetables for food. They had bought a cart, and they had one bull, one buffalo, and two female buffaloes, one cow, and a calf which they got for looking after someone else's cattle. The Board had granted them 190 rupees (one rupee is worth about eighteenpence) and they had brought between them 900 rupees from home. With this money they had bought the cart and the bull (300 rupees) and the buffaloes (100 rupees each). The four acres yielded about 120 bushels per crop (only one crop a year yet, since the irrigation was not very good) of which they sold eighty-five bushels at the government-fixed price of twelve rupees a bushel.

'But that is only if we work very hard,' said the father, meaning, I suspect, that they had to work harder in this dry though irrigated zone than in similar fields in Kandy.

'And we have our annual interest to pay to the Board—on the money we have borrowed from them. That is nine rupees.'

Pressed—for he still had a faint suspicion that I was trying to find out things for tax purposes—he admitted that they also got about two or three rupees a month from sale of plantains. So their total money income seemed to be in the region of one thousand rupees a year; to which must be added the crop of eighty-five bushels of paddy consumed and the vegetables grown for home consumption also.

It is not a princely income for nine mouths, but a marked improvement on that from casual labour in Kandy. I asked them about this.

'Life is very difficult here,' the father said. He said it several times before I could get him to be more specific. The whole complex of living in conditions of which he knew nothing until he came here was a little too much for him, though not, I thought, for the younger members of the family.

'There's the pigs that are always trampling the crops. You can't do much about that, can you?'

I said I had heard that they were supposed to watch their fields and even had watch huts built on the site.

'Yes, but you can't watch them always,' he countered.

You could, but it would entail a certain amount of organization and sustained effort amongst the members of the family.

'And there's elephants that simply walk through the fields too.'

The elephant is a creature of habit. If, in the virgin state of Gal Oya, herds were in the habit of taking a certain path to water, they tend still to do so regardless of cultivation, which they ignore. There were many stories of this instinctual behaviour, and in some places fields had eventually been altered to make way for the elephant-tracks.

I sympathized with him on this score.

'And we haven't any proper place to keep the cow, and round the house when you dig a foot into the ground it is all water so we have difficulty in making a proper lavatory. Besides, there are wild boar too. And there's not enough room in the house for us all.'

I asked him more closely about the way they kept a watch in the hut in the fields.

'Well, one of my sons . . .'

'That's me,' said a young man. 'I sleep in the watch hut with my wife. We have no other place.'

So I understood how they found it difficult to keep proper watch. But when I went with them to their fields I saw that they were not very good husbandmen. They complained of the salinity of the ground—an idea proved by the soil research people to be quite unfounded. What they were trying to explain away was their own inefficiency, their own lack of drive that comes of an upbringing in conditions where you don't have to farm assiduously and well. In Kandy if you have land you need not work too hard to eat, and all of these men had been hired hands in such fields, so they had little training either in the continuous nursing of the land or in the pride of ownership which can breed that approach. I saw very well their difficulties, which were partly of temperament and partly those of a simple people divorced from all they had known at home.

'There's nothing specially wrong here,' one of them said, wondering how to say what he meant. 'But it's not our own place like Wallala.'

By the nodding heads of the rest I saw he expressed a general sentiment. They felt lost here. No old ties of village kinship and village backbiting and village knowledge swaddled them in Gal Oya. They were on their own. Their neighbours were from another Kandyan village and the traditional rivalry between village and village prevented them from making common cause between themselves, even in Gal Oya.

There was nothing here that time and living together could not cure. A feeling of community would develop over the years and a new village community would emerge from what was at the moment a mere arbitrary gathering of people and houses. But the point which I suspected and came to see was a broader one. Land hunger. Already they had built another room on the house and already one son and his family were living in the watch hut. In ten years' time when the children were growing up—in a generation at most—there would be land hunger in Gal Oya, in the very place which had been set up to ease land hunger.

This is the core of Ceylon's economic problem. Land hunger, under-employment, a rising birth-rate which one Gal Oya scheme a year would hardly cope with, lack of industrialization, unbalanced trade due to excess of import over export. It is obvious that industrialization alone or in conjunction with increased area of cropping and increased crop yield per acre will not solve the problem. In an island the size of Ceylon there are limits to agricultural and industrial expansion, given the best of governments. The fundamental is birth-rate. In all the East this same problem has to be tackled. In Ceylon almost no one has taken the subject seriously and there is no organized propaganda for population control. Such a campaign would be infinitely more useful and infinitely less expensive either to the present economy or to the future finances of the island than the efforts at resettlement and expansion of agricultural land. There is no reason against, in fact there is every reason for, their going hand in hand. Until that happens there is little hope of a balanced economy. Threatening shadows of race riot and disintegration of the administration due to overcrowding and unemployment with all their attendant ills loom up. Gal Oya threw those thoughts into high relief. I was saddened that they are so totally unregarded in places where they should be actively considered. A few progressive men in various departments of the Government agreed with me, but not many.

Gal Oya is a partial, temporary answer to land hunger. It is a good attempt, combining not only resettlement on a big scale, but the beginnings of industry in a rice mill, workshops, a technical training centre, and many other things. There has even been an attempt to integrate its new economy with the old one of the Moorish villages on the coastal strip by the lagoons stretching north to Batticaloa.

There are many hopeful things in the valley; and beside them, as if to underline the achievement of the new independent state of Ceylon in Gal Oya, there is one little village of six houses, six families, surviving on its edge.

It is more easy to be touched by poverty than by prosperity. It is easier to portray the evils of society than it is to show the good, the hopeful; but it is pertinent to show both, especially when they are physically contiguous, because they explain each other.

Manthottama was the name of this little survival, and when Tissa and I came to its six decrepit huts there was a woman being led between them by the hand. Her guide was her daughter about seven years old. The woman was blind. A young man of twenty was washing himself outside the smallest of the huts. He had come back to the village from elsewhere so as to support his grandmother who was otherwise without means of livelihood. He had casual work on the dam-building a few miles away. Grandma crept out of the hut, hitching her old cloth over her strops of breasts. She was very old and trembling, rheumy, almost blind, and very deaf. She peered at us and mumbled.

We went and talked to a woman with a lovely face who sat on her door-step with her children. She was shy because she did not have enough clothes to cover herself properly and she held the scrim of her sari over her breasts.

'She talks with a Kandyan accent,' Tissa said in surprise. He asked her how that was.

'They say that our people were driven from Kandy by the British long ago,' she said. 'But I don't know.'

This was probably the suppression of the Kandyan rising of 1848. These people had been pushed further and further in their search for a living. Their names, according to Tissa, were all good Kandyan names and he was intensely interested in them.

Grandma had come over to us and sat in the dirt craning her head to hear what passed. I spent an hour or two there with Tissa who interpreted so excellently that I began to feel the place as well as to know about it. And as we went away we passed the remains of some ancient buildings and a ruin of a small dagoba. And here was the house and preaching-hall of good brick that this poor village had built for a priest to save their souls. And the slab of stone by the Bo tree was filled with temple flowers which they had put there in the morning. The tragic futility of their offering of flowers and brick and mortar began to anger me. And then I could not be angry. I remembered it was their only hope.

There is a place called Lahugala not far from Gal Oya where those elephants which stroll through the crops of the valley congregate in the late afternoon to drink in an old tank. For an hour or so one day I watched them ambling out of the jungle with their cows and babies knee-deep in the lush grass at the edges, the adults throwing mud and grass over the backs of their young, occasionally lifting their trunks to sniff the air. And then we left along a mud track like solidified rough sea, bouncing in the jeep.

Suddenly there was a noise like a trumpet blown very near the ear. I looked back through the open flaps of the vehicle. All I could see was elephant—a great tusked monster of an elephant with little angry eyes, thundering along and threshing his trunk up and down.

Someone yelled: 'Step on it!' And the driver, who by this time had realized what was happening behind his back, did his best. We lurched forward, everyone holding on desperately to avoid being knocked out by the roof of the bucketing jeep. A few moments and the danger passed, not because we were gaining on the elephant but because he gave up the chase. He lumbered to a halt and stood in the middle of the track bellowing after us, frustrated like a big angry child. We got out of the jeep to look at him, and in a moment he sheered off and the sound of his crashing through the undergrowth echoed in the evening air.

It was my day for elephants. Just as we came to the bund of the Sennenaike Samudra near the rest-house we almost bumped into the hindquarters of another one. But this was an amiable monster jogging along the road like an old gentleman out for his evening stroll, and we crawled behind him till he chose to turn off the road.

After a week in Gal Oya I thought I had seen what was necessary, and Tissa and I planned a day off. We drove to the coast and north through that dry seaside zone where the people are nearly all Moors, past Batticaloa where we collected a Moorish lawyer friend of Tissa, and on to Kalkudah. At night we arrived. There was verandah, bed, oil lamp, a disappointing meal (in a country where food is a continual delight); and the wash of the waves across a spectral shore. We sat with a bottle of arrack and good talk turning on the question of love. I began to recount how the concept seemed to have started in Europe with the Troubadours and knightly chivalry, and how it had gone on supported by its peculiar myth, neither continuous with, nor taking much from, the older and less shattering opinions of the Greeks on the same subject. It was now, I said dogmatically, one of the eroding worms in the rose, instead of the rose itself. The East, more practical in the matter, nearer always to the village even in sophistication, talks of love and indeed thinks of it, too, but hardly ever with the fundamentalist attitude of the West. Tissa agreed with me in this and so did his friend the lawyer. They seemed to reserve a romantic corner for the emotion of love, small but definite. The rest was practicality.

It is a subject that makes people talk on, and arrack abets the passing of time, so we woke late on the next day.

The elephant does not live at Kalkudah. It is poor sandy scruffy ground beyond the extravagant set of shore and outrigger and palm; and only the coconut with its leeklike roots finds enough sustenance to raise a golliwog head seventy feet in the air and sprout hard nuts. There is no jungle there, or not now. 'And no love,' said the traveller to me, 'not now. . . .' And the elephant strolls far away and only the monkeys and the colour-discords of birds inhabit the air you breathe there; and a few hundred outcast dogs with eczema and lice, scratching in a passion of itch the long hot days, yowling at Oriental ghosts that their jangled dreams conjure in the singing night.

'After all this time,' said the traveller in a soft voice, 'after all this and all that I'm still in love, in a way.'

'But you're in love with the memory.'

'Even the memory.' He stopped as though his tongue had stiffened with the trance of memory. 'Is love ever unreal like a goddess? Again? The second time?'

'I don't know. I'm concerned with people. I fall in love with people, or

I don't fall in love with people. But *people*—with minds, and with hands that need to be washed every so often.'

'And I with them too,' he said. 'And with much more. With their hopes and mine.'

'And with your memories, apparently. Oh, yes. But don't fall in love with goddesses, even if they seem like goddesses.' I tried to rile him a little.

'Are you in love?' asked the traveller quietly. I thought he was talking to himself. Perhaps he was. 'Are you in love?' he repeated almost inaudibly. And he answered in a minute while an ugly cloud approached the falling sun over the tree by the place where Youssuf the little boy fed the bearded monkeys with their black reptilian faces. 'Yes. Always,' he mused.

I wanted to scoff. But he said, 'It never happens twice.'

Despite the I and the sheets of fine steel that armoured me, I was ludicrously moved by him. Mistrustful but moved.

'Can't it happen again?' I asked.

He looked at me. I had seen those slightly hazed eyes before. Mirrors and travellers have them. 'Ask yourself that question.'

Not now. This first foot on a wild exotic shore made satisfaction too strong to be closed out of mind with the mind's eye that dissects and strips down the mechanism like a mechanic a fine complete roaring engine.

'Come to the point with me,' I said to stop him from talking, and to stop me from thinking and spoiling the wild blood and pulse of muscle and soul that are tuned like the car ready to race from the pits round the track of—of just flesh. I admitted it as we started slowly along the beach to the film-set point where the corny palms of the Orient were standing between sand and sky. All at once I was disillusioned; their little, known, soothing, ordinarinesses wore suddenly thin. They were dull as photographed palms against technicolor sunsets with saronged girls wiggling their sterile hips.

'Why should you be thinking those dead thoughts?' the traveller wanted to know.

'Because it is beautiful in its banality. It has a *rasa* of boredom and de-light,' I said perversely. 'Because in places where life is simple, life is laid bare for you and you wonder about it instead of worrying like a terrier at the trimmings of things.'

'And that is salutary?'

'I don't know. It's disgusting, a real sell, a pig in a gilded poke. . . . People are wonderful, I like them how they are.'

'I like palms,' he said. And maybe he mocked me.

We wandered along. The thin edge of the sea lipped in and out covering his toes but not his ankles from minute to the next. He seemed unconscious of it, and of the grey shadows of crabs which flitted substance-less up to the tide-mark as we disturbed them at the exact margin of the waves. What did they do there, moistening their fine cantilever legs in the tepid froth of saline?

For they lived in the sand and on the smooth floor of their own particular atmosphere, the liquid liquid sea; while we drew in our gaseous atmosphere and inflated our lungs with the means of troubled thought and sometime youth and sometime love.

The traveller hiked on a pace ahead, a pace towards the sea from me. If I could just drown his lambent fire of love's nostalgic scenes. . . . Drown the Troubadour of the twentieth century.

In the seventeenth century an Englishman, Robert Knox, was held captive in Ceylon for many years, with several others from his ship, by the King of Kandy. Knox eventually escaped and, sensible man, wrote his story on the way back to England. Fleeing from the thrall of that monarch, Knox stumbled accidentally on Anuradhapura

which is not so much a single town as a territory. It is a vast plain . . . in the midst whereof is a lake, not natural, but made by art, as other ponds in the country, to serve them to water their corn grounds. . . . Here and there by the side of the river is a world of hewn stone pillars standing upright, and other heaps of hewn stones, which I suppose formerly were buildings. And in three or four places are the ruins of bridges of stone; some remains of them yet standing on stone pillars. In many places are points built out into the river like wharfs, all of them stone; which I suppose have been built for Kings to sit upon for pleasure.

From Jaffna, the Tamil city in the north, which is a south Indian place in feeling and appearance, and where the pre-monsoon aridity makes you gasp for water, you travel south by train: suitably regaled with discussion on the race riots incited by a ridiculous government and resulting in those burned temples and roofless shops in the north and elsewhere. From the intense vigour and commerce of the Jaffna area you come through that plain which was once, in the old days of the dynastic kings, a boundless paddy-field watered by many of those tanks that Knox described, and laced with a circulatory system of canals ingeniously engineered. More than a thousand years ago all this was done, the jungle cleared on a scale in comparison to which Gal Oya today is a mere nibble. The great flat land prospered, and fattened with rice; and paid its iniquitous tithe to the temples and kings and the thousands of Buddhist monks proliferating in the access of piety which in that millennium was the driving force of this civilization.

There could not help, under such circumstances, but be a flowering of art. In fact there came a period of immaculate classicism in architecture which has not been surpassed since in the non-Chinese East, except perhaps at Angkor. Here, at Anuradhapura, occasionally at Polonnarhua to the south and at Mihintale, lie the great statements, the stately periods of Buddhist architecture and sculpture:

Like some tall palm the mystic fabric sprung.
Majestic silence.

That is it. Majestic silence. At the sacred Bo tree, grown from a sprig of that original tree under which the Buddha attained his enlightenment, Knox's world of hewn stone sentinals the ground for ten miles in every direction, carved, ordered, integrated with its sculpture; and now pulling at the strings of deepest peace in you like any other masterpiece of art. Yet this is no isolated temple but a great city, an area as large as central London.

It is a strange beguiling place, the stone forest of its pillars growing half in and half out of real jungle, monkeys chattering in the remains of glorious temples, and the river twisting in the midst of all. The three great tanks surround it, more important than armed might in the hey-day of the city, and, haphazard, a higgledy modern town has gathered in the midst of the old. But the old city was a city of ten thousand monks: only monks. No domestic habitation has survived in all Ceylon from the great age, only temples and religious precincts. The huge dagobas, or stupas, rise even now, after two thousand years, over the heads of everything else, shaped like the breasts of the earth-mother, each entombing a relic of the Buddha. One, Ruanvelisaya, has been badly restored, but the others brood over the land, their solid millions of bricks crumbling and lightly furred with small trees, their bases cluttered with little landslides of brick fallen on the flat pavings of hewn stone. Here and there are *pokunas*, sunken baking pools lined with stone, proportioned with mastery, and carved. Everywhere outcropping rocks like giant pebbles are incised with slots for the tethering of ancient walls.

There is a place called the King's Pleasure Gardens, a fanciful name, where a natural declivity by the bund of a tank has been used to make a pattern of bathing pools and walks and places where you can sit and wonder about the genius of those north Indian people who conquered Ceylon in the fifth century B.C. In the thousand years or more that followed the establishment of Anuradhapura there was a long moment of truth when they looked into the eyes of the Buddha and were somehow cleansed of pettiness—not in daily life but in their expression of the universe which is their architecture. They took the dull plain and made it a prayer, an invocation, a manifest of their faith. They did it with extraordinary dignity, relieving the coolness of straight lines with subtle carving, softening the exact curve of dagobas with an irregularity not in the geometry book; and, above all, landscaping with a virtuosity seldom equalled—perhaps never surpassed on such a scale. The King's Pleasure Garden, whatever it may have been, where—imagine it a moment—water flowed in channels under delicate trees between low-walled walks and at the feet of boulders on whose tops rested small pavilions; and the privileged ones bathed away the heat of the day in those screened pools where water splashed over carved stone before alcoves inhabited by the serenity of the Buddha himself. Beyond, seen from the pavilions, the city of hewn stone resounded to its contemplative silence, and further still the plain fattened with rice whose tithe upkept all this splendour and, initially, even made its bones.

Wander where you will on the grass in Anuradhapura, for miles and miles, and there are stones: fallen pillars with foliaged capitols on their thin shafts; noble half-dozens of steps balustered with carving, each riser supported by a row of little fat *ganas*, leading now to nothing at all but a view of other such places a few yards away. Even in decay the ancient genius for landscaping falls happily on the mind.

Anuradhapura is classical Buddhist. The purity of the Parthenon and of its serene sculptured friezes is there in an Eastern form. The low-relief elephants which gambol on the stone face emerging from an artificial pool, and the great *naga*, the many-hooded cobra, emerging imperiously from another pool at Mihintale, state no less authoritatively than the dignity of ruined temples and the bulges of the dagobas that a golden age of art came to this place, and stayed a little time before it went elsewhere. The incarnate stone of Ceylon Buddhas confirms this greatness.

In the surrounding jungle much more is hidden. Twenty or thirty miles of track menaced by wandering elephant and rootling bears—testimony to whose ferocity can be seen on the scarred faces and mangled shoulders of a few inhabitants—brings you, through a cloud of no less ferocious elephant-flies, through lagoons of smelling *carapincha* and past the fresh turds of elephants and the raw holes of the bears who recently searched there for grubs, to Tantirimale.

People had heard of Tantirimale, when I asked about it. Only one man we could find had been there many years ago. There was a track, he thought. You might get a jeep through, maybe. With axes and sweat we did. And at each stop to clear fallen trees or bush battered down by elephants, the flies, those inch-long terrors, closed in, roaring in their excitement at our smell. We eyed the fresh brown earth in the bear-holes and the fresh droppings of elephants, listened for the alarm of the jungle at the movement of great beasts. And the track narrowed until we were pushing our way through; and the great hands of the jungle gripped us. The feeling that they might crush grew as we went deeper and deeper in.

We came to the place where the trees ended and an elephant-coloured escarpment of rock rose up from the jungle, all bare and exposed. We climbed the slope of it, feeling it might have a trunk to swing round and grip us and cast us away over the tops of trees into the dens of gnashing bears. But it did not. We reached the top of the giant outcrop where, to all horizons, the jungle spread like a rugged carpet, tree ousting tree for a place in the sun.

There is a flight of steps hewn in the rock at Tantirimale, steps which end in a riser half-done, and begin at the feet of a seated Buddha carved from the same rock. Beside him on either hand are carved, incised, scratched on the rock the several stages of his attendant figures which the workmen of those early days never finished. They broke off in the midst, like that last step, half-done, one day: and their work was never resumed. It rests there under the fire of the setting sun each evening, high above the anarchic kingdom of the trees, frequented by strolling bears and stained by birds and the lichen of time. There is a dark magic about the place, a quiet that seems to be about to break, an eternal moment when the long perfection of the place seems as though it might collapse in some unimaginable chaos and annihilate you; when, perhaps, the vegetable kingdom might swallow you all up and take on once more its prehistoric primacy.

In the evening we walked amongst the ruins of Anuradhapura after the enormous red sun had hung a moment between the black breasts of the dagobas and then gone down. The buildings took on their former shape, and a few human forms, half seen in the dark, peopled them again as if it were two thousand years ago.

A girl passed with passionate face between pillars, with silent feet, with a flutter of sari, with a glint of eye. The grasses moved surreptitiously against one another and the little straw hut where someone's uncle sold coloured sweet drinks in the day was closed and warm-dusty-smelling in the air: and shut with its sagging door. The carved figures on the guardstones at the shelves of stairways almost moved at their millennial posts, easing those perfect limbs and tilting their heads in the funny way the Sinhalese do when they are about to talk to you. There was no rice-field here for the traveller to wait by, no anticipation of passionate adventure, no soft breast to pillow his ache on, no soft word to ease him: unless it was the imagined rice of the great days or the breasts of the great mother brooding over the trees or the passionate remembrance of this little bit of human efflorescence in the incomprehensible stretch of time.

The traveller, wayward and partial as we are, impressible like putty or sculptor's clay, did not care to abandon, as we left Ceylon, the outworn attitude of his love from former days. He just recorded his last impression of that masterly impress of the hand that made the temples of Ceylon.

> Come let us sit in the ruined city
> now, as the carmine rose of sun
> lingers like a flower on melted gold
> down the furnace of the passionate sky.

Come let us wander in the strong streets
of this forgotten place where plant is eating stone
where the glance of an impulsive rose
is carved on the lintel of a roomless door
leading through dusk of time to dawn of life.

Come let us touch the fingered feet
of that Buddha sitting between the black and the red
between stone and fire between earth and sky
inward with immaculate calm of eye.

Come let us die the passionate death
now, as the trump of violent day
echoes irresolute in dusk:

Come die with day amid those muted
columns of stone still cooling like skin
now, beside the yearning temple
whose face like a breath befalls the evening air:

Come let us walk in the fading light,
come, on those dual sadnesses, descend
into the cave of interregnum which is night;
come taste the wine of splendour's end.

For—
all this was once a noon, an age
powering with its heat the abandon of men,
towering in stone like a lithic wish
sprung from their hands, flowering:

Come touch your face to flowering stone
put feet on the soft solidity of step,
and fingers—caress that perfect cameo
of rose, and eye explore this moulded shadow
the deeps of that intaglio.—No bone
of you but tingles for their truth.

But the eye beyond the portico of stone
the plangent rose descending the hour
the death embalming the time
of day when noon struck fire struck soul—
this moment comes to burial;
the eye will soon pass the lip of the world
and drown down in the universe of night.

Shall we now linger by the classical façade
whose spasm of beauty ebbs into dark
as life bleeds away in trickling tears?
Dare we wait the moment of aubade?

Come!
We turn. There is a child
playing with an ancient stone
on which is carved a god, a doll
the size of his hand.
We stand. He smiles.
He has made a pattern with his finger
in the sand. . . .

# IV. Singapore and Malaya

BY NOW we were very far away and long ago from home so that Europe no longer seemed real in letters from friends or in the paragraphs of sometime papers that blew across our tracks. Increasingly those missives and those newspapers seemed even foreign, because we felt we knew more about tropic than about temperate zones of the world. Like an evolving animal whose environment is reflected in the colour of its coat, we were taking on the colour of the tropical world in our mental skin. It is then you can begin to see the English, the Europeans (but especially the English since they are your own people), in the way you see a tribe in unfamiliar terrain. You watch them with your mental eye as you watch the people of a tribe, with the curious objectivity of a zoologist observing the activities of an ant-hill. That marauding party of Anglo-French fighter ants, which Eden sent out, went to Suez about this time, and through the giant lens of the air between them and us we watched their sortie with involved detachment. Even watching ants, you tend to take sides. . . .

The traveller was still shaken a little, still a bit sore about love and about the way he had been forced once more in Ceylon to adjust the wopsical hat of his old romanticism in the face of a different love that came from closer knowing. He was now suspended between rival concepts of love and life—his old one, and his new one which was too new and too uncomfortable to wear unconsciously. And in the world of countries we were both suspended, blowing here and there like a wind-sock in the blasts of many cultures, none of which seemed at the moment very much our own. Hard to swallow the fact that it is difficult to know very much about any world at all—much, at least, that is significant. Everything played fast and loose with us and all the seven varieties of *rasa* replaced each other with kaleidoscopic bewilderment in our churning heads.

Now we were making our way to another little island in our past, to Singapore where at the surrender of the Japanese in the Second World War we had encountered our first Chinese civilization and rubbed emotional and intellectual noses with our first Chinese people. Between

Ceylon and Singapore stretched the sea and the sky, now cloven by many ships and ranging planes, now no longer the fabulous ocean and air peopled with serpents and fright-started birds that it was to the Chinese, Arab, Portuguese, and British travellers in ancient times—as indeed it was to us ten years ago on that first pilgrimage to the Orient. Mechanization means little sometimes.

Coming to Singapore was like returning to a house, a village, which used to be home. You know it will have changed, but the heart doesn't really concede the fact and is surprised, even shocked, to find the house redecorated and the village transformed. The heart is a romantic and a nostalgist. People who live in houses and villages are not.

These ten years, unsuspected by the world outside, and by me, Singapore had been metabolizing, as places do, on its little leaf of an island, with the secret inevitability of a chrysalis. Now it was nearly a butterfly. Nearly. That is the idiocy of nostalgia: and the madness of travel; whose madness is the madness of music. Both have time, which is rhythm; and quality, which is melody like the metamorphosis of places. So the traveller is maddened—like the Greek grasshopper 'mad with music'. Not with the music of nineteenth-century torrential symphonies; but with something like an extended fugue whose multiple voices enter and re-enter many times, often in strange guises, tangling in ordered fashion like the strands on a loom that is singing and clicking and agitating with its own peculiar music. Metamorphosis is the music of mankind. You must not object if now and then it grates a little on the nostalgic ear. It may even be working towards resolution. At this moment in our travels we were not much of that conviction.

The music peculiar to Singapore is commerce. Not for one moment could the city exist without the flux of merchandise which pours from the ships of all the world into its quays and godowns, and which later pours out again like those printed notes on pages which come from the instruments of the orchestra, all sorted out and parcelled up in miraculous ways, the several surprising subjects of the fugue, to slip off into the responding wants of other Oriental places. Singapore is the shop on the busiest corner of the East.

When I first saw the place the shop had been closed by the Japanese for three whole years, its sources of merchandise and its customers had vanished. The city was almost but not quite a commercial corpse, and the owners were just returning to view the remains. The task of reviving it, of breathing commercial life into its lungs, was just beginning. One thing was sure: even revived, the body would never be quite the same. Resurrection always means a new sort of life. As months passed this new, harder, more closely competitive life began to shape. But at first, except amongst the returning bosses who had everything to gain by energy, and amongst the Chinese importers, there was a vast apathy in the people. Years of malnutrition, worse

than that suffered by the poorest section of the population in the old pros-
perous days, took their toll. Moreover, the whole machinery of commerce
had fallen to bits and there was at first no way of earning a living to buy
food, which was scarce and dear. Even the buildings, decaying with neglect
and high humidity, reflected accurately the picture of people in and around
them, their faces peeling and crumbling, the faces of old broken people. The
arrival of the Forces all clean and well-equipped and rough and homesick,
swarming and fornicating over the town, injected a little money and a little
spurious gaiety; and those who benefited most from the money and the
gaiety were those who least required help.

The rest, the mass of little stringy old men who cart crates on their
sallow shoulders, the innumerable patient black-clothed women with faces
of tired madonnas, the wan children, lived on in their misery and their
overcrowding, as people do in adversity, with a marvellous animal strength
of will. The river was stinking and choked with broken junks and sampans
on which whole families live out their lives; and past whose rotten planks
the slow foetid water bore inflated corpses of Japanese soldiers, dogs,
suicides, and the victims of old scores paid off in the immunity of troubled
times. They moved slowly downstream; the money moved slower, down
from the pockets of those who had it to those who had not, who lived in
the boats.

Then we had to help the thousands of Dutch who poured in from the
prison camps of Java and Sumatra—men and women and children broken
and beaten and diseased. Whatever their crimes in Indonesia their punishment was too heavy for the onlooker to bear. And the hell of Changi Jail
along by the beach to the east of Singapore debouched its prisoners in scenes
of Dachau and Belsen. To the classic infernos of Germany and its medieval
prototypes were added slow tortures of endemic Oriental disease, flesh
which crept with putrefaction made more horrible in the burning sun. That
terrible gamut of disease peculiar to the old Orient rampaged through those
places, through Changi and through the camps of Sumatra. Tuberculosis,
malaria, beri-beri, pellagra, untreated syphilis eating away the organs
and collapsing spines, huge abscesses, hookworm, and the rest. The babies,
collected by an English woman I knew who had just rejoined her Chinese
husband, died in ones and twos in the makeshift hospital which she set up
of her own volition; and nothing we could do with vitamins and nourish-
ment and antibiotics would save them from the legacy of their mothers'
starvation pregnancy. Those milkless mothers, sinking down here and there
with a terrible listlessness, dying in the waiting-room.

In the centre of the island some of us found a small prison camp where
for some reason the Japanese were holding a dozen Javanese—since at
first there were not sufficient Allied personnel the Japs were allowed to
control minor matters. Here in a few huts those dozen men lay in their own

dirt with the lice and pests crawling over them and drinking their blood
and their sweat. They lay, too weak to crawl to the door where the Japs
had left bowls of rice ('... in accordance with the International Regulations',
as they said). Until a few days before, one man had been able to get to the
food and had brought it to the others. But when he could not, the rice
mounted up at the door, eaten by ants and stray animals.

When we blew a tyre one day on the road between the city and the north
of the island my Malay driver halted a column of Japanese who were marching past in charge of their own officer and made them hold up the back of the
car in the broiling sun until he had changed the wheel. He removed a wrist-
watch from the officer. I did not stop him. His insignificant vengeance found
its response in me though I had not suffered.

During the year that followed a semblance of order was put on Singapore
and that slow-moving money filtered down a little and more people had
enough to eat. And then I left for the strange shores of England against my
own will. The divided heart is a heart hard to live with. You can't live with
people for long without being bound to them. It hardly matters what people
they are, but with a natural liking for Oriental people it is harder still to
leave them. I also became fond of the Japanese, years later, in their own
country.

All that was long ago and as far away as the England which now in its
turn again felt strange round the great corner of the world. Singapore was
nearly a butterfly, shimmering with the gilt of commerce but bearing underneath its surface the seeds of another larva. Each place, each way of life has
its own horrors. The easements of commerce make a few more to point the
indigenous ones. But the Chinese with their incredible resilience seemed in
the intervening years to have effaced the suffering of the past. Or almost, if
you discount a legacy of stunted teenagers. No amount of resilience makes
up for childhood starvation.

Despite the disappearance of that brutal instrument of human torture,
the rickshaw, the streets of Singapore are still humming and cluttered with
life. In the back streets and alleys of the purely Chinese parts still lurks the
recognizable Orient of the past. Scenes of Conrad and Loti and Maugham,
of those eulogistic essays in childhood books called *The Story of Sea Trade*
and *The Romance of Rubber*, together with the vulgar superficialities of the
travelogue, lie before you, engulf you: and finally absorb you. But so do
other things. The bulgy cars of bulgy Chinese with bulgy bank balances
are not to be seen in those back streets, nor the sedate Morris of the European
with pale wife, and their paler children climbing on the back seats. The
stylish European frocks of Chinese office girls and daughters of the Chinese
bourgeoisie here give way to the traditional *cheong sam* and to the shiny
black cotton jacket and half-mast pants that flap round the shanks of men
and women of the working class. Those European perms and stiletto heels

of the city, of elegant restaurants and dance-halls, that smooth American-style suiting in pale blue or pale grey are here the wooden sandal that clip-clops along the cobbles, the cheap cotton, the dragged-back hair with bun at the nape of the neck, the singlet and Chinese trousers of the coolies. Close buildings festooned with poles of washing push people together, and hundreds of stalls decrease even further the space to live and to walk in. The crowded space is laced with radios screeching Chinese songs and jazz, streetcalls, lorries as decrepit as the British Empire, with bicycle bells and the honking of horns as futile as cries of Commonwealth. Add the unceasing fugue of the alleged nine tones of Cantonese conversation, which—like Italian—is sensuous enough in its music for continuous rhetoric—and the darting of a thousand children from every door and pavement, and the feeling is warm and passionate and squalid and lovable. You've got to be tough there.

There is a wealthy Chinese in Singapore who has a lavatory made of *cloissonné* and there are many beautiful Chinese women who have forgotten how to speak their own tongue. They live outside the town in gardens of fragrant flowers with many remnants of Ming and Ching art or expensive collections of European furniture imported at great cost. They have their society which is not without interest, a society on European-Singapore lines with cocktail parties and bridge and neurosis and children who are a problem because they have too much money and little incentive to work. The traveller and I are always in and always outside this society—in it because we have to do some of its chores not to be churlish, and out because we can't keep it up. But eating in the streets at the stalls is another matter. The sight of a Chinese family having a spree meal there—all nine of them and seven below the age of ten, and they probably have no lavatory at all—is more warming to those cockles of the divided heart than all elegant society. Like the French and Italians, even ordinary Chinese are fussy about what food they eat and how well it is prepared, and some of the best food in Singapore in the lower price range is to be found in the streets where you sit on a worn old stool at an uneven table and order a course from several different stalls according to the speciality of each. The traffic is threshing and jiggling past and the call-girls from the house over the way are tripping down in their tight dresses slit to the hip and going off in tri-shaws to an evening's assignment. The noise is deafening. But that is no detriment for Chinese who have always had to live in it. Like those naked electric-light bulbs under which they often sleep blissfully, a fusillade of sound registers not at all on the Chinese mental ear. And the family tucks into savoury bowls of this and that and picks its teeth with contented relish after all is done.

Amid the resurgence of commerce, with its new bridges and modern buildings, air-conditioned offices and inner-spring mattresses in the new Singapore, Chinese life remains curiously and doggedly Chinese. Even the well-to-do, when they have a big dinner, have a Chinese one for preference. And in the wilderness of glass and aluminium façades, flashing neons, and self-service stores, there resides unchanged the boisterous vitality of the Chinese—and occasionally the slow beauty of Malays (for the Malay is a reluctant convert to the West and in danger of being effaced by the Chinese who, in commercial things, are not). It would be better for European children if they had a book called *The Romance of Chinese Vitality*, that extra-ordinary quality quietly throbbing now as it has for thousands of terrible years through some of the worst social and environmental terrors in the East. Such a book would give a truer picture of what goes on and what to expect. Chinese vitality is like the Chinese face which wears better than others in its spare fleshly rhythm until the moment when it suddenly shatters —as if you had dropped a Sung pot—and fragments into old age. Then, shard-like, the face is almost indestructible, carrying within itself (for the perspicacious observer) the history of its genesis and times. Their vitality makes them an appalling people—baffling in their indefatigability; and a lovable people because their human warmth is never far away. The imagina-tion of the Elizabethans and the slogging qualities of Germans are built into tight Chinese bodies and combined with a sort of frenetic intellectuality which is and was the gift of neither European type.

Malays are sweeter. Both men and women. Graceful, slow, full of eye, sensuously limbed. Like their language which has one word for a light flapping sound (*menggelepek*), and another for a heavier flapping as of a sail (*menggelepak*), and such delightful onomatopoeia as *sepui-sepui* for the sound of a soft breeze—they are poetic in a sensuous way. Whereas Chinese are bounding and cacophonous, and, when poetic, entirely philosophical. (Only a tiny fraction of Chinese poetry deals with romantic love.) There is a whole world of difference between Confucian and Taoist ways, and those of the Prophet of Islam when he strays into the Far East.

Suddenly you realize it is good to be back.

'You will gather,' wrote the traveller one day in Singapore when we had been eating in the market and were back in the flat and he felt the urge to share his emotion with distant and doubtfully comprehending friends, 'You will gather that I'm happy.'

I paused for the astonishment of that friend who would open the letter in the winter of the soul in England. Travellers are distrait, excited, sufferers from ennui—seldom happy.

This must be the first time [he went on], apart from the hedonism of com-mencing love affairs, that it has happened in an at all peaceful way. Maugham, who was a curiously deficient sage when it came to talking about the East, got it right for the wrong reasons when he suggested that the East was a *must* for the young. In his day you lived as a European, and even nowadays you ought to. But we live with Chinese and wonder about Europeans like a coolie wonders if the same female appendages lie hidden beneath that ravishing European dress as a great lady of a great Tuan walks past from her car. Today I see you as a young woman of your tribe!—You in England! Perhaps I'm East-struck like a kid in London or Paris might be stage-struck. Like him I neither know nor care. Suddenly I'm intensely released and sane and airborne on a Chinese air. . . . All Europe is a collection of barbaric tribes!

'But why here, specially? And now?' I asked him. 'When we have known all this before in our other life ten years ago?'

He thought for a moment. 'We have a cage in our place. I feel I have escaped, almost. Escaped from the English rot.'

'And what about the Chinese rot they have for a cage here?'

'Yes, yes, of course. But it's a village cage not so chromium as ours and not so . . . You can see how the English middle class *are* here. More clearly than at home. You can see their . . . lack of values except money—when they rule here—how they rule in England, how all the Western world is a middle-class cage.'

'And,' I suggested, 'you can see the downright sweated labour exacted by the Chinese middle class here.'

'Yes. But . . .'

'Do you actually know what you are feeling?'

'Not exactly. But I seem to know the Chinese better than the English I know at home.'

'And by inference you diagnose the Home English malady better?'

'Something like that,' he said. 'It's not ready for your analysis yet.'

And I couldn't get another word out of him. You mustn't squeeze the juice from an orange till it's ripe.

Then we took off for Borneo. When we came back to Singapore there was an emergency. The desire to escape from one of those cages the traveller was talking about—the cage of sweated labour in its polite modern forms—had stilled the throb of the city. The throb of its commerce at least. Not the throb of its heart. Officially described as tense, the situation was electric. In curfew we drove from the airport in a bus with wire-mesh windows— 'Another cage—they are all supposed to protect,' said the traveller sardonically—through police barriers, through deserted streets where neons flashed on the rain-soaked paving with not an eye but ours to see them. The police grip took us all protectively by the throat of our lives and shook us a little with controlled love. And took the opportunity—as the Chinese had ten years ago in troubled times—to pay off with a death-kiss a few old scores of its love.

It was all over in a week or so and things returned, superficially, to normal. But we sensed the bomb that is smouldering under the cage of Singapore. The fuses of all those bombs under remnants of Empires are getting shorter since China, since apartheid, since the long dream of the Orient has come to waking.

But back again in Singapore there was suddenly time between this and the next thing, and nothing much to do but enjoy the place and the people, and live in a leisurely way. Staying with Fong, a solid Cantonese only very superficially Westernized, it was easy to enjoy life. Everyone else in the block of flats is enjoying his and hers. The mornings are enlivened by the desperate efforts of a young girl on holiday from school to learn the art of the piano. Not a note on the printed score escapes her attention, each is struck in and out of time with those little ruthless Chinese hammers of her fingers, with never a glint of feeling. The only thing she knows for sure is when she is wrong—which is most of the time—and, persevering by nature, she repeats and repeats until it is less wrong. In the evening there are two trumpeters, one passable and the other learning. 'The Roses of Picardy' is not a melody you care to listen to very often even when well played, even when played well on something other than a trumpet—but this is the tune chosen by the trumpeters. Hearing them, and not to be outdone, the pianist, sitting doubtless lethargic and wan after her morning effort, is galvanized into a renewed burst of hammering at Czerny in a key which never accords with the solid C major of the Roses which are forcing their strangled way from the trumpets of Picardy. Last of all, the trio having exhausted itself, the lanky youth with the sniff who lives across the corridor takes his courage —and what is worse, his violin—in both hands, and renders a few uncertain scales and an occasional 'Pop Goes the Weasel'.

Through everyone's open windows comes the accompaniment to this music, the staccato flushing of the lavatories—lavatories of the unresponsive type requiring a long and vigorous thrashing before their orgasm is reached and the welcome deluge descends.

It is not easy at first to cut out, hard to ignore the infantile screams whose stimulus is the aberrant pin escaping the folds of the diaper, to ignore the ting-a-ling bells of itinerant hawkers and the cries of the Indian men who tend cows which pasture on the grass at the back of the block. But in a little while you get used to the abundant life of others going on right in your ear, and I have felt elsewhere lost without it.

Fong has a shop in Oon Chan Street, and like all the other wholesalers and importers in the street he deals in foodstuffs. Fong buys onions and garlic and other dry vegetables from China, and his shop, as you struggle in from the mêlée in Oon Chan Street, reeks of them and of the corn-cob-shaped rope and sisal bags in which they are contained. The front shop is divided like a maze by wooden partitions about three feet high and in each cubicle sits a Cantonese in singlet and creamy shoulders with an abacus and some scruffy account books or order forms. The whole shop lifts its grinning head and flashes its gold teeth as you enter, and Fong comes out

from the back shop with a bowl of liquid in his hand. He left the flat earlier
than usual that morning and went to his doctor—his Chinese doctor—
who prescribed some medicine for him. This brew, already boiled up on
the charcoal stove in the back, is in the bowl, black and heavy as school ink.
You try a sip and it is acrid and leguminous, and Fong makes a face as he
drinks; and you go into the back shop. Here there are two ornate Chinese
throne-beds or bed-thrones of black wood inlaid with mother of pearl,
from which a couple of dozing employees dislodge themselves with goodwill. One of them makes some tea for you. Fong sticks to his medicine.
Fong is neurotic because he is a well-to-do Chinese and doesn't quite know
what to do with his life. It is quite a common symptom of 'plenty money'.
He owns part of a race-horse too and loves to gamble both on horses and at
cards. He is lucky, and superstitious, and extremely generous. It is hopeless
to take him out to lunch. He always manages to pay. We talk sitting on the
thrones with the best shoes of the employees in a row by the wall and their
clean shirts hanging like white fans from nails on the other wall. Periodically the phone rings in the front shop and a machine-gun-fire of Cantonese
bursts out, followed by a diminishing flow of conversation—presumbly
about the substance of the call. Then the shop settles back into its seeming
torpor and the contrapuntal clicks of the abacus resume their descant to the
low murmur of conversation and the occasional crushing of paper. And Fong,
who never seems to do anything, gives an occasional word to one of the
employees. He enjoys talking, his small dark eyes quick to notice everything as they dart about in the plumpness of his face and beneath the escaping
brush of his carefully slicked hair. He is discontented with his life and enjoys
only perfecting his cha-cha-cha and buying more L.P.'s for that expensive
Hi-Fi set in the living-room of the flat, entertaining his cousin from Hong
Kong, driving a high-powered car with the radio on, endless talk in his
sensuous Cantonese voice, and all forms of gambling for big stakes. He
sometimes wants to learn French and go again round the world in search
of happiness, but he is afraid of being lonely and stays put with his Cantonese
friends, with whom he is also lonely—but safely lonely. He sounds, when
you come to break down his life, one of the people you wouldn't want to
know. Yet he is worth knowing and you count him one of your friends,
perhaps because he is aware that the most satisfying thing would be interesting work—and he has none. Most people are not aware of that. As a
person he feels intensely Chinese, but he lives in a Europeanized world
whose values he only accepts on the surface. An excess of money has
divorced him hopelessly from the mass of Chinese in Singapore, and he
moves mostly among those whose wealth is commensurate to his and who
are also Westernized, also neurotic, spendthrift. One of his best friends, however, is an intellectual Chinese whose intellectuality leans towards socialism,
but because it finds so little answer in thought amongst other intellectuals

in Singapore, is still idealist and flabby, and drowns its frustrations in whisky now and then. Kong, his name is, and he ranges in sometimes, like a wolf without its dinner. With me he will discuss ideas, with Fong mostly gambling and girls, and other men's beddable wives. Neither of these two is deceived by Western values which remain alien to them, but both succumb to them for lack of a coherent system of Oriental values. It is part of the malaise of the East in the mid-twentieth century.

'Also,' comments the traveller, 'you would say Fong hangs too much on the hope of a romantic love—just as I did.'

'As you still do when you haven't cerebrated the idea out of your head temporarily. Yes, he does.'

'I can carry on for you. The idea of romantic love is foreign to Chinese life. It is a borrowing from the West and doesn't fit in Oriental ways of living and Oriental social patterns. . . . Yes?' The traveller mocks me.

'Correct—with the proviso that romantic love has always existed in China. It was never thought of as the inalienable basis for matrimony, but rather as what happens to the soul of a young man when the marvels of the world and women first impinge on him and he goes mad with joy and beauty and hope. After that they are quite realistic about it. They had to be, mostly. The woman was required to be fit and willing for work to be a satisfactory wife.'

'Which is a more reasonable concept?'

I suspect I'm being trapped. 'Which as a basis is a more reasonable concept,' I say, cautiously.

'I agree with you,' he replies, looking out on the world with a better-give-up-all-that-youth-nonsense-I-suppose look. 'But I don't quite feel it in my loving bones.' There are moments when I love him.

But we had had our fling—flings, indeed—which had been unsurpassable and ecstatic, and disastrous when you now think of them as permanencies. So we were in a position to be seeming wise.

'I don't feel I'm quite immune yet—to the madness,' said the traveller with a sort of shamefaced hope.

'I hope you never will be. Just that when bitten you will know what bit you.' There are moments when you feel very wise indeed.

Malaya is a country without any special flavour. What it had has been knocked out of it during centuries of colonial rule, and the beating-up has intensified since the war. There is nothing much left to show except thousands of acres of rubber trees, vast tin mines, a subdued and apathetic population of Malays and discontented Indians, and, in 1956, a web of armed posts and landing strips spun by the Army and the Air Force to catch the 'Communist Terrorists'. Even the little bit of charm that lingered until after the war has now disappeared and the country has reached *Merdeka*—Independence—without quite knowing why, under an ultra right-wing leader beloved of the British governing body.

For eight years or so we had been reading the episodes, or at least those which were printable in England, of the Malayan campaign as its tactics and strategy were gradually adapted and changed and the running war intensified against those C.T.s, as they are called by everyone. And by courtesy of the R.A.F. on this visit we went here and there in the country in bombers and transport planes and in helicopters to see what went on. First to Kuala Lumpur, the capital, we swept in with all the ease and power that money places at the disposal of its sacred law, and touched down on the efficient acres of the airfield between lines of parked bombers. Rows and rows of warplanes of many types, hundreds of men, all the devices of modern aerial destruction, and a few special weapons such as the loud-speakers fitted in place of bombs for broadcasting discouragement to the 'terrorists' below in the jungles, great bales of leaflets to rain a literary fallout on the unsuspecting villagers. The Ops Room was humming, its walls lined with maps spotted with flags and coloured pins, full of cups of tea, abracadabra of R.A.F. terminology, and crews coming and going in their flying suits parcelled with long shining zippers, helmeted in black leather with rubber ears. I wished I had been a small boy again to enjoy the glamour that small boys find in the soldier game.

Soon we were in a helicopter, as in a lift from which the building has fallen away, and lurching over the trees, dandling between furred hills over a world of exuberant jungle. For days it was Ops Room waiting, helicopter sorties, drops into jungle clearings where surprised Malay soldiers welcomed you as you ducked out under the beheading blades of the machine and scuttered away to safety over the whipped grass. Often the soldiers were expecting their food supplies and not a correspondent, but they took it very well and showed off their little zoos of jungle beasts collected in the long empty hours of waiting for this and that duty.

Living with the pilots and crews of aircraft, talking to soldiers English and Malay, it was difficult to remember that they were not playing soldiers but fighting a close difficult stealthy war against people they hardly ever saw. I was amazed at how many thousands they were and at how few were the 'terrorists' whom they stalked; at the millions of money poured into the armed attempt over seven or eight years to eliminate so puny a foe: at the fact that an idea in some places is stronger than an army. In the end they never succeeded in capturing the affections of the village people and in the end they won from sheer weight of numbers. In Cyprus they lost, in Malaya they won. It was difficult to remember they were not playing soldiers.

One operation I followed in detail, marvelling somewhat at the way I was allowed to see all in the Ops Room and fascinated by the tight complexity of the timing and co-ordination of the various stages of the attack:

hopping here and there to see the ground batteries trained on that spot beneath a cliff where it was thought an enemy hide-out was located, hearing the orders from H.Q. on the field radios, taking-off for the spot in the serene skies of Malaya with all the passionate beauty of the tropical jungles spread unsuspecting below. Seen from a plane circling not far away from that cliff, at the precise moment planned, the sky yielded up a formation of bombers soaring nearer and taking shape; yielded up their stream of bombs falling diagonally down for ages and ages. And the jungled cliff-top suddenly erupted in smoke and rubble as we sat craning our necks from our plane; and the shattered cliff fell hundreds of feet on the land below. Accuracy was perfect, and by the time the blast shot up and swayed our wings the bombers were far away in the other reach of the sky as though they had nothing to do with the deed. When the ground forces got to the spot they found plenty of traces of a hide-out. But no terrorists, dead or alive. The intelligence services of both sides were about equal, and all that effort and might was wasted, like a hammer used to swipe a flea.

Those days with the forces in Malaya were for me full of sadness. You can't hold the childishness of people against them, not when you remember your own. The madness and badness of the world is no greater these days than before—only more concentrated and more codified so that people at large have no idea at all what their co-operation in this and that means, no idea what their simple and innocent actions (like unloading the bombs on the hide-out), their childish convictions, entail. Under the emotive words 'Communist Terrorist' the powers that be classed all those who opposed the British rule in Malaya; and the ordinary soldier with no particular axe to grind simply accepted it as truth. It did not occur to many that they were fighting and killing for rubber combines and tin magnates back in London, for the good money and sons at public schools of the planters in Malaya. Or if it did, they said it was better than communists. And every printed page of all the newspapers in the world that they could read was on the side of the angels. Those thoughts, more than the rights and wrongs of a tangled situation, are full of sadness; and the traveller whose life is full of madness finds another species of it which he calls badness for lack of a better word. We are a little island, England, with a very great past, with centuries of ideas that were forward in their time; but we have no present idea that is forward in our time. It is normal thus: all history tells you it is inevitable. But we fly in the face of history. History is the brutality of outmoded ideas.

It was a curious time for us in Malaya, uneasy, sad; you can't grasp an unintelligible idea however hard you try. Perhaps the populace has realized that. The symptoms existed here and there. Apathy, cynicism, the crumbling of the old British code in colonial places, the nabob beginning to do his own chores, the subject people seeing him at it.

Visually Kuala Lumpur, the capital, was always a curious place. About

the turn of the century there was an Englishman called Hubbard who was
let architecturally loose on it to do the important buildings. He suffered
from a lack of architectural ideas and a certain whimsy. He remembered,
probably, that the Malays are Muslims, and fired by this stroke of genius
his thoughts turned to Granada and a mixed bag of Middle Eastern mosques
and citadels. Unfortunately he had his way. From the railway station min-
arets come not the expected call to evening prayer but an occasional puff of
train smoke, and through its Islamic portals crowd not the Faithful, but those
who need to catch a train. Down the road in the main square where the
Tudor-bethan club (not Hubbard's) dozes on the greensward, a great Moorish
fantasy rears its mock-Whitehall, architecturally somewhat between the
Houses of Parliament and the Alhambra. But fortunately there are not too
many of Hubbard's creations. An architectural vacuum ensued, and, since
the war, has been brilliantly filled by municipal and foreign architects who
have put up some of the best buildings in the East. The fire station is a small
poem in concrete and the Federal Building is also intelligently excellent. But
perhaps they are made more splendid and spare by the demented leer of
Hubbard's mosques and Caliph's palaces across the road.

Socially Kuala Lumpur is still in the vacuum from which its architecture
has passed, that indefinable place between old and new conceptions rather
like the 1920's in Europe when the impact of cynicism, jazz, cubism, and
new money for new classes made for some a desperate revel of the years.

Shall we go with the rubber broker and his girl? we asked ourselves.
It was a half-promise which we felt we had to keep. So we went to the house
and were filled with whisky, and dinner which was sausages on an elegant
table served by a white-clad Chinese servant. And then too full of whisky
we went out in the car to pick up the broker's friends whose common need
of alcohol, and only that, made congruous their diverse personalities. We
went on a pub-crawl of the town. But it was some kind of a night when the
pubs were deserted, all hollow and potential, tricked out in chintz and sick-
coloured walls and green suburban lino to make it like home. Impassive
Chinese behind the bars quietly juggled with abacus, concealing their smiles
as the Straits dollars tinkled into their tills.

Standing on this and that foot, with glass in hand and the desiccation
of whisky in the mind, it was hard not to recall student and navy days when
a world which lives unsuspected inside the world you know swarms up like
the vernacular of a known language, comprehensible but unlikeable and
strange. Half-world. The old half-world of student days when you drank
with a bravado in places which both attracted and revolted you, when the
taste of spirits was still pleasingly obnoxious and the drinking set fascinating
enough in their imagined viciousness, when the bitterness of gin and the
lassitude of hangovers gradually became less horrible than the sense of your
own and their futility; and you veered away and forgot all about it.

In Kuala Lumpur it all recurred, the regurgitation of an undigested meal in the throat. And we were soberer and soberer as the bars passed and the whisky descended. And sober amongst the drunk we gathered sadness and became despising. The fifth or sixth bar was a Japanese bar, a crowded room with a frieze of mask-faced Chinese tarts powdered deeply so their eyes looked cut-out holes in the flesh. They wore tight *cheong sams* exposing their functional thighs through the slits. This was why it was a crowded place. And the other reason was the proprietor's son wandering about in tight trousers collecting beer mugs and brushing the section of the English who liked to be brushed in passing. Everyone was sure of everyone else's function.

But under all that everyone was there for alcohol and to lose his aching self. A plump little Eurasian woman of forty-five sat on a high stool with her soft back against the bar. On either hand a man sat, elbows on the bar, drunk. Her skirt gaped at seams under my eyes as she whispered confusedly in my ear and now and then broke into a warble of half-remembered song. I rather liked her because she was so hopeless and soft put against the tarts. She was amiable, she devoted herself exclusively to me, assuring me of her most respectable relations in Ceylon; until I said I had just come from there, whereat she looked affronted as though I had said a dirty word or pried into her private life.

'I was married to an Army major. A major counted then. Lovely time . . . lots of friends. . . .' A little line of sentimental song. 'Married so young. He just snapped me up, dear. But you know,' she looked round as though seeking privacy, but really attracting an audience, 'you know, he was *terribly* jealous.'

'Listen to Betsy!' said one of the drunks, waking. He wagged a thick finger an inch from her desperate bright eyes. 'I know! We all know what happened to you, ducky. You took too many weekend trips to Singapore, didn't you now?'

The glamour of this memory made her smile with purring content. She nudged me as if to . . .

'You know how it is . . . they're away so often and there's nothing to do. . . . Lovely time. . . . And Gerald . . .'

All the bar was gone for her in a rosy moment. In fancy she was desired again and her fat thighs had thinned out to their old elegance, and the beds of Singapore were hers to choose from. She took my handkerchief out of my breast pocket and dabbed the watery corner of her eye, and I bought her a drink quickly to keep her going in case reality should rise all ghoulish, in case she should remember tomorrow when she must go again to the houses of the English to sew for them where she had once been invited with the major. . . .

Two roughs like greasers from some ship were crashing round, trying to help each other to the lavatory. They kept knocking people's drinks over, apologizing. 'Sorry, mate. Didn't see yer. Buy you another little drink. Everybody. Drinks!' Arm wandering compass-like to pick out the Japanese son of the proprietor. 'Hey you! Sonny-boy, little girl, tight-pants! Drinks for every—eryone!'

But his mate said: 'No. No, Jock,' coaxingly as to a child. 'You had too many now. We all had too many now.' And he smiled round at all the people. Then they remembered the lavatory and crashed round again as big as sixth-formers with mild blue eyes and foreheads creased like the foreheads of boys. . . .

'And the parties we used to have! Oh, the parties . . .' Betsy was saying.

'And the major laying the cook-boy's wife.' One of the drunks turned his head and winked heavily. But she didn't hear him.

'But now they're all little boys,' she went on. 'Just little boys. . . .'

Groups of four National Servicemen were sitting in the cubicles ranged along one wall, two facing two across the beer-pooled tables where dead matches slowly swelled. They were silent and pale, following with eyes one of their pals who had picked up one of the Chinese tarts. Some played a silent game with a moistened paper napkin placed over a tumbler with a coin lying on the wet membrane. With cigarettes they burned cautious holes in the paper until the moment when the coin, no longer adequately supported, fell into the glass. And the last man had to buy another round of beers.

At a table sat a Chinese girl and her mother, flashily dressed. The girl drank from a pint of lager, holding a handkerchief under her lip, and ate between times as though something depended on it from a bag of potato crisps. They talked earnestly to each other and took no notice of anyone else. They were waiting for something. In the end they left, edging fastidiously between the drunks and bowed to by the proprietor's son.

I was still listening a little to Betsy and buying whiskys for her and ignoring those little provocative glances that slid downwards over me. They were perfunctory, for we were far away in the old days on rubber estates, at dances in Raffles Hotel, and the price of brandy and servants, and how young I was and I didn't mind coloured people, did I? Then the blurred glint came into the eye again, more automatic than hopeful.

The pick-ups round the walls lingered on, sipping with a funny delicacy at orangeade, their eyes singling out for future reference those who were *amateurs* of the proprietor's son and those who were not. And Betsy, swaying wildly on her perch, said a tender farewell when we left. I wondered if anyone would buy her another drink and hoped they would. And the greasers were singing somewhere off, in the lavatory perhaps.

We moved on at sickening pace in the car driven with one hand by the broker while he fingered his girl with the other. He was sure he was sober.

And we came to a place of jostling people where in the street outside too many lights pierced the eyes and crude posters flaunted the mockery of advertised sex. We went into a building like a large garage, hollow tin roof and concrete floor, whose walls bulged with the music from a band, and Malay boys and Chinese youngsters danced madly. The baby-faced R.A.F. boys were there, too, pale as suet.

Rock-'n'-roll had just swooned into Kuala Lumpur and the first fling of it was inflaming the kids. An inspired Chinese trumpeter screamed his way through tune after tune, mad, blood-pulsing, perfectly and correctly depraved. His genius was irresistible, his trumpet yelling like animals mating, coaxing its controlled frenzy of sound through the bodies of the dancers who flung and gyrated rapt and mystical, hardly knowing what they did. The moment of near trance came for most now and then, when the insinuating rhythm mated with their own physical rhythm and they moved on the undulation of its involuntary waves and were no longer entities but a group being.

The traveller would have liked to be twenty with rock-'n'-roll, for he felt at that age the same despair to which it is an answer. He felt then more abandonedly the exultation of being a body with other bodies, as if all were attracting magnets swimming in the sweet flux of sensuous space in the embittered world. But now his despair had gone. He said it had gone.

They danced on the dusty floor with light verve, with the muscles of the groin singing and the grey squid of brain glistening and feeble on the flesh-hot shore of jive. But the English boys, jazz-crazed and girl-starved, jived with each other in a corner by the band, and some of them, overcome by who knows what, had given up and passed out on the platform where they twitched like fish that remember the sea. And others sat near, with eyes fixed stonily, and slapped their thighs in an unconsciously allusive way.

Midnight, or was it later, came. The band played three lines from 'God Save the Queen'; and everyone went out. The hall enlarged, resounding with a few catcalls. A smell of dust from the concrete blew about as a back door opened, and it seemed that a line of double-deckers might thunder in for the night.

So we moved on again through the evening which got worse like Kafka as it went. Another murderous drive into the country, somewhere, to a place called Lake Gardens where volumes of loudspeaker thumped the eardrums and the lights defied the night. We sat at a dirty table under tawdry bowers on rocking chairs under neon fluorescence in the midst of yelling people, gaming machines, small boy waiters in ill-fitting suits, and a battery of juke-boxes the loudest in all the world. We shouted because the juke-boxes played several tunes at once—'Annie Laurie', waltzes from bits of Tchaikovsky, Sinatra's 'Nancy with the Laughing Face'. Edge-curling, baffling.

Doubtless the cicadas and the bull-frogs were noising on the lawns around. Certainly a few outshone stars were trying their best to twinkle. But the moon had taken her lamp elsewhere, outclassed by our violent emitter.

'Useless to be highfalutin about it,' said the traveller. 'You got yourself into it, boy, as they always say in the movies. Now get yourself out. Or get something out of it.' He sat very still, looking round him bewildered like a child. 'The depravity of it, like pulling the wings off flies. Honey from juke-sex. . . .'

'My half-world. Adding up to nothing. Not depraved enough to satisfy. Like posters animated.'

All those Chinese and Malays had somehow thought it worthwhile to ape the drinking and amusement habits of a bunch of expatriate English whose ideas stuck somewhere between the wars, and somewhere in their teens.

We took a taxi without anyone noticing and went away, the desiccated little granules of the brain still bothering about it, about a certain despair that the West brings to the East.

K

# V. Borneo

$B$ORNEO is another world. They still exist—worlds which our commercial rapacity and our idle wanderings have only lightly touched; where, mercifully and mercilessly, we have left things alone. When you first saw the shading and clouding of a TV screen as it drew its banal picture from space, there was a magic in the moment: standing in the cabbage patch in the garden at home with a bit of red glass before the childish eye and watching the moon totally eclipse the sun's molten eye, there was a child's magic, something dawned with the darkling sky: when the great zeppelin came low over the street and you happened to be standing on a stool at the window and the world seemed overlaid by the great animal belly of it, there was fear and magic like close contact with a brood sow in an agricultural show: when the arrogant masculinity of peacock strutting near suddenly erected its blinding fan of a tail and the feathers flicked your gloved hand, you took off the glove and kissed it for some strange childish magical worship. Borneo is another world like all those moments. And as in all of them you have there the immediate tremendous opening of the heart and trembling of the mind as the otherness of it eclipses your little snivelling self, overwhelms your parcelled-up little being, and makes you no-count, a little unit who may or may not manage to live through the wild antiquity and the simple logic of its men and jungles. You search your heart not for its meaning but for a shred you might call your own, for your identity which is suddenly lost.

There are masochist travellers who write books, who revel in the labyrinth of their own self-finding. And there are some who, revelling, are more concerned to find others—and perhaps as afterthought and dreggy by-product, themselves, enlarged, diminished, softened up, fined down, or whatever. Absorptive soul-barrel-scraping masochists of travel are not finally very interesting—they might as well have done it at home. They are the type who, if Lyons Corner House sold Lysol, would go and commit their suicide there. The traveller and I, always ill-assorted, none the less belong, both, to the outward-going view of people-then-self-then-things.

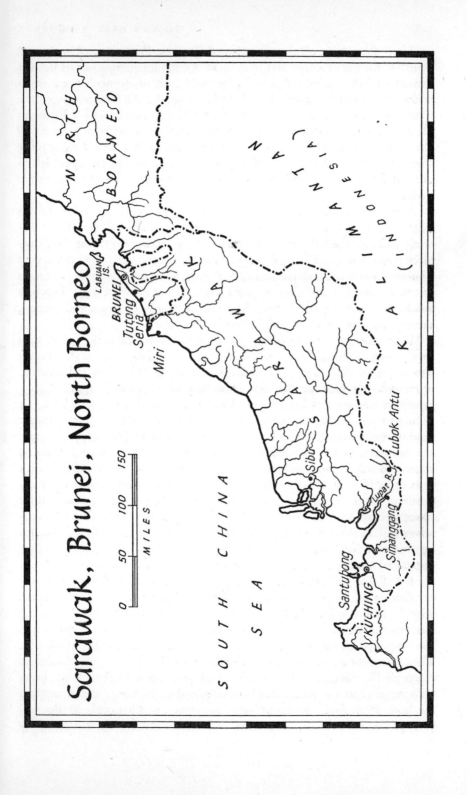

Sarawak, Brunei, North Borneo

Until the war, in all the centuries of Chinese, Portuguese, Dutch, and British trading exploration and settlement, the mountainous heart of Borneo was almost completely unknown. The 'wild man of Borneo' was a myth neither proved nor exploded. When they came to the headwaters of the rivers the detailed maps gave up and contented themselves with a Victorian blank which, in a more fanciful age, might have been filled with a picture of the wild and woolly Borneo man of the cartographer's imagining. Flying over the country it is not hard to see how this core of the great island escaped digestion while the coasts were for so long exploited by maritime traders.

From Singapore you come first to Sarawak, the largest of the three British territories in Borneo. The coast is almost uniformly flat. Only distantly through the halo of the morning do the mountains thrust their own black tropical drama. Falling from their feet the coastal belt, often more than a hundred miles wide, slopes gently to the sea, a fearful living tangle of trees for ever elbowing and clawing for a place in the elixir of sun. Through this kingdom of vegetation wriggle ochreous volutes of rivers and streams, carving the green mass of jungle into jigsaw shapes.

It was an immense morning, as we came there, calm sky piled with foamy clouds in irregular cones and crossed now and then by streaks of fawn like single strokes of water-colour. Immense, placid, warmly brooding, primevally leguminous; the sky encircling all imaginable space with a rapturous gesture and keeping it radiantly around this rampant land. To think of man here was unfitting. How could he *be* in this writhing Medusa head of mythological earth? Here and in the swamps of the upper Amazon are the heads of the two-headed Gorgon of the world whose feet are in water and whose soul springs and tentacles out in a passion of vegetable growth as if to turn little questing men to stone. And indeed the most primitive of the settled people in the far interior, the Kelabits, believe that for transgressions of their code the final catastrophe is petrification of themselves and all their belongings. When I learned this, long after, I recalled my own first vivid horror and fascination at those huge stretches of moronic vegetable, wrestling eternally for life on the scalp of Borneo.

But all this wilderness of life decaying, falling, rotting, feeding with the enrichment of its own putrefaction its multifarious spawn, comes down with the rains through the long muddy rivers to the sea, to a gently curving innocence of coast, to the long arabesques of the shore where it bleeds into the ocean and its corpuscles settle in yellow patches at the fluvial mouths. The blue sea is stained green there with the green blood of the green Gorgon's chlorophyllic chevelure. But her life does not ebb with the blood. Long millions of years the jungle has been fulminating, building, and destroying the land. Even forty thousand years ago there was a people in Borneo, perhaps several peoples, with a defined civilization, vastly overawed by

death like the Kelabits of today, and perhaps like them excruciatingly concerned with the journey of the spirit in the afterworld, a river journey—for
they are mostly river people.

No sooner arrived in Kuching than my whole desire was to get on the
rivers, and we took a coastal vessel downstream from the town to the South
China Sea and the long beaches of immaculate sand. Turning east we sailed
slowly coastwise and then headed for the mouth of the Lupar River and
wended a long morning up to Simanggang where the river ceases to be navi-
gable by any but smaller vessels. To this point the river is wide, soft-flowing,
more grey than yellow, the banks far apart and their jungle no thicker than a
European forest and almost as sedate. You pass small traders, rusty iron tubs
of boats on whose sides the lick of paint has been the most infrequent caress.
An occasional black Chinese junk heaves up ahead, also ancient, derelict-
seeming as though some tide (that Bore which Somerset Maugham makes
the dramatic focus of his story *The Yellow Streak*) had dislodged it from
a quiet hole in the mangrove swamp and set it adrift for the sea. Simanggang
is the place of 'The Yellow Streak', the memory of Maugham still execrated
quietly by those older locals whose skin, though fiery with a million stengahs,
is called white.

The romantic in us, the traveller to far places (and also—just think!—
the Empire-builder of the past in topee and baggy ducks) leaps for joy-
thrill when he is bundled into a long canoe with his bags and baggage and
taken away by a native crew towards their native country, all defenceless
and quivering. It is a sort of romantic rapine that befalls him and his spiritual
nerve-endings go into tremor at the thought. So off we went up the river with
a handful of amiable Iban lads and an outboard motor doing the work of the
paddles which lay in the bottom of the boat. A slow going it is. For the trouble
with mechanical appliances like outboards is that they are insensitive to their
environment. Their blades never feel the twist of creepers whose tendrils
lie just submerged and wind round the shaft. The motor gives the protesting groan of a child who knows not what ails him; and the paddlers turn
off the gas and heave the whole stupid contrivance from the water and
unwind the vegetation. Then off we go again. The paddle might be the more
laborious means of going, but every paddle is the end of a man's arms, and
feels encumbrances. The lookout in the bows signals like an old-fashioned
motorist left or right as we head for a log like a crocodile with only its
snout above the water—water which now after a spate of rain in the hills
is thick as soup and yellow as the tiles on a Ming tomb, the Imperial blood
of the jungle.

Jungle closes in on you in the swelter of an afternoon. Rocks startle the
water into foaming white, small islands part its golden-yellow hair. Thicker
and greener and more secret come the great trees, and the banks are lethal
with crocodile snatching every week or two a girl or a child who is washing

or playing in the honey warmth of water. You begin to see little landing stages—mere posts on other posts edging a yard or two into the flow—where slips of boats nose like sardines with eyes in the reeds. And you begin to see the villages and the people—the girls big-naked-breasted, bodies like pale soft porphyry, and men caught as they come from the water unclothed with limbs of Egyptian alabaster, cupping their genitals in their hands for modesty. They have skins of butter-gold, heads of straight hair black as lacquer, and, typically, a classicism of Oriental feature, bones moulded by sculpting gods.

Far up at a settlement whose name signifies the Place of Departed Spirits, as dusk is falling and the yellow rose of the sun enlarges down the sky, the journey comes to an end. Here is as far as canoe can go and here there is a white man, with an Iban wife and several Iban children, who officiates for the Government far away in Kuching. As you step ashore here the great peopled silence of the Borneo world makes itself felt in the air. There is no one about. Your noise, your English vowels, sound inopportune. Sitting in the living-room of the bungalow while supper is prepared that tremendous night population of the jungle air invades the room—soft moths of a dozen species, mosquitoes twanging their little guitars in the ear, pebbly beetles of frightful shapes, small caressing bugs that stroke their languid way over the damp surface of your skin, tiny ticks like sandflies which give their presence away only when they clench their jaws on the first few layers of the epithelium in search of blood; bats circulate the ceiling and need to be ignored—not easy at first—and cicadas and mantises stray in to the window sills or spot the walls while you watch them to see which way they will jump. There is something acutely terrifying about this milling abundance of insect life at night. You are always glad that you are not alone, that there are other human beings at hand to help you against the insidious kingdom which seems—just as do the legions of the leguminous world—to threaten human life. There is that creeping sensation that you may go slowly mad in the face of relentless moronic growth and reproduction, the insensate growth hemming you round with the drunken inevitability of a claustrophobic nightmare. You are glad there is company.

The company that night was about twenty Iban men all ages and types from the neighbouring longhouses, whom we invited to come and drink with us. To be honest they were rather urbanized Ibans, having been in contact with the blessings, mixed and pure, of this outpost of Empire. They liked whisky better than their native *borak* and wore, for the most part, shorts of the Empire flappy pattern reaching flag-like and khaki to the knee. Most of them were much tattooed in the Dyak fashion, some with an elaboration of decorative motif very pleasing to see; the most unusual of which, as tattoos go, is a column ascending from the root of the neck up over the larynx to the underchin, dark and broadening as it goes, rather

like the head-on view of an elephant from its trunk to its crown. My
interest in tattoos was nearly disastrous, for one of the older men turned out
to be the local practitioner in the art and thought a rose on each shoulder
point would make a good start in life for me.

At odd moments when my host was not interpreting for me I found
myself sitting back slightly outside the scene in the room. The floor was
littered with Ibans young and old, each with a glass in hand, each in his
own particular stage of inebriation, animation, or other complex reaction to
the surroundings: the insects were falling in their death-throes from impact
with the lights and writhing on floor and on heads and clothes, and bats
wheeled through the dim area next the ceiling. Everyone talked at once—it
is no prerogative of civilized parties—and peered at the collection of photographs which we had with us. From that mixed bag of portraits of people
and pictures of places—Moscow, Nigeria, England, France—the Ibans
slowly abstracted the ones they liked: the snow falling on the Red Square,
a Nigerian beauty, people in Cannes. Surreptitiously one or two of them
began rolling the pictures and stuffing them inside their clothes to keep.
The old men had faces from which the statuesque had quailed before a
lifetime of *borak* and garrulity. The young boys, certainly not virgins—
for after the age of sixteen it is rare—still retained that clear bloom of
youth, the almost Chinese cream of their faces moulded strong and supple
under the strange haircut. The head is shaved except for a pudding-basin
shape falling high on the brow in a severe black fringe and just below the
farthest-back bump of the skull, barely touching the tips of the ears. You
think of monk and schoolgirl combined when you look at them. Their
ears, slit in childhood and subjected to increasingly weighty ornaments,
depend, in the old men, to the shoulders and farther—long tape-loops of
paler flesh sometimes dangling a heavy brass ring. In some areas the upper
gristle of the ear near the tip is also pierced and through it sticks a leopard's
eye-tooth, but this I did not see in the Ibans. This fashion of heavy earrings
makes life difficult. When liquor gets the better of an Iban a hasty and un-
controlled shake of the head may knock out the wearer: so they tend to
remove the worst of the jewelry before parties. It was a moderately drunken
evening. All the best sources from Tom Harrisson downwards tell you
that Dyak evenings are.

The morning took us to a longhouse. Suppose you extend the principle
of the open-plan house to embrace all the houses of a single village, compress
all the houses side by side into one structure and remove all the intervening
walls, place the whole on stilts about ten feet high with a rough-and-ready
stair at each end—and you begin to have an idea of what the longhouse
looks like. It is a social experience of the most extreme interest. There are
many varieties of longhouse, altering from district to district. The Iban
ones are a little more subdivided than others, for each married couple has

a cubicle with a door leading off the main communal stamping-ground in which to sleep in private. But otherwise everyone lives and dies together on the bamboo poles that are floor and under the rafters where you keep your fishing tackle and spare clothes, and where you couple with the girl that takes your fancy. Much more than a village, the longhouse is a community; everyone in it has some direct concern either in work or in kin with others; and when dark falls most of the inhabitants are at home with each other, eating, talking, children and dogs playing games, women cooking on the open fires.

It is said that the Ibans are the most mercurial and violent of the Borneo peoples. I was surprised in a way to feel that they were degenerate in the sense that they seemed largely to have lost their belief in old tradition without being in the least positive about any other. This is probably not their fault, but neither is it very appetizing to observe. Just a flavour of the old is preserved in custom and more especially in the sort of nature of the people.

There was a muted sun sweating through the heavy sky in the morning as we walked from the river bank to the longhouse and climbed the notched trunk that served as stairs to the end verandah. It was a silly time to arrive for they were all out in the fields and only a few old people and children were left. Entering, the long vista of the living space recedes away, the long bamboo pole floor catching the light here and there from the openings in the left wall, the striations of the rafters sagging here and there with loads of unidentifiable things stowed on top. Below floor pigs were snorting and hens cackling and pecking the dirt. A naked child with a dirty bottom squinted in inverted position through the cracks to observe the livestock. But it is dark in a longhouse, difficult without flash, which falsifies and flattens everything out, to take adequate pictures. An old man was making a fish pot to use in the river, sitting tremulous in a shaft of light from a door weaving split bamboo with extreme slowness and absorption. He may have been deaf for he did not hear us come and we watched him for a few minutes sitting there with emaciated fingers fumbling a little but threading by dint of perseverance the one wavering splinter past the other. Above his head hung a net full of blackened skulls, human skulls, the relics of former head-hunting days. I would not have thought they kept these remains so casually and perhaps it is not usual, but there they were, the symbols of many a former triumph over evil forces threatening the house at one time or another. For the getting of a head was not a casual affair done for mere barbarity, but an essential step in warding off some impending catastrophe which for this or that reason had come on the community and was easily divined by everyone from the omens.

Towards the centre of the longhouse was an area occupied by the head-man and his family, the aristocrat of the community, a dry little man with large eyes who rolled cigarettes and offered them round while his wife, surprisingly, made some tea and poured it for us. She seemed younger than him, her breasts not yet dropped and stroplike. With many children they sat in an unconscious family group not unaccustomed to visitors these days, but still a little agitated in the backs of their minds by such foreign bodies. I was content to be there and let the conversation take whatever turn it liked, while the strangeness of their living conditions sank in a little. The cocks tethered outside the doors of the married cubicles scratched at the shiny bamboo and crowed warlike cries at each other, straining and scrabbling about, ready at any moment for a fight—the purpose for which they are kept. They reminded me of fighting bulls in Spain, surging with pride and anger, symbolic of primitive masculinity which lingers on in the midst of human tameness in human society.

As the evening comes and people come back from the fields the uproar begins in earnest. It is never still in a longhouse at any time of day but when the whole community is there and the children and the dogs all stamping about on the wincing bamboo floor, arguing and chattering, barking and belching, life revs up to a noisy frenzy. This is apparently much enjoyed by all since no one ever makes the slightest effort to abate any of the din. For a European it would be exhausting to live long in such a place. Yet to understand the complexity of this society, as of any other, time passed with its members would be essential. All round the world the traveller and I kept promising ourselves that we would stay somewhere for a very long time. We knew we wouldn't, really; financial considerations need to be thought of. But we returned eventually to Europe even more rootedly convinced that to do so is the only way, and with an even stronger desire to put theory into long practice some day.

For all those twenty or thirty families living in the longhouse on this upper reach of the Lupar River, life is still a precarious matter. Their main crop is dry paddy, and the soil is poor—often unusable because covered with a six-foot layer of peat on which nothing much will grow. It sounds easy enough to fell a patch of jungle as they do in Ceylon and to plant there, but if it is acid peat no paddy can be sown. The margin of safety is commensurate with the adequacy of the rains and their proper timing in relation to sowing; and in this primitive agricultural context that is small margin indeed. So all those people in the longhouses are poor people. They do a little rubber-running over the Indonesian border a few miles away into the hills, carting down the dirty sheets of latex on their heads and selling them to Chinese from the old junks after a long trek downstream. Otherwise there is no outlet for spare energy to be turned into cash. These days some emigrate to the coast to the oilfields of Brunei and the refinery, but for a communally living people this is not a satisfactory solution at all. Still, if we have not, in Burke's phrase, 'turned a savage wilderness into a glorious

Empire'—and now never will—at least we have left well more or less alone. Sarawak under the white Rajahs, the long line of Brookes who owned this land for many a year, suffered perhaps less than any other British territory from officialdom, missionary misguidedness, and the petty tyranny of paltry Englishmen.

Since the country was taken over from the Rajah Brooke, and his cranky but light administration replaced, the missionaries have flooded in and made thousands of cupboard converts. Most of the missionaries seem to be the puritanical put-pants-on-the-niggers type which must make for some comical readjustment in the Dyak mind (not to mention the Dyak life with its apparently licentious but really quite strict moral code). I would have liked to see this in operation. The combination of comedy and tragedy is perhaps seldom the highest art, but it is often symptomatic of transition periods in life. It would be interesting to see how far the chill waters of Christianity can curb the passionate alcoholic sessions of nights in the longhouses or those wild parties when the whole community goes to visit another similar one. And how do the missionaries cope with the male custom of inserting a metal crossbar through the flesh of the penis to enhance the sexual activity of the women in coitus and increase satisfaction? How, when you alter the details of a way of life, do you prevent the intricate pattern of the rest of that way of life, which is totally bound up, from creaking at the joints? Removing the obvious abuses has so often in the past led to dislocation so far-reaching in other apparently unconnected branches of primitive society that the society has disintegrated. The improbable concept that you can found a new society (supposedly a better one) on a spiritual basis, when the former was founded on a material one, still activates the missionaries of Churches in primitive lands; and the good they do is, ironically, always and only material.

We left next day, the tyranny of dates placing its huge thumb on our mental necks. Shoved off from the banks by Ibans who had to be warned not to give us their usual parting practical-joke gesture of over-turning the canoe. Leicas and typescript assort ill with the yellow waters of the rivers. Down the jubilant river in the sunshine with the flux of life and death of vegetable Borneo substantial as minestrone in the water. We wished a little that we had never come up for we had had only a sip of the Ulu (as they call those backwoods). And when we got to Kuching a couple of days later it was dark and rainy, and the next day was Sunday.

You are awakened by the sound of bells. Momentarily the disordered mind places its body in England. But full consciousness soon clears away all that nonsense and, from the tree outside the window which is dripping creepers from its branches, it is obvious that you are in the tropics. The bells, now registered more precisely, are the worst you have ever heard. Hard to decide what makes the sound of them—perhaps that same local electric current which produces the garbled tones of the organ that follow their truncated carillon. The church—cathedral, indeed, for it has a bishop—is opposite the hotel, is new, resembles a garage with ecclesiastical overtones. Raymond Mortimer on a visit to Kuching is said to have likened it to a Finnish telephone exchange, which is the last and the most adequate word on the subject.

Kuching is a sleepy little place at the best of times, but the feeling on Sunday morning is one of repressed activity. The earnest Chinese and Malay Christians (some of the dullest) are in the concrete church. So is the bishop, you imagine. But the aura of his faith has taken the guts out of the morning and the people off the street. Those spurts of sad and sentimental hymns conceived and cherished in Anglican England waft now and then across the padang where a few tough Chinese pass on bicycles with dependent cigarettes and snowy singlets. The shops down the street are semiclosed, the docks are dull as the ditchwater river under its swags of raincloud. A few Malay women in their best batik sarongs and gauze pink tops wander along past the deserted market where we used to drink cups of coffee amongst the coolies in the hot of an evening. One or two sturdy but quiet kids stump past the hotel with green nylon shirts, and a Chinese funeral moves by equally quietly (doubtless in deference to the bishop's imposed peace) with a flutter of paper money and some gauds of paper wreaths. You have a premonition that once the final hymn has wended its way to the vague God above the rainclouds, and the not-too-numerous congregation emerges from the contraptious portals of the cathedral, the whole of Kuching will intake a big breath and let out a yell.

There are minor signs that this is so. Opposite the church across the green is the cinema and a little queue ready for the first round of a film so unspeakable that it was doubtless cynically made for the South-east Asian market. The release of the congregation sensibly augments the queue. The quiver of a gong on the air means that the Chinese funeral has reached its cemetery sufficiently remote from church to risk scaring a few devils peculiar to the Orient. A waiter swears in Cantonese as he drops an ashtray in the lounge. One or two people drift into the refrigerated bar. The surplice of the Christian morning is slipping and showing a lively area of body. By lunch Kuching is back in a comfortable sarong and the clouds have lifted and evaporated like the sound of a hymn in the limitless pagan bliss of the sky.

In Kuching I wanted to see Tom Harrisson, the nearly mythological character who was dropped into central Borneo in the war and thereafter organized the whole of the Ulu and its almost unknown peoples to resist and exterminate the Japanese. He is now Curator of the Museum, one of the best little museums in the East. His reputation as a fiery character, often formidably right when officials are wrong (he describes himself as egocentric to a degree), made it something of a blunder on my part to have asked to see him before I had evinced the slightest desire to see the Chief Secretary of the Government. But much the best plan in a strange place like Borneo, after collecting all the official information and familiarizing yourself with the bare bones of history, administration, economy, and local custom, is to find someone who is spiritually tuned to his surroundings and not merely roosting there on a telegraph wire whose other end is in England. Tom Harrisson seemed just the man I wanted. But he was down at the mouth of the Sarawak River at a place called Santubong.

Surprisingly I managed to talk to him on the phone across the mangrove swamps, and astonishingly he suggested he send his boat up-river to fetch me. It felt like St. Peter sending down with a pass for the Gates. Early next morning in the museum when the wild chromatic birds that the Kenyah Dyaks carve had hardly opened their painted eyes from sleep behind the polished glass of their cases, the boatmen were waiting to take me to the wharf. These two lads—from their conversation—held Tom Harrisson in the awe which had been his portion with the people of Borneo when he directed the fantastic campaign in the jungle, which still makes his name passport to many a Dyak heart. They placed us in the boat as the sun was rising and the water glazing in first light of day. And we set off with the stream and a dawn-shattering roar from the outboard. The wharf was still dozing, with rusty little trading vessels tied up there, its uncertain level spiked with meccano derricks and random-strewn with the little huts and sheds and claptrap of unloading. A quarter of a mile away lie jungle and swamp and isolated atap houses on their stilts on the black slime of mud, boats nibbling in the shallows, and herds of little monkeys chattering and fleeing through the tops of the trees. Like all the north-coast rivers of Borneo the Sarawak winds in loops and lovers' knots through swamp before it reaches the sea. Almost as an afterthought it forks in two at the mountain peninsula of Santubong, widens and flattens, spiked with stakes for fish-traps like the roller of a musical-box, and relaxes after its long jungle journey into the placid South China Sea.

Ah wonder! to be speeding down the river, light as a walnut shell but sentient, discovering every moment accidents of sky and tree and collisions of water with the budding rose of sun—as shattering to your soul as the natural accident of a painting by Piero della Francesca. But Vlaminck is the man who should have painted the rivers of Borneo at dawn and sunset with his conflagration of colours; yet he is too small a painter to release the delicacy of this river violence. Is it only the stone-boxed townsman in the traveller whose soul rushes out from itself, like the expanding universe, at first vision of such natural splendour? He feels a sort of emptiness in his overfull love of the scene as the fragments of his shattered soul flee each other like outer nebulae into the curvature of limited space. By comparison the Paul Klee patterns of the fishing stakes and the pin complexes of bamboo platforms near the river mouth, where they hoist and lower the nets, are no more remarkable or moving than pins in a paper that grandmother used to have; yet a moment ago these were delight to the eye. It is like those wild sky days in England when the moors and the firmament speed away from you towards the apex of some triangle in infinity and the breath goes out of your lungs and you have to put face to earthy grass, lips of the spirit to breast-mother whom we all used to worship in the infancy of our race, to be entirely human again. For in a way to be human, and especially to be traveller, is to be lost sometimes and to feel the puny body of you that attempts to contain its soul, and to need the actual contact of the actual earth. The traveller sat in the boat, now and then staring at his hands which were real or at the keratinous skin of the boat-boy's feet which were also real— because at the time nothing else was. Like a fabulous tree which is said to flower but once in a thousand years the world is flowering on the river in the dawning conflagration of a new day and the traveller knows suddenly that here in tropical places this is what makes the ache in his heart—that the tree flowers not once in a thousand years but many times in every day.

It seems at first a deserted swamp through which you meander with the river. But why are there so many boats poling, paddling, chugging by? And so many people in them crowding out of the thatched leaf-shelter aboard as a wisp of cooking smoke trails astern? The long *perahus* with knife-sharp bows and stern cleave almost wake-less through the water, and tiny dug-out canoes wide enough only for a slender pelvis miraculously balance on the current, edging out from clefts in the mangroves. It is a populous swamp. Here and there the roofs of houses on stilts just back from the banks resound to the voices of unseen children.

Nearer to the mouth where the river forks on either side of Santubong's sugar-loaf mountain you can begin to smell the sea. The fish-traps multiply like models of molecules, some with their wind-sock nets hoisted—so you know the tide is flowing and the fish not slipping downstream with their endless gullibility into captivity.

The estuary has silted up and the village sleeping at the foot of the mountain lies upstream of the mud-and-sand bar in a grove of coconuts.

Tom Harrisson was sitting in what appeared to be the dining-room of a solitary house on a promontory. On the table were the remains of break-fast, a mass of papers, a small dictaphone, heaps of potsherds. He wore an old pair of black swimming shorts the waistband of which underhung his belly and made the garment too long in the leg: and on his top half he had a transparent nylon net shirt. His big feet were bare and his head grew a very small shapeless straw hat of indefinable origin which he wore both in and out of the house.

He shook hands.

'Have a look round. I'm busy,' were his first words, obviously true.

He returned to the table and the two local clerks who stood there with anxious looks and bundles of papers. He reminded me of a man who in similar circumstances said: 'Talk to my wife. She knows *nothing* about archaeology!'

We went out to a verandah and sat on rattan chairs whose substance had long been invaded and riddled by termites. The green grass ran down to the sea a hundred yards away and the sun shone benevolently, and I never wanted to move again. But with Harrisson around to be still was reputed to be impossible.

In ten minutes he came out with a couple of bottles of beer and bawled for glasses. He began to talk volubly and at large about what was going on, ranging from the survey of native fishing and the three hundred types of fish caught for sale in Borneo—to the whims of government and the excavations of a Chinese cemetery which he had found on a headland not far away. His volubility is far from the vagueness of the politician. It is incisive, slanderous, scurrilous, backed by a muscular intelligence which makes all he says alive and excites your enthusiasm about the subject—whatever it may be—that he happens to be talking about. His weak chin, to which he refers in print, is living proof that a weak chin may refer to only the smallest part of the character of its owner. Perhaps in a sense it may be the stimulus to that abounding ego, also memoralized in print by its proud possessor, which has done something in Borneo (to say nothing of elsewhere), whose repercussions in the field of South-East Asian prehistory are certainly profound. But in 1957 the discovery of the caves of Niah was yet to come and neither he nor I knew that forty thousand years ago there existed a people whose paintings on the rocks are older by far than Altmiara or Lascaux. But at Santubong—

'We're making this survey of the fishing. For the Government. All those papers in there,' indicating the chaotic dining-room with a swipe of the heavy arm, 'deal with that. I dictate it all into that machine. Damnably sensitive—picks up every unprintable word I say, and the typist woman back in Kuching has forty fits every reel I send her.'

Some hens and chicks had strayed on to the verandah and were pecking about our feet. Harrisson suddenly became conscious of them.

'You—bloody—Dyak—hens!' he exploded, setting each word on its outraged stool. 'Shoosh!'

The epithet applied to hens was meaningless to me. Later on when he was telling me how all those old friends of the war days from the backwoods —the Kelabits and the Kenyahs and the Punans—came sometimes to Kuching and automatically treated his house as they would their own longhouse, drinking up his spirits and making themselves completely at home even when he wasn't there, I realized its comic force.

But the work which evidently captured his imagination, and mine, was excavation of Chinese cemeteries situated on promontories along the coast. We heard about this as we wandered upstairs glass in hand to what might have been a lounge but was even more cluttered than the dining-room with bits of pottery, metal implements, corroded gold trinkets, jade *pi*—all of Chinese origin from the three sites in the vicinity. Only enthusiasm can make such a rapid injection of information stick, and I find myself even now remembering a lot of it.

'Off you go!' said Tom Harrisson suddenly. And he yelled for one of his clerks to take us along the beach to the site where his wife was supervising the excavations. Off we went. You obey Tom Harrisson without question.

Nothing in any case could be finer than a stroll along the beach in mid-morning. The sand is littered with blackened husks of fallen coconuts, running with spidery crabs. Fronds of palm and runts of mangrove punctuate the smooth yellow and in rock pools minnows hasten on their errands from side to side. The sand is firm to the foot, crunching with shells, its surface broken in detail by worm-casts and the miniature deltas of seepage. It was hot and the clerk, just returned from an expedition to the 12,000-foot mountains of North Borneo, turned his mind to the cold caves in them and how they slept there under the dark rush of a million bats and swiftlets swarming crashproof with their supersonic echoes above the beds of guano, almost pinned by the cold fingers of stalactites. He was a bright lad, entrusted with recording every fragment of the early Chinese settlements in Borneo.

The upshot of the excavations was the pushing back by a couple of hundred years of the dates for those settlements previously thought to have begun in early Ming times. This in itself is a major contribution to archaeology.

The site where they were working lay on a peninsula, much of which had obviously been eroded by the sea, so that what was left of the burial ground was probably a very small fragment of its former extent. The headland was rock with a thin topsoil easy to dig. The complications were not terrain but the owner of the ground adjacent, who complained bitterly and frequently that his garden was falling into the sea as a result of the excavations. As this was manifestly true he required continual pacifying.

Grubbing in the earth were Harrisson's young German wife and a few Malay boys, sifting the top six inches of a square yard of soil with their bare hands. And amid the labelled sticks marking every other square yard as though the archaeologist had put them up for memorials to shadows of the past which had lain there, a noble Lord hung around studying the birds and dying for a cigarette. On the shore were two Malay women chipping mussels from the rocks. It was a peaceful scene with just that touch of the bizarre which gives a peaceful scene its bite.

Leaving the party to its picnic lunch we went back to the house and lunched—a bird shot by the noble Lord—with Harrisson. Not for an instant did the spate of his commentary let up; intelligent, amusing, informed, ranging into the corners of things like a detective in a suspect's room. In the tropics it is a rare treat to bump into a cultured man. A treat not relished by other expatriates in most tropical places. Tom Harrisson with his ebullience *and* culture appeared to enjoy the disapprobation of the white community at large. It is a pleasure in which I would willingly join him . . . as comment on the community.

In the midst of the meal a wary little man in natty creased shorts arrived. 'The headman of Kampong Santubong,' said Harrisson. 'Don't tell him you're journalists or he'll bore you to death with complaints.'

We neither liked nor trusted this man, but he took us down to his village where he had a comfortable Malay-type house of wood on stilts like the others, slap on the beach. It was afternoon and the village slept—literally and atmospherically. The tall poles of bamboo (more exciting Klee shapes) stood somehow immanent on the tumbled sand between sea and row of village houses, nets falling dry and ginger from them like the setting for an unrealized play. A few dogs panted under the houses. One dazed child in falling shorts stood contemplatively fingering the nets and occasionally butting his heel into the sand.

Most of the thousand villagers live by fishing, helped out in their spare or hard time by tapping the old rubber trees on the side of the hill behind their houses. Rubber is a kind of economic stop-gap in foul weather or times of elusive fish, and the inferior latex yielded grudgingly by tired trees is sold in the market of Kuching for even less than it is worth. But by externals at least the village is well off. Houses in good repair, no squalid children, and few of the ragged faces and ragged clothes that signify long poverty. There is a school and a mosque, and the water supply is clean and fresh, trilling down in several miles of bamboo pipe which had just been replaced over long stretches.

The place looked simple. But the mosque sported a coloured pin-up on its wooden front wall, and most of the houses were decorated somewhere on their interior walls with portraits of the Royal Family almost as faded as the institution of monarchy itself—but apparently cherished.

As we were walking through and pausing to admire the sweat of a man chopping wood at this unseemly hour of heat, the village suddenly woke up; and turned on all its radios. Someone, I forget who, was giving a speech in Malay and it was possible to continue your walk and hear every word from a succession of radios. Suddenly I realized that the tall single bamboos here and there were none other than aerials. The school had gathered after the siesta and all the children were in the water learning to swim from a tough little Chinese. Over the roofs the nets soared up on their trellises unmindful of the radio waves and faintly moving in the springing breeze.

We took leave of the headman, and motor-boated over the estuary to another village described by Harrisson as 'very young, a sort of natural child of Kampong Santubong and acutely jealous'. Here the main source of income was the durian, that fruit of repellent smell and luscious flesh. In season the durian's choking pungency must hang like a gas-cloud over the estuary and the village—but it was out of season at the time I was there, and only a few heaps of husks added their accent to the sea air. The sand is white in this village and the important people were crowded into one house, balcony fluttering with beautiful women, to assist at a circumcision ceremony. The ultra-modesty and retiring disposition of these Malay women dissolved a group perfectly composed before I was near enough to photograph it. They just melted into the dark interior of the house with a fusion of electric colour, leaving darkness in the window which had framed them.

Nothing strange in Santubong. But the traveller is conscious of it in a strange way.

'When you take a boat from Paris to Rouen, or Charing Cross to Greenwich, Rouen and Greenwich are obviously sure that they exist in the context of each other and of all their neighbours.'

I began to wonder what he was getting at.

'But in places like Santubong you arrive and they are lost. They aren't anywhere at all. They're unconscious of themselves, like an English village in the sixteenth or seventeenth century. There was a road to the next place and the fishing and the crops and the people who were mostly related or known to everyone else. And outside the horizon all the world and God and the Devil and the whim of the weather and all the fables in the books and the stories of childhood—all these things were striding over the world away in the unthinkable distance. And after all it didn't really concern you except for making some more fairy tales and doing the right things in the religion now and then.'

I thought it was more concrete than that.

'No,' the traveller insisted. 'They're almost totally lost, without knowing what it is to be lost. What else, do you suppose, gives such a place such a quality of sweetness?'

'And that's why travellers like islands?' I said. 'Islands which are the acute stage of the lost village.'

We returned to the awareness of the world and the self and the history and the attainments of races which is culture in our own sense. Tom Harrisson was brandishing his packages of blasphemous tape-recordings which we were to take back to Kuching to that stung spinster who did his typing. He

L

walked down on his big bare feet to the boat with us and stood pondering
while the boatman removed his clothes and dived into the water to clear
some entanglement of weed from the propeller. And then we were off with
the sun glistening on the wet back of the boatman and the clouds gathering,
and the wind and sun and cloud and throb of motor commencing the
evening *son et lumière* on the river.

The tide was full now, risen to the sharp line across the mangroves below
which was nude stem, and above leaves; and the nets were all lowered into
the water in preparation for the ebb and the foolishness of fish. In the
interval which comes over things before dark the water glassed over and
flattened and began to take on its night mystery. The whole fling of the
sunset sky cried across the surface in blood and lemon with reflections of
cloud like the wings of ruffled doves—the sky of the thousand-and-first
night which flares each tropic evening. If your spirit is not made of
nylon, your eyes bubble polythene and your brain of latex foam, you
cannot fail to be moved. Moved to exactly what, is sometimes hard to say
outright.

Kuching begins in winking oil lamps from those swamp dwellings.
Silent boats, unlighted, slip past, sometimes with a great pale eye painted
on the bow surveying you through the humid air. And the wharf comes up
at last blazing with electric light; but less real than those flickers of little
lamps in the leaf-walled houses.


'One should rehearse one's life from time to time,' said the traveller
after it was all over and we were safely back in the air-conditioned sanity
of the oil-field hotel. 'It's like being in a play with a record-breaking
run. The tendency is not to notice what you're about as the months go
by.'

'We nearly had it, didn't we, today?' I murmured with a summoned
smile.

'Yes. And I thought suddenly that I hadn't had the time to remember
which act and which scene I was playing. That was the worst part for
me. . . .'

Not that the particular day's adventures had added much to the story
we were acting out.

'Perhaps it didn't add a word,' the traveller demurred, 'but there was
plenty went before, that I'd been gabbling through without following the
plot—let alone the inner plot. My particular terror at the moment we came
down was that all my life should be wasted because I hadn't had time to
sum up.'

'And you would go to your grave, like a virgin, not knowing?' I teased.

But he was too shaken by the escape from his own little hell of not having done the addition to rise to banter.

At least we knew about oil—a little—after a few days with Shell at Seria. The higher flights of thinking on the subject are special to economics and politics, dangerous ground like oil-fields themselves, and are best left to those who reap—for the time—the profits.

'You see—the points in travelling, or in life,' persisted the traveller, 'are nearly always made long after the event. Don't you think so?'

'Like the benefits of a major operation. The patient is unwell immediately after, but gets better?'

'*D'accord.* But don't take it too far. Travel is adding. Not excision of part of you.'

'You absolutely sure?' I said, mostly to myself.

To the potting shed of semi-useless knowledge we added in Seria some jars of boiling oil. It may be that we had an idea that there were forty thieves inside, but we kept mum about that—as nice guests should in the machine of a host's well-run house.

They had sent the helicopter for us to Labuan Island in Brunei Bay where we landed from the plane from Kuching. A brief drive over the sky took us with great ease to the small airfield and the town of bungalows, the derricks (which we learned to call rigs), and the miles and miles of silver pipeline snaking by the road.

I was rather surprised. Previously I had thought of oil-fields as areas of ravaged land piked with steel like the stumps of trees after a battle. But Seria was nothing like that. The long rectangle of it has been neatly cut out of coastal jungle and swamp, nicely flattened and drained and civilized, brainwashed of any lingering savagery. It is all seemly. Each of those bungalows is girt with a fine lawn and a garden where domesticity of washing-line and flower-border prevails. There are white children playing on tricycles and the family car sits at the gate. Here and there is a small enclosure, fenced off as though it were holy ground, where some piping loops about and dives into the earth to suck up the oil: or there may be a little engine there, regularly elbowing up and down to drag the oil up from a well that no longer has enough natural pressure. You have to drive quite far from the centre of the garden suburb to find the fuel plant where oil is partially refined, roaring angrily under the sun. But even here there is a thought-provoking view of it past a new mosque built by the company for the Muslim workers. Further away—right on the edge of the jungle, as if they had been placed there to frighten it back like watchfires in night encampments—there rise three flares from the flutes of three pipes taller than the trees. With little imagination they turn into wild blossoms blowing in the wind. But they are not. The poisonous gases and other waste products of oil burn off here and the power of the burning quakes the ground and shudders the air. It is calculated, they say with a touch of nonchalance, that the energy wasted here in heating the already overheated air would run the main gasworks of London. But the state of Brunei in which Seria lies has no industry to utilize this enormous potential. It is impressive wastage. The thunder and the trembling of the ground cause you to reflect on those forces that so evidently seethe just beneath the thin crust of the world we stand on.

Briefing from the chief oil geologist—a cultured Frenchman—enlarges the wonder, and those thoughts tie in with the genesis of oil.

Oil is a secret substance. It gathers in secret places. It is hard to win. Millions of years ago in the toddling years of the world an astronomical number of unicellular organisms lived and, operatively, died in the natural course of things in the warm sea. They fell to the sea-bed and gradually formed a layer. The layer thickened slowly as more and more organisms piled up, and was covered by a course of silt or mud. It is the kind of thing that should be happening off the Borneo coasts today, but owing to the changed state of things is not. The world is growing old. We are not now laying up stores of oil for the future. In the course of geological time the stresses and dormant fires beneath the earth's crust which are continually synthesizing and breaking down, exploding with many times the force of the biggest hydrogen bomb, bending and fragmenting the outer wall of the sphere—these forces made oil from the carcases of the organisms. It is completely believable.

There are records of black substances oozing from the skin of the world which go back for hundreds of years—in some places in Arabia this leakage burns, and has been lighting the desert since antiquity—but it is only one hundred years since people began to think there might be some way of using oil commercially. The science of oil began then. Into it and from it have poured some of the largest chunks of man's wealth in that century of technological revolution.

So many millions have been spent on oil. It is surprising to learn that amongst all the ingenious methods evolved in all branches of the industry, none has yet been devised whereby the presence of oil can be predicted with complete certainty. Only one in ten holes drilled laboriously and at fantastic expense into the earth's crust on the advice of the best experts, the best instruments, produces a drop of oil. Only one in twenty-five produces oil in commercial quantities, and only one in about a thousand indicates by its abundance that there is probably a substantial oil-field in the vicinity. So you need a bit of capital behind you before you embark on the oil business.

In Seria it seems that the major pools which have been tapped from the land, including those which lie a little under the sea and are tapped by drilling on an incline out to sea (deviated, as they call this method), have reached their maximum output. There is evidence of a slight decline in the production of the field as a whole. Exploratory drillings in the vicinity have proved unsatisfactory and attention has turned to the sea, since those deviated wells under the shallows have struck good pools. (A pool is not a pool in the literal sense. Another image shattered. Oil doesn't occur free in gallons but hangs like water in a sponge, droplets of it clinging in the crevices of limestone layers or in the sandstone deposited on those unicellular cemeteries of old.) Seismic, gravimetric, and other explorations of the geological basin at whose edges oil has already been found on land, suggests that it extends twenty-five miles out to sea to an area called Ampa Patches, a number of cloudy yellow blotches caused by proximity of the sea-bed to the surface. A well was being drilled there.

You reach Ampa most conveniently by helicopter, although heavier stuff than humans must come by ship. The perspex bubble containing you and the pilot like two goldfish in a bowl takes you up from Seria into the air, vertically, until you begin to wonder if it is not a hazardous leap. And then you drift out in the general direction of Ampa rig which is a mere black dot on the diseased skin of the sea. Nearer still the platform appears about as big as a stamp, and landing on it with a safe quelch of the balloons which replace wheels is quite a relief.

The rig was near completion and the drilling machinery was coming from shore the next day. We put on our steel helmets against falling ironmongery and ferreted around in the steel labyrinth of the place. Most of the space is taken up with accommodation for the workers, water tanks, a galley, stores, and general amenities of an island community. It is an artificial island standing on stilts in the sea, based on the hope of oil. A three-million-pound hope. The economics of oil resemble those of the roulette wheel—the bank, the cast dice of drilling, and the exultant gusher of a win—for Ampa may produce nothing at all but a little salt water; and the three millions will have been thrown into the sea. But the slight chance of oil in plenty is financially worth while, for the gambler has lots of capital to load on his dice, and the bank is potentially unlimited.

On this curious platform, with our little travel-bubble resting diaphanous on the landing area, were the riggers—a bunch of tough Scots, Irish, and Dutch, with whom we had tea and seed-cake in their mess—and a crowd of Iban workmen welding and bolting things together, their tattoos smeared with dirt and oil and their ready smiles breaking above those patterned larynxes and between the floppy pierced lobes of their ears. Everyone said they made good workers and were quickly trainable in crafts of various types. Later I saw the technical school ashore where the young ones are put through their apprenticeship.

It was an interesting afternoon and we finally took off again with the mail for ashore, and circled round the rig to get pictures of it from several angles. Rising at last to over a thousand feet we made for home with the late sun shafting low beams over the sea like a spotlight on a display of

silk. In the clouds it was getting cold, but as we emerged the air between
was warm again; and crossing those rifts of space lent a kind of daring to
flight. A plane moves too fast and you are too closed in to get the thrill
of being a bird—or a bubble—in space. In a helicopter you're right up
there.

Coming in to land the engine exploded at three hundred feet—bang!
Deathly smell of burnt oil. Silence. We are falling, tumbling, in silence.
Like a shot bird.

The ground comes up dizzily. Details focus in your transfixed eyes. The
blades are hardly revolving above, and the perspex is thinner than soap
film between you and the hard rind of the earth below. Crunch and rending
and clatter. Stomach driven up to the root of the neck. You tumble out with
the pilot yelling, 'Get clear!'

Silence. Then the sounds of earth, of birds in the trees, the merciful
grass beneath your feet. And the contraption does not take fire. It's a total
wreck, but your trembling legs still carry you, intact.

It is not nice to be dead, tremendously joyful to be alive, to realize you've
been given time to sum up the play of your life. The thoughtful traveller
was preoccupied for the rest of our time in Seria with the excellence of
living. Rather less than half his thoughts were on the winning of oil, on the
complete township of twenty thousand men and wives and children in
Seria, on its shops, cinemas, playing fields, clubs for all the social grades
from the top executive's new palace to the beer den of the local labour
force. We ought to have been thinking of the meaning of oil in its larger
context, and of the way the social hierarchy is established on traditional
lines in this oil oasis. We should have taken more notice of the fact that
conditions are not bad there for the people, and that the profits from oil,
this being the twentieth century, are at least to some extent invested in
goodwill in the form of welfare and various pursuits not directly productive.

But soon another idea impinged. The oil royalties, to the tune of 100
million dollars, which accrue to the State of Brunei every year. Immediately
we wanted to be off to Brunei town.

Shunning the offer of another helicopter we elected to drive along the
shore, there being no road—along that long yellow beach I had seen from
the air. The sand is hard and smooth as an expensive road. The sea,
gently rippled, is cooling in the morning air and warming in the morning sun,
sparkling. A fisherman, thigh-deep in the sea, gathers and then casts his
net. We stop to chat to a group of Malays who are sitting in the water
by their boat. Their propeller had come off and they had rowed inshore and
sent one of their number to find the spare. Two of them were making sand-
castles to pass the time. They have no guilt about wasting time. To right
and to left of them the epitome of beach stretches into the horizon, un-
complicated by sign of man—fishermen belong to the sea. You could wander

here for days, or sit and build castles in the sand, renewing the tired springs
of sanity: or maybe speculating about oil.

At a little place called Tutong where a river cuts the shore you ferry
over on a wooden 'boat'. Thenceforward there is a road to Brunei town,
through jungle where atap villages nestle with their little paddy stores on
stilts.

There's a nicely casual air about the dilapidated Rest House in Brunei
town. It sits on the edge of the river estuary with an old Chinese temple on
one side, and on the other a backwater where gravel from up-river is unloaded in small baskets from shapeless boats. The proximity of Kampong
Ayer, the Water Village, sitting on the flow just opposite, would make it
hard for the traveller to court the immaculate with a straight face. And in
fact you don't have to bother with a clean shirt for dinner, or even socks
at lunchtime. That awful era of the starched shirt in the jungle, worn as
shield to personal and national honour, somehow by-passed Brunei
altogether. No one is any the worse for the omission.

Brunei is a tiny state ruled by a sultan, advised by a British Resident and
staff. The annual income of the State is nearly one hundred million dollars:
the population is around sixty thousand, and the total area—90 per cent of it
jungle—is 2,226 square miles. The classic story of a Brunei schoolboy, who
suggested on the basis of simple arithmetic that if the Sultan divided this
income from oil equally amongst every member of the population for a
few years no one need ever work again, is so manifestly correct that a
Welfare State has been established. At least when I was there the beginnings
of it were going forward. From the planners' point of view Brunei starts with
some advantages. The town itself was almost completely razed by bombing
in the last war and an entirely new town has been built in the post-war
climate of town-planning. Properly untidied by the fact that this is the Orient,
the planned town is not bad. The few old houses left give it a little accent,
as some of the old churches add a point of comparison in Manhattan. The
old Chinese Temple, too, was charming; but its roof fell in with a resounding
crash while I was staying in the Rest House, and by now I expect it has been
cleared away.

The Sultan is a fervent Muslim and a fairly wise man. Apart from a few
soul-mates in the sultans of the Persian Gulf where oil lubricates the state
economy to a commensurate degree, he possesses the smallest and probably
the wealthiest little parcel of territory in the world. His neighbour Sarawak,
with dozens of times the area, has a mere fraction of the revenue pouring into
Brunei.

The Welfare State, however, filled me with disquiet; not because it is a
bad thing, but because it seemed to be so ramshackle, arbitrary, and subject

to whim and venality. There are old-age pensions for the asking, but some-times to get one you have to bribe the source. In many places I saw new schools, excellent modern buildings, beautifully designed and executed. Education and school meals are free. Some of the schools were teaching, and I spent a delightful morning in one in Brunei town itself, where hundreds of pupils were happily and efficiently organized in their sparkling classrooms. But there are others, empty and functionless because of the insane nationalist policy of Brunei for the Bruneis, which at the time prevented the importation of teachers from Malaya.

Suhaimi, a young Malay from the information department, was my guide in Brunei. I was maybe lucky on my travels in finding so many people who did more than they need have done to help. Maybe there are more good people in the world than some travellers seem to think. Suhaimi was certainly one of them. He was in his twenties, married to a beautiful Malay woman, and they had one baby of which they were extremely proud. They lived in a house which they had somehow made charming, where we ate the most delicious Malay food outside the land of its origin. Usually it is a little awkward when the men sit down and are served at table by the women of the household, a little constraining to the European. But the happiness of Suhaimi and his wife in their life took away any such feeling from meal-times in their house. Grandma was always hovering in the background with the baby in her arms, handing a spoon there and a fork here and smiling in the quiet well-bred way of one who is content with her lot and wouldn't have it otherwise.

With Suhaimi we pottered about and talked to all sorts of people, and we explored the Water Village. As you cross the river from the town side the promontory where the Residency sits on the sole piece of high ground in the neighbourhood stands apart beyond the Yacht Club and a few European houses. It is very isolated from the people on whose destinies it advises, and after a lunch there I was glad to be staying nearer the heart of things. Beyond is more estuary eventually leading to the pot-shaped Brunei Bay. Smaller coastal vessels can get to Brunei town but there is trouble—everywhere on the Borneo coast—from silting. Rumours of a new deep-water port for the State of Brunei were rife when we were there, but it has not so far materialized.

Across the water the village stands on a forest of stilts. It is said to have been there for about a thousand years—not of course this same village, for timber rots quickly in the warm water and humid air, but probably one very similar in looks. The original reason for building in the water was un-doubtedly security from attack, but now that reason has long ago evaporated the village community stays on. They have gathered such a tradition of living in this way, a sort of inarticulate love of their place, that all the efforts of the Government to move them to prepared plots of land on which houses had been built for the inhabitants, failed to budge them an inch. And the expensive site to which they were supposed to move was deserted and forlorn when I saw it.

As ever the traveller's sympathies are divided over Kampong Ayer, pulled by the evident sense of getting the villagers on to terra firma and away from the dank unhealth of the stilt houses, and pulled sentimentally and aesthetically by the sight of them where they are. Eventually they will move in dribs and drabs of their own accord as times move on and social pressures tend that way in them. Eventually all the world will get itself into some sort of idealized suburbia, whose uniformity I fear. But perhaps the easy-going but very definite identity of the Malays of Kampong Ayer will not be erased so fatally as I felt mine would by such a move. Likely enough they would invest the new houses, boxes that they are, with their unconscious individuality (as Suhaimi and his wife had done). But there, across the river, they still are.

Imagine then the scene. A spread clutter of low thatch and wood huts on a thicket of rickety stilts, shored up, crutched, leaning, patched, the result of a long make-do. In the early morning as dawn turns into pale blues and blue-greys and as these flush with airy orange and the closed night sky opens up to the brilliance of day—the Kampong stirs. The fishers return from the night sea, coldly, and the nets are soon being hoisted on tall poles so that they rise above the rooftops like ghostly Crusaders' tents. People begin to move with muffled clatter about the verandah's loose boards and along the cat-walks that lead between this and that place. No walk is very long, so there are soon many other boats shoaling like fish in and out and round the stilts. Much that goes on in the village is hidden from the outside by its situation and by the fact that you need not emerge into the open water except for shopping and fishing. So it is primarily the exits and entrances of the people which are laid bare to the watcher from the Brunei town bank.

After the smoke of cooking fires has been trailing up for a while the children begin to arrive in boats—some from scattered houses elsewhere, collected in a water bus—at the school which is merely a larger building a little taller in the walls than the houses of the village. With their satchels and slates they leap like monkeys up the ramp to the school. Some of the smallest kids come in their own canoes, paddling with an assurance and ease that I envied. And you think how we coddle and cosset our children in the West. I couldn't discover if children often came to grief in the aquatic hazards of Kampong Ayer, but because of the lack of such information I guess that they don't.

Then the housewives looking at their stores come to a mass conclusion that they must do some shopping, and set out in dug-out logs, in coracles, in any sort of floating thing they have, across the river to Brunei—every one of them extinguished under a yard-wide straw hat the shape of an upturned cup. Their faces and shoulders are thus modestly invisible as they drive the stout little paddles into the water, but a continuous backchat of conversation goes on between them. Meanwhile the men are going to work, or mending nets, or scratching their bellies as men like to do in the early sun. And the transport boats, long *perahus* slim and dark as sharks and laden with merchandise to the water-lipping gunwales, stream out and in, propelled by outboards and spotted with passengers taking a cheap ride.

The younger women coming ashore sometimes exchange their female-snuffer hats for Chinese orange paper parasols which lend their splendid skins a vital glow so you could eat them. But they are very shy, walking with grace which makes a jolt of the sight of an English wife.

The silver-smiths and other craftsmen—joiners, makers of nets, weavers who are mostly old women—are getting going in the hen-coop huts of the village and the younger children are swarming on verandahs chasing the hens and poking sleeping fathers who are relaxing after the night's fishing, falling over cooking pots and disturbing aged aunts who are preparing vegetables for the midday meal. The planking on all sides as you penetrate through the water alleys is a-rattle with feet, and people are washing with black hair streaming over face and creamy shoulders in the water below, clutching the uncertain legs of their houses and taking a swim down the alley and back.

This, you see, said the traveller and I to each other and to anyone else who might be around, is what they want to clear away. And we looked at the bathers in the river which is also sewer and at the water rats skittering up the stilts—and also at grandmother tending a tin tub of flowers on her life-long verandah . . . and we were glad we didn't have the job of forcing the evacuation.

Brunei is a boom-town. The very idea contains within itself a warning. For booms are generally shortish-lived. With oil—as opposed to gold—for substance of the boom, prosperity may last longer. But with oil you can't tell. Still, within limits of Muslim and Oriental thought it is a forward-looking little state. As with a provident man who suddenly comes on great riches (the budget surplus in the current year was seventy million dollars), his actions are for the most part guided by his humble past. Only his occasional dreamy fantasy leads to some indulgence. And this perhaps explains the new mosque.

Along with the agricultural research stations and the new roads comes the mosque, in the same package deal. You have to allow them this. Recently I heard that it was opened, but at the time I was there the work was only about half-way done. But certainly it was the biggest mosque in South-East Asia. The tower was already up but not completed, and as we puffed upwards round its spiral staircase to the top, two hundred feet above the ground, the panorama of the town revolved below. The great mosque domes shimmered in the sun and the workmen crawled about like insects on the bamboo scaffolding; the river shaped itself as it does on the maps, at the feet of the mosque, and Kampong Ayer across the way looked somewhat askance at the massive piles of ferro-concrete rising towards the face of the Prophet. When the tower is done it will have a lift so that the muezzin will have breath to send the call to prayer through the microphone and loudspeaker system when he gets to the top. The walls of the mosque were to be faced with Carrara marble which, they told us, was already cut and waiting shipment from Italy. The central chandelier which I saw in store weighed four tons and cost ten thousand pounds—a sort of war memorial to the fluorescent tube. And the carpet to cover the main hall of the building was being woven in India—the largest carpet in all the world, they proudly said.

One day it would be fine to go back and see how all these improbabilities fitted together. Like the State of Brunei itself there's a sort of crazy logic about them. You keep a warm place in the heart for both mosque and State and for the fortunes of the people and the dank, sunny, friendly Kampong Ayer on its mended legs in the river.

# VI. Bangkok, Hong Kong

Unintentionally in Siam, we were unprepared. Casually arrived, so, casually, we met people and saw things; and the one life which you or I must lead, because it is our own, was partly laid by as others settled haphazard on shoulders and head. Those wopsical hats again. Sometimes you even have to don one, for the same reason you turn on the cold tap when running a hot bath. More comfortable.

Dining with an American and his wife in their home (their word) surrounded by Japanese paper lanterns and Thai bronzes, with negro music unsuiting the air and ice clinking in a glass jug as Walter mixes martinis using dry sherry instead of vermouth—there it was all American-social-confidential.

Walter is pleasant Italianate-hairy, deodorant-clean, intelligent in the way expatriate Americans are (so sure they're citizens of the world at large). And his wife very cool in those transatlantic clothes which never, never make woman more feminine but only boyish. There she sat, efficiently elegant, assured in her curious appraisal of Thai life—an outlook so insular in its American way that it jutted into the whole room like the front of a lorry which has crashed into a parlour. Undoubtedly inside both of them were sensitivities, whose focus I didn't quite find, hidden carefully by a send-up humour and the not unkindly New York iconoclastic wit which amuses for a short time. And the servants, whom they were quite unable to manage, moved in and out of the room doing useless things, and we never had what we wanted at any moment. It was an evening of civilized banter touching on things deeper and then recoiling because we knew we had nothing in common—and our intense civilization forbade us all to handle prickly topics on which we wouldn't agree.

Yet the previous night, coming in from the country to Bangkok, was warm-cool and moony. A star-crusted navy blue sky floury with light hung over the spurs and obelisks of the temples. The canals reflected brightness between maps of weed, and houses of wood and tin—the jungle of Thai living—were bleached by the light. Vistas from the bridges looked ghostly as photonegatives. Thai faces, upturned, floated pale and glazed along the dark hazard of the roads. Silent tri-shaws slipped past with hooded passenger, waxed thighs of pedalling driver and purr of tyre on tar. By the roadside were secret houses night-shuttered beyond small moats of canal, over their humped and rotting bridges, treed with palm, studded with an occasional oil lamp. Occasional shapes of reclining figures, moon-waxed and forgotten, slept in draped sarong on verandahs in the music of insects and the stillness of a distant voice. If the Buddha himself had been incarnated suddenly there, on the road, in an incandescence of nirvana—no one but Americans would have been surprised.

This heals you of evenings shouted over the nightclub band, of ill-cooked dinners in refrigerated places where digestion falters and Estelle the millionairess like an old irascible goddess eats only broth and dry toast. She took to us because for once in her life we were people who didn't want any of her money (although I must say I wouldn't mind some). It is the tragedy of very wealthy people that they are forced to select their friends on the basis of money. They end up knowing other millionaires and their wives, which somehow doesn't solve the things friendship is supposed to solve. The traveller, who inclines to think people are more lonely than they are, was genuinely shocked by the isolation of Estelle. And perhaps he was right.

Estelle was on a bit of a world tour and we casually got tied up with the Bangkok part of it. Stumping through some Siamese temple she was like an aged deity from another religious system. (Commerce, after all, has its own mythology.) Sitting in the boat as we wandered along the *klongs*, as they call the canals, she resembled a figurehead from an old ship. So old, so commercially wise, that dragged-back hair barely covering the scalp, those surprisingly soft talons of her hands bearing one ring. One ring one inch square; all of it peerless sapphire. On any other hands you would have suspected it. But Estelle had a necklace of twenty sapphires nearly as big, set in diamonds. One morning she appeared in it at breakfast complaining that her neck was sore because she hadn't been able to undo the clasp and had slept with those expensive rocks.

God knows why they built Bangkok where they did: humanity produced Estelle, God knows. In the old capital at least there was firm ground round the river, but here it is swamp and silt, on which most of the city is perched on stilts like Kampong Ayer in Brunei and Estelle on her millions. But the tremendous sophistication of the Thais and their delicate civilization has made much more than a village of the place. Coarsening in the business sector with its Western-style buildings doesn't really detract from the delight-ful muddle of the older parts of the city where wood is the basic material: nor does it detract from the humanity of the millionairess. Just as in Venice and Kampong Ayer, life happens on or beside a canal. But the Thais are neither so elegant in feeling as Venetians nor so lost in their little world as the people of the Water Village, so their city is more surprising than both; and Estelle in her way is more fantastic than any of them.

From the steps of a mouldering hotel on the river you can hire a boat and move off at once into a world of water and wood. The river itself is majestic—fit for the Royal Barges—but the town over on the opposite bank is homely under a morning sky the colours of transparent fish. Life goes on in a quiet daze as soon as you edge into the small canals from the teeming river. Between palaces and temples the *klongs* poke gently into the backblocks and the slapping river waves give way to smooth water. It is suddenly intimate, close-packed, swarming with domestic life. Sounds of bumping sampans, and of voices that were lost in the wide air of the river, here come into focus. The canal is a corridor between houses, the roof is sky and branches of fine trees, and the sun is still yellow and tentative, reflecting from the water into the shops and houses which all lack a front wall. When you build a set for a film you omit one of the walls of the room. So do the Thais. Their teak houses have their teak feet in the water and no front to cut them off from the neighbours. You live and die in each other's pockets. The mango trees are fruiting beside the houses, and the warty jackfruit. The nude kapok hangs its eliptical pods on thin branches like the last few leaves of a winter tree in Europe, and the rose-apple overhangs the water, its tea-rose fruits shiny as cherries, sweet-watery, brushing your head as you meander along past the house where a sewing woman with an antique Singer on a crate works intently with half-made clothes festooned on a line across the back of the room. Next door is the dye-works, festooned also, but with cloth which is all black and hangs on tall trellises, oozing a little jet into the canal.

Life is various, exposed, genial, in the *klongs*. Here it is not offensive to know your neighbours' business. It is impossible to ignore it.

In the sunlight and the dappling of foliage, colours are warm. The dusty red-brown teak of house walls, the rotting black teak of piers, the caulked black of sampan hulls, sage-green of leaves and silver of bark, and the paving of yellow-grey mud-viscous water—these are the setting. Spattered on them are motes of crimson and blue and white and worn-out black of laundry hanging up to dry. The flash of gold teeth at entrance to betel-stained caves of laughing mouths touches delicate pinks of Japanese eating-bowls. Piles of hairy coconuts and stacks of crinkled paper in Chinese lucky red lie in boats tended by youngsters whose heads are tufted like coconuts but black. A thin man in dungaree blue goes by in a boat set out with cakes and sweets, all coconut-white, succulent with peanut and garnished with calligraphy of icing in green and sherbet-pink and lilac. And behind him comes the water-boat with its three large tanks like galvanized dustbins wallowing with fresh water at one *tical* the kerosene can. In a shed are skeletons and shells of new boats, their satin of planed wood studded with white points where the nail-heads have been puttied up. Then grocers' boats, and canal-side restaurants where plastic tablecloths hang limp and nasty. House upon hovel upon house . . . and from a barber's shop emanates a strong smell of English lavender, the only familiar note.

The Venetian austerity of water and stone, that encounter of princes, is not here. Nothing can make wood a princely building material.

Embedded in a tangle of Thai naval sheds where slender youths with fawns' eyes and crew-cuts lounge navy-fashion on the decks of outmoded warships, you come on a sort of hangar back from the canal where the Royal Barges lie. The pomp and dash and delicacy of them is Louis Quatorze idling on the pavement on moving day beside the milk bottles and delivery vans. They are like refined dragons, gilded, fitted for ninety oarsmen, prowed with the Garuda, which is bird and man, or with the tall phoenix which is neither swan nor eagle but the spirit of both.

Back on the river all manner of boats swarm down on you. Curly sampans like black bananas tilt alarmingly on the waves, full of emaciated figures in black with felt hats like upturned tulips, and nearly naked men wearing straw pie-dish hats paddle at the stern. Bigger boats—hulks and junky junks— pass piled with brown rice from the country for the mills where men in blue shorts and scarlet headcloths work in a flurry of flour and sweat. Angry little yapping boats spring through the water straining at a lead on which two or many more barges drag laboriously. In all the larger vessels families are sitting under the tin canopy eating, while the washing flaps in the breeze. They look precarious. The essentials of their life are around them—pegs hanging with best clothes, the stove in a kerosene tin, boxes for seats, bucket for drawing water to wash, the coloured picture of the King. The children are in antics on the heaps of cargo and yell and wave as you pass. No one thinks they might fall overboard. Now and then the older boys dive into the river and clamber aboard your boat to take a ride with you. Then, grinning, they suddenly leave again and swim to another boat going down-stream to where they live. They seem happy as porpoises. Hardly a boat looks new; they are all old shoes of boats, shapeless and friendly. The upper-works resemble hencoops perched on a scrap-yard—charming, tottering, makeshift, surrealist, with people making water over the side and men shaving and mothers airing their babies by the tiller.

Three hundred *wats*, or temples, they say, are scattered through Bangkok. I would have thought more, and didn't attempt more than a few. You see the big ones above everything else—stone and strange, flashing, decked with daemons, bristling against the sky. But they have another quality. Outside India Buddhist and Hindu temples are soft as well as exotic and fanciful. In Burma, Indonesia, and in Thailand you see them. Female and sprightly, delicate, with lithe arches and complexity of roof on top of roof, they preen themselves like birds in a special paradise of their own from which one is rather excluded. The gay formalism of Thai dancing is implicit in the temples of Bangkok. It is surprising because you are so little accustomed to the temple as a place of gaiety and exoticism. The astringent melancholy of India does not transport with its religions. But Hindu and Buddhist fantasy easily leaps the oceans and in the exuberance of South-East Asia translates into a particular poetry. The temples of Thailand have a lyricism. They radiate a message which provokes not reflection but simply happiness.

The conceits of an old religious architecture and an imported religious system are here—elaboration of motif, turning of motif to other function, surprise juxtaposition of flowers and figures, of dragon with soft though geometric shapes; gilding and gilded scales, ceramic mosaic but also mirror mosaic. Chinese superstition, the old animisms of South-East Asia, the Indo-Javanese tangle of mythology, mingle at random with the imports from India. Except for the specialist there is little point in dissecting the components of Thai Buddhism. In Ceylon it is held in great veneration—but considering the dilapidated state of the religion there, it is not surprising; and there are historical reasons, too. But Buddhism in Thailand seems even more of a pastiche than it is anywhere else, at least on the evidence of its temples. All this chaos of decoration and mix-up of origins is, however, controlled by a delicacy as creative as it is purely Siamese. Chinese daemons fifteen feet high—taken as payment for Chinese commercial debts a long time ago—guard the entrance to a temple where a fine withdrawn Buddha sits like an Asian lotus in his bland omniscient dream. But unlike God he is very human. He is made of real flesh—by some chance it is gilded flesh, or petrified or lacquered—but very flesh. He has the long ears of aristocratic women, the fine hands of princesses, the wax-smooth war-round limbs of Thais. He is almost female—but absurdly male. The whole look of him cries Asian, cries flesh. Not fear. Nowhere is the Buddha a jealous or a carping God. Most especially not in Siam where he is worshipped as elsewhere, despite his own word that he was not a God at all. If you do not say 'I am master' maybe you stir a different kind of obedience.

In the commercial city of Bangkok a coating of concrete covers the pliable wood of the East. Lacking our history, our three thousand years of European thought and the jealous God who sprang alarmingly from outside into its midst, the Thais have only a dream of the West—if a compelling one. Until the war they largely escaped our depredations and almost wholly escaped our religions and our government. So life is much more haphazard (to our eyes) than that of Colombo or Singapore. The riches of tea and rubber are not in Siam, and their absence has left visible some of the beauty and the sores of a small Oriental country and its people. In a way Thailand is more exposed than any other such country to the two lode-stars of the commercial West and the success of the new China.

With the poor people there is little politics. With the aristocracy the

West is the bright star. Yet a Princess with whom we took tea in her house told me quite seriously that in the bombing during the war the Post Office, a new building much decorated with garudas on its façade, escaped damage.

'It was miraculous,' she smiled. 'You can see why we think well of our garudas.'

And some of her friends who were with her on the wide verandah of the house, between luxurious rooms and garden where the spirit house on its pole stood not far away, smiled too in agreement.

The Princess's husband owned most of the dangerous local buses. They were very wealthy. A small private canal led into their garden. Estelle sat smiling, too, in her Paris couture, her pearls, with her substantial handbag containing a cheque book that could buy us all up reposing on the cushions beside her. She played with one of the children, looking into the childish face as though reviewing with a sort of dispassion the process of her success through life since she was such another little girl—but a poor one in a European slum.

Another day we spent five hours shopping with her. We sat in a shop looking at Thai silk and as she bought several hundred yards of it a beggar stood with his nose pressed against the window, watching. Outside, when she was getting into the car again, she turned and looked along the pavement where the beggar had gone.

'That man doesn't get enough to eat,' she said, with her dispassion. I thought she had not noticed him.

Later, in a shop where they sell antiques, she spent easily and largely. Writing the cheque she turned to me.

'I like spending money,' she said in that faintly guttural accent of hers. 'The only thing you cannot make is time.'

And when the transaction was completed, except that she hadn't handed over the cheque, she said to the dealer:

'Now you give me a present, yes?'

And the little Chinese, lips quivering into a sickly smile, fished up some trifle and presented it to her.

Finally that afternoon, with the entourage all but dropping in the heat, perhaps less resilient because they were not having her pleasure of spending money, she sat down on one of those china tubs which the Chinese love to put in their gardens.

'Run for a Pepsi,' she said off-hand to one of us. 'I'm thirsty.'

It was the only sign of fatigue she showed.

The Siamese Government has recently been seized with an attack of Buddhist conscience mixed with national self-consciousness. They have begun to restore the ancient monuments in a big way. Excavation by trained archaeologists is always a worthy task, but reconstruction is somewhat more suspect—especially in places where the profusion of material to hand may

M

lead to confusion and arbitrary results. In Ayudhya, the ancient capital of Thailand, something of the kind was going forward.

It was not mere traveller's sentimentality, nostalgia for *temps perdu*, that raised our mental hands in useless protest. The essence of a ruin, when it is the ruin of a beautiful building, is precisely that it is a ruin. Restore it to a semblance of its original condition and you have at once posed the awkward question: What shall we do with it now? For now, complete and in functioning order, the building in all its beauty looks at you and asks: Where are my people? The priests, the devotees? *They* are not restored, for they were mortal and decayed beyond the powers of restorers; so the building hangs there in the fields like a bride whose groom has fallen dead on the way to the nuptials.

But worse than the academic restorer is the pious one. From fuzzy photographs I conceived a passion to see a reclining Buddha near Ayudhya, a forty-foot marvel of peace. And coming through the maze of warm crumbling brick which everywhere covered the ground where an old palace once stood, stumbling over pieces of carved stone and tiny perfunctory castings of Buddhas, I suddenly saw it recumbent beside a tree whose hundred stems embraced a wall and were crushing it in a slow vegetable clinch. For a moment I thought they must be putting up some fair or other with a forty-foot reclining Buddha at the gates.

'It was decaying, you see,' said the interpreter. 'They were very worried about it. So it has been preserved in concrete.' He looked with satisfaction at the butter-yellow monster from which all the meaning had shrunk beneath a layer of insensitive concrete. Pilgrims were sticking little bits of gold foil on the surface.

'You see how they attempt to cover the Buddha with gold!' he went on. 'In some years from now all will be golded. . . .'

One could not doubt it. But they were gilding a lily already dead.

So much has been excavated in Ayudhya that there is not museum space to hold it all. In the remains of a temple there are superb bronzes all jumbled together in an iron cage, and some Buddha heads stuffed like miscellaneous shopping in a bucket. Walk along some of the tracks and there, amid plantations of banana trees, stand stone Buddhas contemplating among the ragged leaves. At their feet are fallen heads which any European museum would be pleased to have. It would be simple to tuck a couple in the boot of the car and drive away. It might even be a service you performed in so doing, for these serene marvels in stone will surely not long survive the cupidity or the iconoclasm of the passer-by.

Ayudhya is disintegrating in a slow vegetable explosion, and simultaneously reforming in parts under the hands of misguided authorities, as trite as a film set. Happily there is so much of it, and so much that probably cannot be restored, that some of its marvellous echo will perhaps go on sounding softly through the years. The modern town adheres to its flank by the bend of the river, all shacks and floating homes. In gardens the spirit houses are festooned with purple, lime-yellow, green and red paper, fluttering; and an indigent father sits in the shade reading a newspaper and rocking a cradle by means of a long knotted string tied to his toe. In a shack restaurant while we were eating excellent Thai food—pork, sweet fish in pink sweet sauce—the children came to beg with hands in attitude of prayer. They were silent and sad-smiling, not importunate. An old woman, paralysed, doubled up, dragged herself along the pavement in sitting position. She used one hand to propel herself and the other, limp and deformed, trailed in the dirt. Her face turned towards us momentarily as she scraped past our feet—half idiot, half tortured, the face of one who is always ignored.

'I reckon I've ten or fifteen years to live yet,' the hefty Australian said philosophically, 'and I don't intend to leave much in the bank after I'm off.'

'I'm helping him,' said his wife cheerfully. 'I helped him quite a bit this morning.' She patted a hold-all stuffed with purchases.

Estelle would be the ideal wife for him, the traveller reflected. She would help him even more. He felt he ought to introduce them. Trouble would be that she would make so much more with what riches he had, that there would be no catching up with the earnings.

But the Australian, having said his say about his money, looked rueful as though in some ways he regretted the feel of money running out of his hands. He wasn't there when we saw the old paralysed woman. He was a nice man, and his wife was a nice big-breasted woman, but it wouldn't have mattered if they had seen her. Estelle would have summed it all up and looked back in momentary pity; for she came from a place where they knew about such things. Australians do not. Estelle would have known the hopelessness of the circumstances of poverty. Quite naturally Australians do not.

In Hong Kong I met a young New Zealand couple on their way inexpensively to Europe. I had known them slightly in New Zealand. They came to the hotel one night after their first two days in the East.

'I can't get over the poverty!' the wife said. She was really moved to horror. 'You don't know what to do. The *details* of it are so dreadful. That's what gets me down.'

The details, the reality was what she was trying to say, are what get you down. The reality of great wealth, too, I was about to say to her. But I didn't. She had enough to cope with. I never met her again. I would have liked to meet her again when she had had time to think it out a little. But maybe nothing much happened.

The Orient can be very hard to live in. One day it's impossible. The next, the thought of leaving for the West is almost unendurable. That poverty, the peculation, apathy, the abysmal degradations of mystic rituals

controlling every act of life—those details can drive you to the door of the
airline office with money in your hand for a ticket to Europe where all that
is in less degree or better concealed, or easily circumvented because you
know the ropes more perfectly. In some Indian city not long before we
reached Hong Kong, the traveller said:

'I've committed myself. And be damned to the isolation of it.'

'But now . . . ?' I said to him. 'I mean after these last couple of years since
Hungary?' The Left of the world seemed to me to be turning on itself like a
nightmare sleeper on his moonlit shadow.

'It's inescapable,' he said firmly.

'Is it? It feels true. But when you contemplate your life . . . committed,
I mean. Isolated more than you know from the majority.'

'It's they who are isolated,' he said.

'And you who will feel it. You the romantic, the lost in beauty.' Most
of me agreed with the traveller. 'I'm always committing myself. And after
a time I have to do it all over again. The earlier dedication, unity, or whatever
you may like to call it, didn't go deep enough. Things happen and you
realize there are further expanses of life in relation to yourself which your
committal is too restricted to embrace. So you are forced to recommit
yourself.'

'If you look at a very small child, without sentimentality, as if it were a
small parcel of hope—which it is, and nothing much more—then you are
committed for evermore,' said the traveller very quietly.

It was too simple not to want to detect a flaw. But I had just given my
bag to a starved boy whose shoulders poked out of holes in his dirty shirt.
He carried the bag to the door of the airways terminal. He couldn't take it
further because if he had they would certainly have kicked him out again.
He had carried the bag about ten yards, I suppose. He set it down carefully
and adjusted the tie-on label so that it hung straight, and tried to look as
though he had done something special, with extra refinement of porterage.
A crush of people blocked the plate-glass doors at that moment and I had to
wait before I could go in. The boy looked at me with a sort of pleading
solemnity, as though to ask me to remember he had done his best. His held-
out hand was tentative. Not entirely his muscles, but the need to which his
life had conditioned him, held it out. I searched desperately in my pockets
which were full of air tickets and receipts and pens and inoculation certifi-
cates. I found five annas and five rupees. I gave him the lot and snatched
my bag and dived into the terminal. I caught a glimpse of his face. The
wonder there was practically unbearable to see. Eventually when I came out
again to get a taxi I found he had somehow taken my hand and I was carrying
my own bag. He stood radiantly smiling as we drove off cringing into the
seat under the weight of our immeasurable riches.

'You see,' said the traveller rather sadly. 'You're committed.'

So, at the door of the airline office in the Orient, you hesitate as the air-conditioned cold inside puts its clammy hand on your throat: you take a quick scout round the frustrations and assorted discontents of your spirit; they somehow begin to seem less important; and you turn away, stowing the money back into your safest pocket, and take a stroll in the pulsing warmth and fierce smells of a back street where life and death are more real in their ghastly and homely way than they ever were since childhood in Europe. It isn't exactly true, of course, that they're more real, or that you think they are for more than the emotional moment. Order is properly meted out in the West, more or less, and you are fixed in your caste there, or in whichever you have arrived at by various means. Order is properly meted out in the East, too, and the Orientals are fixed in their castes there, or in whichever status they have—the fortunate wealthy ones—managed to escape into. It is only you, the occidental, who in the East are fundamentally outside every caste; and, with a little trouble and empathy, inside every caste. Maybe it is that which in foreign places vitalizes the traveller and his more analytical half.

Maybe, too, there is a sort of sensuality in us that responds to the particular stimuli of tropical climates and their subtle violence. The word 'temperate'—whose overtones are temperance, not warm enough to do without a pull-over, rather chilly in the sea, fruit crop chancy this year on account of little sun, rooms shut most of the year against the cold—the word in that personal context is not attractive. 'Tropical' is. Even its overtones of running sweat and utter fatigue in the limbs, doubtful food, smells of excreta, bestiality of man to man, don't cast the slur that logically they ought. They make you think of the people who are driven together by the extremes of climate and derivative environmental conditions in a way we are not in the dull temperate belt. Between extremes of human experience a delicate, fascinatingly tremulous equipoise teeters through living in the tropics. It evokes the thing we call beauty—but beauty that is wanton and subtle at one time. It evokes cunning that does not contrive scientific things (but can and will). You either respond, or you don't. It may be as simple as that.

In South China, where it is only sub-tropical, something of the same feeling exists, and there are other reasons for it. In Hong Kong, also sub-tropical, it is gone. Now that is an interesting thing.

A week of rain. Every morning waking to the sound of rain, opening your eyes to the curtain of rain falling between the roof and the floor of the verandah, feeling the air heavy with moisture and completely odourless. Now and then the sky brightens a little and the rain stops. You go out because you must go out to relieve the monotony of hiding indoors. Everything is drenched with water. Traffic swishes past like speedboats in the running streets. Clothes hang limp, sodden faces of buildings drip water on your head. All the offices are alight inside, the office workers scuttling about or sitting bemused at their desks leafing through papers. The junks in the harbour begin to hoist sails in the hope of drying them a little, but the sky, and the distance where the dragon-back of hills separates British from Chinese territory, scowl like the face of a disapproving god. Even the sea has lost its vitality, beaten with tiny lashes of rain like a man put into a torpor by the rain of bacteria in his blood. People in bookshops, European residents and tourists from the liners on cruises, are searching for something to read. The sellers of cigarettes and papers on corners of streets tentatively lift the oilcloth covers from their wares, shake the water off, and fold them inside out. For once umbrellas—the English city black and the varieties of green and yellow varnished paper—are furled, and the vestibules of restaurants stain with pools of water draining from them while the owners eat.

It darkens again. In the distance thunder growls like a war and people upturn their heads to inspect the sky, which assures them of nothing but that it holds a lot more water yet. You begin to speculate what it is that holds so much water in suspension up there, to suspect that you didn't learn properly about it at school.

But in a way the rain is a good thing. Yesterday the papers said several million gallons fell on the island and its little scrap of mainland—Kowloon and the New Territories—but the reservoirs are still almost empty. After the exceptionally dry few months past it takes a lot of water to make the authorities sleep easy in their beds. Long ago in a drought they had to import water from the Chinese mainland. But that was before the revolution in China and they would hate to ask now.

Water is one of the smaller problems in Hong Kong. A few more reservoirs here and there, a little ingenuity, continuance of the present rationing system for a time, and the thing is solved. The great ache in the otherwise heartily thriving commercial body of Hong Kong is the refugees.

If there is one thing worse than being born to a life of semi-starvation in the more rigorous parts of the earth, it must be to be born in a refugee camp, or to have to live as a refugee. In Hong Kong you would be one of more than a million and a half wedged into a few square miles of mostly mountainous territory where the local inhabitants already numbered one million six hundred thousand. Only 12 per cent of those three million people live in the New Territories, and the remainder are jammed together in the thirty-six square miles of Hong Kong, Kowloon, and New Kowloon.

There are not many reliable figures from the past to tell you how many refugees were pushed here or squeezed out from there in revolutions and cataclysms of their fellow men. But perhaps never have so many quite helpless people arrived in so small a place with so little hope of escape from it, as came to Hong Kong.

They arrived in a city lately recovered from the Japanese and reclaimed for Queen Victoria—or something as near to the social conditions of her dreadful reign as the local British could manage. They poured in from the deep cautery of the Chinese revolution and stood in the unfamiliar place with lost looks.

Or most of them did, for they were mostly peasants. But there was a proportion of scholars who disagreed, frightened bourgeoisie, and a power of bastards padded with the treasure they had been filching over the years from the mouths of those lost ones who came in the same broken junks and scrambled over the same hills—over the black scales of the dragon that separates Hong Kong from China. And they all ran in the fuddy-duddy streets of Hong Kong with their spacious arcades and rotting stucco, past the windows of the English mandarins who were sitting inside sweating and money-grubbing under the fans, past the stately homes of Englishmen stuffed with the treasures of Peking which their fathers and uncles looted before the time of Sun Yat-Sen. Every Chinese uncle and cousin in Hong Kong was inundated with relatives, begging food and a square yard of his burning roof to pitch a shanty on, a corner of an overcrowded room to lay the baby down.

A million and a half. Milling distracted and weary over the little settled heap of Hong Kong. By now it is an old story and the flood of refugees has been regulated by law until it is only an illegal trickle stealing in on boats down the China coast and disappearing into that multitudinous yellow bosom of the Hong Kong populace.

The condition of the city is not as bad as that of pre-war Shanghai. But the social structure is identical. Therefore the evils of it are similar—both acute and chronic. It would be untrue and unfair not to praise the people of Hong Kong who, through the Government, have done so much to better the conditions of that appalling host of Chinese who came as refugees. They have done a lot. Officials will point to the free distribution of food, the dreadful barrack blocks which have been rushed up in Kowloon, the extensive medical services, the colossal sums of money which the revenue of the Island has disbursed. And they will proudly—and in the case of the late Governor—tartly point out that all of that money has come from internal sources and none from international funds. You are tempted to retort that there must have been a lot of surplus money in the hands of the ruling classes, that they could be so lavish. Lucky that there was, for otherwise that searing misery of life in Hong Kong which even today hits you like an angry hand, inflaming the cheeks of your humanity, would have been more terrible than it was. They have done quite a good job. They needn't brag about it. They had the money to do it. Besides, there's plenty more that remains undone.

We were going to China when we arrived in Hong Kong. We were coming back from China when we arrived there again. That puts the life of Hong Kong under a powerful searchlight. Astringency is the quality of one's reactions—even after a year or so has passed. The great mass of

China proper lies just across the border, an hour's drive from the jetty where you disembark from the ferry at Kowloon. Whether you think it looms or grins in your direction depends very much who you are and how much money you have. There are many Chinese in the Colony who incline to think it wears a certain smile. Rather more of them than the Hong Kong English like to believe. There are of course Chinese in large numbers who are more English than the English in outlook, and a few pseudo-intellectual English who are more Chinese than the traditional Chinese in theirs. There are also the majority of English who don't consider the Chinese at all except to pay them wages. But really in talking of attitudes one can afford to ignore the extremes and consider, largely, the middles who all have ties of blood with people still in China. They freely correspond with those relatives and large sums of money in remittances, in the Chinese filial way, find their way across the border quite legally to many a village and town in China. Despite the prevailing wind of anti-Chinese propaganda many Chinese have returned over the border to China—and more are still doing so, probably more than the statistics admit. In China a young man or woman with keenness and ability is sure of a good free technical education and a job that, in terms of other people's jobs, is well-paid. He is sure of neither in Hong Kong. I know many young people in the Colony whose lives prove this statement.

We still have the maimed beggars in Hong Kong, the lethal rickshaw, children toting the babies on their backs, a frightening tuberculosis rate, children of eight who work as room-boys in hotels, television which only the rich can afford, restaurants pouring with sumptuous food, and people waiting in the hope of a scrap of food, like dogs.

The Island usually called Hong Kong is actually named Victoria. Vertically it is a rough cone, and in plan diamond-shaped. A road more or less follows the coastline all round, and the sides of the cone—the Peak— are festooned with switchback roads leading up from the town on the north shore, to the palatial houses of the well-to-do. The nearer you live to the top the higher your income, the more mildew you collect in the winter and the more splendiferous your view. The rich can afford in an esoteric fashion to live on a view—that it consists of the mainland of China is neither here nor there.

To the south lies the original Hong Kong—the Chinese characters standing for Fragrant Harbour—a little fishing port now called Aberdeen, tight-packed with junks and sampans, the homes of a large population. The Empress Dowager, the last of the Manchu rulers of China, a crafty old woman, was once voted a large sum of money with which to build (for the first time in China's history) a fleet. To her the idea seemed a dull one, thoroughly anti-traditional, so she spent most of the money on a stone boat which she caused to be set by the shore of the lake in her Summer Palace. It is a charming object, much frequented by the Peking public on

Sundays in the fragrant spring which comes to that harbour in the Western Hills. Naturally, all the commercial vulgarians of the East have reproduced it in this or that material for some purpose or the other. The latest mock-up is the Sea Palace at Aberdeen, floating picturesquely in the midst of the crowded fishing-fleet. Inside is one of the best restaurants for sea-food in the East, on two floors lavishly garnished with fluorescent light, teeming with Cantonese waiters and, in the morning and afternoon full of Chinese playing Mah-jong so that the place echoes to the clicking of the bricks. Alongside is moored the kitchen boat, all white mosaic walls and fiery furnaces where delicious food sends up the odours of a gourmet's paradise. In the morning you find the manager buying from a fleet of local fishing boats the ingredients of the evening's meals—*bêche-de-mer*, foot-long sea-slugs, fish of all kinds with names such as Green Coat, Golden Fin, Two-beard, Yellow Dragon; and the whole gamut of giant crustaceans. The chefs are grouped at the open end of the cook-boat preparing the vegetables and fish, while an eager crowd of poor women and children wait for the scraps they discard. It is a strange contrast, those thin kids and the nourished cooks who are entirely indifferent to the preciousness of the food they let fall.

And leaning over the gilded dragon which serves as balustrade on the dining deck of the Sea Palace, the diners are peering down into huge floating tanks where the fish are kept alive. A coolie stands there with a nylon butter-fly-net and catches the fish you indicate as it swims all unsuspecting in the green water.

An Englishman standing beside me one day, a man with the proper sporting instincts, lamented the unfairness of this scene.

'Look at them, the silly clots,' he said, referring to the fish. 'Not a dog's chance!' Then a marvellous yellow and black fish took a leap for freedom from the net of the coolie and plunged into the surrounding sea. 'Bloody good! One lucky sod's got away! Now that pleases me a lot.'

At night when the Sea Palace is glittering with light and tinsel and murmuring across the water, the boats of the fisher-people lie small and smelly and dark round it. As you are rowed back to the shore in a curly little sampan by a Chinese girl whose other work is in bed, small homely scenes float past—the family eating under the tarpaulins in the light of an oil lamp, the children curled up in corners asleep. An occasional fish comes up for air with a short plop and the moon of Hong Kong hangs above a frail lace of cloud.

Drive homeward up to the Peak and stand an hour or so there looking down on one of the world's fabulous sights, the whole spread magnificence of the great harbour between the Island and the illumined carpet of Kowloon across the water. The cliffs drop sheer at your feet and Victoria stretches from left to right, from tall banks and offices, restaurants and nightclubs, away along to the straight streets of Wan Chai which is the Chinese quarter. There the lights are densely packed in an ordered galaxy of neon of every conceivable colour, the runnels of streets liquid ribbons of light. Here and in Kowloon live the mass of the people, sleeping and eating and being in a vast pullulating mêlée. It is a crazy place. To spend time there is like taking a walk through a disordered mind. All the images of life are there, alive and kicking each other, mixed, jumbled, inter-existing. An aura of merciless hardness is one of the qualities you sense there. The survival of the fittest Chinese. But it is nothing like the hopelessness of an Indian town. The Chinese actively like to live in a big group (let us not enquire whether this is conditioned by the fact that in their history they have almost never had enough to manage not to); and they seem not to suffer from that 'perpetual state of sub-conscious irritation in the mind' which Tagore postulates as a deep influence on Indian character, and which shapes the pattern and feeling of life in India. The Chinese are an altogether more placid people at heart, excitable but governed in excitement by their own strange ethical calm. Somehow they are always much more at home with the rest of the world than the Indians, and they seldom have the Indian's sad bitterness. Even in the refugee villages in Hong Kong you don't find that dire extremity of the spirit that stabs you in an Indian village: because the Chinese have a massive resilience, collective and also individual. Yet curiously their suicide rate (and not only in Hong Kong) is one of the highest of any people in the world.

If there is one factor which may explain the divergence of the Chinese character from that of most other tropical and Oriental peoples it is perhaps that they never took to a religion en masse. Even Buddhism, the most popular of the great religions in China and the only one to take some hold, never swept over the country with the violence of Christianity in Europe, or Islam through the East. If anything controlled Chinese life—ever—it was a subtle mixture of the conservatism of Confucius, mixed with a little Taoist magic and proto-science, and a dash of nice other-worldliness from early Buddhism. Obviously that sort of code is not likely to shake a state or a spirit to its foundations. The eclectic, however delightful, and even reasonable, is seldom a shattering experience.

Something of this, then, it may be, makes of a Chinese slum a different kettle of fish from those of India. The barbarities of one or other cult of Hinduism which underlie and stultify (and sometimes magically electrify the spirit of India), which to the outsider make life there now repellent and now dear, don't exist in the Chinese huddle. The poverty, the rags, the disaster of funeral expenses and bizarre marriage customs and the impoverishment of whole families as a result, are certainly present and obvious, but somehow that Chinese ebullience—result, you might suggest, of the lack of a fundamentalist religious outlook—rides the life-storm without falling into the voiceless and piteous horror of the worst of life in India.

Yet, knowing this from experience, you are moved to a shudder of pity and to anger by a valley back of Kowloon. There is no flat land there to put your house on. The shacks on the slopes are like cripples helping each other to stand up. After the rain the ground has collapsed under the feet of some, and sad piles of old plywood and rusty corrugated iron mixed with canvas and bits of roofing-felt cascade down the slopes. Here and there whole families were salvaging from it the more solid pieces, so as to start again somewhere else. It is men, Thucydides remarked, not walls that make a city. Even a shanty town of refugees. The kids are all daubed with dirt. The single well is several hundred yards down the valley. From it a procession of women and boys come and go with wet washing and buckets of water.

From the brow of the hill above the valley, if you cared to get out of your leather armchair in the Hong Kong Club and take a look, several breakneck paths descend among the leaning huts. The air stinks of urine and the view from most doorways is the packing-case wall of the nearest house a yard away. When you are bowling skittles along the fifty yards or so of polished floor in the clubroom set aside for that activity, it should come to you that some people don't have enough space to lie down, that your bedroom window does not look out across urined mud at a verminous packing case. Faces peer at you from windows in old tea-chests. A man is propping up the corner of his undermined house with a bit of a branch, and his wife is standing by, fearful that it may totally collapse. In front of a hut where some flowers are growing in a kerosene can you may pause to wonder that they care to bring extra water from the well, so far away. At the end of a blind alley is a dark cell. Through the doorway a taper is lit before a small shrine of some Chinese sort. Dimly, beside his shrine, apparently more sincere than the Sunday-best congregation in the churches of Hong Kong, an aged Chinese with wrecked face is mumbling the words of his intercession to a god who passed with his own generation.

And then, above, on a square yard of terrace commanding a view of the valley, there stands a madonna of palest anaemic skin, nursing her miraculous Chinese Christ-child. She is posed there in her private paradise. A helicopter, indifferent as the morning star, hangs above her head.

There is a large cemetery no more than a hundred yards from the valley. It is convenient. But I'm not sure that it isn't reserved, like the Hong Kong Club, for Europeans only.

Hong Kong is an excellent example of colonial capitalism, and, in this latter day, of its sop to the subjects of a paternalist regime. The system has been officially described as a benevolent despotism. Benevolence is a word somewhat suspect when you find it used of the largesse scattered liberally among the poor of Hong Kong. For the distribution of these huge sums was partly made in self defence and partly with an eye to the main chance. After the war Hong Kong had to turn into an industrial city-state. '. . . economic survival was due to the expansion of, and revolution in, its industry; and this was made possible', says an official handbook with candour, 'in some measure by the three gifts which some of the refugees brought with them from China; the first a surplus of labour, the second new techniques from the North coupled with a commercial shrewdness and determination superior even to that of the native Cantonese, and the third new capital seeking employment and security'.

The loss of the trade with China, which in 1938 made up 75 per cent of the colony's total, made a very uncomfortable hole in the pocket of British business there. The upheaval in China which caused this produced at a single stroke both the problem and, as the handbook admits, also its solution. A super-abundance of labour that has no other outlet is necessarily attended in this type of system by exploitation of labour for its cheapness. But there was, and still is, one fly in the ointment—the existence of China over the border. For every Chinese, except those whom the divorce of extreme wealth has separated from their own people, looks to China as even a comfortably marooned man does to a sail on the horizon. So in Hong Kong the Government had to make things more or less bearable, or they might have had a revolution on their hands. To put it in such terms is not all the truth, nor is it maliciously intended—merely that these are the basic conditions over which all sorts of benevolence have acted. Benevolence is a nice name for charity, and charity is too often the insurance, the cheap insurance, of the rich and safe against the evil time of discontent. No amount of official fingers pointing to those huge blocks of resettlement flats good and bad, to the manful job done by the medical services and poor relief, to the expenditure freely made from the colony's pocket, should obscure the fundamental mechanics of what happened in Hong Kong. What has been done is on the whole good for the refugees. But it is even better for capital investment.

'Do you see, my son,' the holy Maël exclaimed, 'that madman who with his teeth is biting the nose of the adversary he has overthrown, and that the other who is pounding a woman's head with a huge stone?'

'I see them,' said Bulloch. 'They are creating law; they are founding property; they are establishing the principles of civilization, the basis of society, the foundations of the State.'

Hong Kong, unfortunately, is not the only Penguin Island in the East.

But those million and a half refugees. . . . Let's not suppose, as people glibly do in Hong Kong and elsewhere, that all of them knew what they were fleeing from. The rich ones did, and they brought their capital with them, as the government handbook gratefully memorializes. The mildly well-to-do were frightened that they would be levelled—that basic fear of the bourgeoisie. The intellectuals fled because they were Chinese intellectuals—which is to say ultra-reactionaries fitted for life by reading all the best traditional Chinese poets who were bucolic scholars of the feudal type. And the mass of the rest, the voiceless many from the disruption and horror of the Chinese countryside in the old days, why did they come? Because they were afraid of the communists? Yes, some. Because they were conservative and feared they might be worse off when the old rulers of villages had gone? Yes, some. But most came to Hong Kong, I think, because they had nothing at all to lose, and because they thought they might be better away from the stagnant provinces of South China which were their home. That same resilience and vitality which have altered the face of China in the ten years since the revolution made them gamble on the chance of better things, even in the unknown. For it *was* an unknown; but less unknown than a new political system. And the history of China is one of repeated destruction of the land by revolutions and their armies, of peasants moving off to some other place. They were not to know that in the new regime in China they would at least have enough to eat. Probably no one actually starves in Hong Kong, but too many have too little to eat while the great enterprises of commerce build costly office blocks.

At night you can see into those empty offices. A few dim lights reveal the acres of vacant floor space. And at night you can see into the equally big housing blocks where hundreds of thousands of the more fortunate refugees live. There the lights reveal no floor space that is not crawling with Chinese like bees in a hive. And in the shanty villages here and there on the more impossible hills the oil lamps in old cigarette tins are flickering. Thank God for the rain, you think, for once or twice a fire started by those lamps has made thousands homeless overnight.

But in the strong heat of day the harbour and the wharves are teeming. Here is the dirt, the smell, the confusion (more apparent than real) of the Orient. Here are the coolies bursting their blood vessels under yokes of heavy produce, here is the swindling, smuggling, spitting, and camaraderie of people who have to work altogether too physically hard in the heat. It is hackneyed in literature, though too often used as a mere backdrop to the important loves of the whites. What is it, then, that disgusts under the fascination? If you are neither a mad dog nor a true colonial you tend to look at the impassioned movement of the working people on the wharves and in the boats with real empathy. You know very little from personal experience about back-cracking work like this, but expanding the little you know over the long days from puberty to death tells you what it must be like. And you have only to look at some of those faces to know the rest. Those families who live out their lives in the boats: the young good-looking girl with her baby tied down to the deck, heaving on the oar of the junk, her clothes stained with sweat, her arms corded, feet calloused, face showing already the furrows of age; her husband on the quay, bent under the dead weight of the huge marrows that come from China, his gold-capped teeth bared in the effort; his or her mother, that old brown scrap of screwed human flesh squatting on the high stern platform of the junk, also pulling on an oar, or cooking or washing, or sometimes tending that pathetic plant tied to a post there. The family live on that bit of deck aft, while the good wide part of the junk is given over to the cargo of pigs in baskets, which cover the hold with their ordure, or to onions that make the air tearful as it floats back.

Their life is probably a little better than it was. But to leave change to chance in a changing world is cruel and bad. These people have very little defence against the adventures of the rest of the world—its moneyed adventurers, its opportunists. Their expectation and hopes are small, but if by chance they had more, these would be frustrated. Their heart-tearing struggle with weight, and for life, in the sun, the brevity of their youth and the quickness of physical old age—are our indictment.

We chanced on the mortuary one showery morning in Kowloon; in the middle of the traffic at a T-road where shop upon small open shop lines the pavements under the coruscated stucco and lucky-mirror mosaic of arcades. The sides of the road were spattered with huge wreaths, fifteen feet high, of nasty paper flowers, leaning against the shop signs with the colours trickling into each other in the damp. One of them bore a little photograph of the deceased lady, a thin old woman, with her name under it. Sitting on the pavement, feet in the gutter, were the band in dirty white uniforms with peaked caps, smoking and conversing. Their bashed trombones and horns, various cymbals, Chinese gongs and drums sat beside them beading with rain. They wore a lugubrious look, for they are professional funeral musicians and the melancholy nature of the job and its frequent repetitions has produced a mixture of the sepulchral and the bored in their faces.

The coffin, a curly shape peculiar to Chinese coffins, was carted unceremoniously out of the mortuary doors between the remains of discarded wreaths from other funerals, and dumped on the road. A red pall covered it, on which were two Chinese characters—not the name of the deceased, but of the undertaker. The relatives and the professional mourners, their heads draped in white hoods, came out after the coffin in varying degrees of affliction. It was difficult to tell which was real emotion and which mere humbug. A woman followed them with an old tin containing incense sticks which she distributed to the mourners; who lit them from matches or cigarettes, whichever was to hand. Then all began circling the coffin, about fifty of them, children and grannies alike.

The band, meanwhile, had gathered its yellow bones from the pavement, given a preparatory spit and taken a last drag at its cigarettes, and was now lined up fronting the mourners as they revolved round the coffin. A small crowd, mildly attracted by the lackadaisical dirge, gathered. Cars and rickshaws and lorries were passing all the time honking even more loudly as the crowd thickened. Various rickshaws waited their opportunity to draw the wealthier or more ancient relatives in the wake.

The circling petered out and a relative scolded a professional mourner for not doing his stuff properly. Everyone knelt in the road facing the east and the coffin. Then the advertising pall was whipped off and a couple of coolies roped the coffin and lugged it away to the hearse—an aunt-like vehicle in black wood which would delight the devotees of rococo and Rolls-Royce. The hearse moved off at a spanking pace, hooting and scattering handfuls of paper money, and disappeared in the chaos of Kowloon streets. The band took the head of the procession, followed by mourners with suitably bowed heads, by the large wreaths. And the rickshaw trade brought up the rear.

It was all over. The passers-by sloped off and rain began to drip down again. Men at doors of shops went in for a glass of tea or a bottle of Coca-Cola. The scabrous wall of the mortuary stood totally exposed in the tears of rain. The paper money was sopping up the rain.

A youngish woman picked up a piece of it, put it to her mouth, then touched the sole of her shoe with it; and threw it away. No one seemed to know what this meant to her, or whether she was just crazed.

Another funeral was forming up and new wreaths were coming out of the mortuary. A few relatives congregated for their own corpse, and another band began to get ready.

The rain falls heavily now, bouncing off the black oilskin hoods of the rickshaws and plastering the singlets of rickshaw coolies to their chicken-thin skin. The Peak over the harbour disappears behind its modesty of cloud, and the wives of the wealthy who live up there are phoning up their friends and saying, Do come to dinner on Thursday week. Isn't it *frightful* weather! We're having such trouble with the mildew on things. . . .

# VII. Fiji

The sprinkled isles,
Lily on lily, that o'erlace the sea,
And laugh their pride when the light wave lisps . . .

Not Greece, as Browning wrote, but—at this stage in our journey—Fiji.

'In a way,' said the traveller, who knew the lines, 'they fit better in the Pacific than in the Aegean, don't you think?'

There is sun, we found, almost perpetual sun, in the Islands in December. Coral reefs encircle the gorgeous necks of the Islands, bounding the aerial view of their milk-green lagoons with a fine thread of surf; and all round lies the lapis-lazuline sea, the monstrous voluptuary Pacific that engulfs the boss of earth under an unechoing arc of sky. 'A sight to dream of, not to tell!'

Such a heap of nonsense has been written about the South Sea Islands that, like Cook when he sailed clear through the latitudes where the fabled Southern Continent of contemporary fancy was supposed to stretch, you would hardly be surprised if they didn't exist at all.

But in fact they do: and Paradise, thank God, is not to be found there.

Not in Utopia—subterranean fields,—
Or some secreted island, Heaven knows where!
But in the very world, which is the world
Of all of us,—the place where, in the end
We find our happiness or not at all.

For Paradise is really one of the most stupid, pathetic, and boring of all ideas. If you ever met it in the world it would be essential to write a long, long book describing in the minutest detail just how things were there, so as to show once for all that only nitwits could be happy in it. Apart from lunacy, there is no escape. There is only the journey into other experience, deeper, that is, into one's own understanding and closer to other people's hearts. The dilemma which forces you to consider escape is only solvable in that way.

Once that is firmly embedded in the head, that seepage of sentimentality called the romantic view dries up a bit and you can start for the South Seas without misgiving.

'Did you?' asked the traveller with embarrassing innocence.

'Of course not! Don't be silly.'

'Oh.'

'Of course not. We're just clearing the air of South Sea Mist. Which is pink, like tinted spectacles.'

'Is it?' he said. He mocked me a very little.

'Yes. Decidedly.'

The mist dispersed, momentarily, you can look back through the recorded past of the South Seas and find almost nothing but Gauguin in painting, and a handful of salted mariners in writing and travelling, that is not loaded with Paradise.

But then ruminating on all you have read and heard—and wished—the mists seep through again. . . . There are simplicities you never dream of. You are led away, protesting but willing. Like the shock of bared flesh the Islands hit you in the yearning belly. You want to explore the sensuous resilience of this flesh in the blue bed of the Pacific—as if for the first time making such an exploration. Passion, that simplicity, flares up by the minute, inflating from neat balloon to lolloping bladder of a thing at the will of the slightest South Sea zephyr. You can fall in love with the Islands as if they were women; each breath of theirs becomes a sirocco, each of yours a passion of tingling anticipation lethargizing and driving at the same time. The stretched senses seem capable of unlimited further stretch, and the being capable of deeper and more disastrous committal without need of more reason to urge it.

'Aiyee!' cried the traveller. 'It must be a disease.'

'The infection called Paradise. Something like rabies mixed with moon-light.'

It was seldom hard to best the traveller. He clung still to the remains, the pink misty relic, of his former view. The journey was slowly telling on him, dispersing haloes, rubbing out pious and unconsidered inscriptions on the iconography of his thought. But there is an irreducible naïveté in all of us, and travellers, by virtue of the marvels they encounter, are more prone to its charms and its poisons than others.

Consider, before we go on to cast our souls away on the Islands, I said to him gently—for maybe I was treading on dreams—consider how the people first came here. There they were, established on the shores of the great continents, the land which stretched perhaps from China through what is now Indonesia and was one piece with Australia; and the other land which is South America. They were living by the shores east and west of the great ocean, fishing daily, making short shore-wise trips because in many places to

N

sail may have been easier than to walk. And later, much nearer to our own
time, when the Indonesian Archipelago and Malaya were separated, the
people were sailing from one island to the next, island-hopping, trading,
planting crops here and there, fishing in favourite spots. Over centuries many
hundreds of millions of little journeys must have been made, quite safely
and between places which the eye could see, or between places which were
a little farther apart than that. It was quite safe—until the storms which
spring from nowhere, from the sudden wrath of the sea, and whip their
chastisement across the face of the world, blew those outriggers and their
men away.

Sometimes the boat would contain pigs or other livestock being trans-
ported from one to another pasture or brought back to the village for
killing. Sometimes there would be a few children aboard, taking a ride with
their father for the fun of it. Even there might be a woman or two, coming
with you to help in some pastoral or domestic task, or to prepare the meal
while the men were at work on the island away from home. Now and then
there would be a mouse or two, or a rat, crouched among the odds and ends
at the bottom of the boat where it had gone the previous night when the
boat was beached in front of the huts by the shore. And there would be
coconuts of water, quite a supply of yams and taro, and the meat and
vegetables for the meals the women would cook in the intervals of work.
And surely there were cooking utensils, implements for digging and cutting, and the means to make fire; while someone, doubtless, had taken along
a line and a fishing hook carved from bone, even a spare one, to get a little
supplement of fish in the waiting-times.

Consider, then, that a storm blew up occasionally while some of those
frail-looking, but really sturdy, craft were plying to and fro; and they were
blown away for days on end—it happens quite often even today—into
fearful distances.

> Roll on, thou deep and dark blue Ocean—roll!
> Ten thousand fleets sweep over thee in vain;
> Man marks the earth with ruin—his control
> Stops with the shore; upon the watery plain
> The wrecks are all thy deed, nor doth remain
> A shadow of man's ravage, save his own,
> When, for a moment, like a drop of rain,
> He sinks into thy depths with bubbling groan,
> Without a grave, unknell'd, uncoffin'd, and unknown.

But a few sunblistered, half-dead men, after days of drifting at the whim
of current and breeze, came to land. Summoning their last strength they
navigated the jaws of the reef and stumbled up the unknown shore. Where
they were they did not know. How to return was utterly beyond their
powers of navigation. How to live, to start again with the little community

of the boat, was something more within their range. With the valiance of men in despair, with the hope that seems implanted in men to defeat their utter hopelessness, they set about their life in the new island of which they were the only human inhabitants.

They may sometimes have been lucky—for currents and storms in the Pacific are remarkably constant in strength and direction at various seasons of the year. They may have found other men already settled on the island; men blown like them from elsewhere, perhaps in the same generation or the one before, or many tens of years ago so that all they recalled of their homeland were a few old men's tales of it, together with the special crafts of their forebears.

If that boatload of castaways were men alone, they lived until the last man died solitary and crazed with his final loneliness. And then the island's population was again extinct. The little land waited in its fastness of wind and tide the accident of another voyage to people it again.

All the tales of miraculous voyages, accurately planned and deliberately embarked on, which abound in the imagination of romantic writers on the Pacific, prove insubstantial when you come to look at facts. Early European discoverers, on the other hand, describe time and again tales the local people told them of men who arrived from some unknown place and stayed on because they could not tell where to go that was homewards. Those Europeans also tell of desirable islands where life would have been easy, which were unpopulated and showed no sign of past human habitation. They recount, too, congestion and misery on other islands whose barren coral barely supported the crush of human beings. Analyse the winds and currents, the thrust of seasonal drifts from the continents and archipelagos—even from major Pacific islands towards others—and the explanation of Pacific population resolves its own riddle without recourse to superhuman feats of navigation in prehistoric or even historic times. And if a doubt still exists in the mind it is enough to remember one simple fact— that several of the early European travellers, with the aid of sextant and compass which no indigenous Pacific voyager had, were quite unable to find an island that they had visited some time before. Remember, too, the sanity of Captain Cook who, against all the romanticism of the times, postulated accidental voyages as the means whereby the Islands were peopled.

The story of those ten thousand unwitting fleets, at least of those few that hit a land, appears then clearly on the screen of history. So does the fate of the others, the majority, those thousands of little boats and their accidental crews which tell no more tale than the drop of rain to which Byron likens them, which vanishes in the enormity of ocean.

When they had established themselves and increased with the passing of time, the islanders evolved their own particular cultures, variants of those at home and adapted to the new circumstances—though retaining echoes of the originals. And with the advent of Western men in ships they began to decay; the sometimes fierce, sometimes happy, way of life they had made began to disintegrate under the blows of our technical civilization (or such of it as we brought them). Finally we bought or seized them, and in Fiji almost wiped them out, first with measles and later with influenza. We implanted there an alien group, Indians imported as semi-slave labour for our sugar plantations, who, with the toughness of Indians, themselves increased. Now they outnumber the Fijians and outclass them in political and commercial astuteness. Having divided, albeit unintentionally, we still rule, balancing the pans of Fijian and Indian the one against the other, balancing land ownership traditionally invested in Fijian hands against political and monetary capital stored up by the Indians.

But forget all that and arrive, a mere observer, by midget plane from the international airport in the north of Viti Levu, the main island of the Fiji group—at that broken-down field near Suva, the capital in the south. And trundle in a broken-down bus into town. They drop you on a corner nowhere particular so you have to tote your bags along the road to the hotel. You enter by the street-level bar and past the dining-room where potted palms reign if not supreme at least with a Victorian frown. Upstairs there is a fat old Australian woman whose life has been spent at the desk. She sums you up with a quick, motherly, but down-to-earth look, and takes you along the long linoleumed corridor from which all the bedrooms open and on whose other flank are the showers and zinc bath-tubs and the wreaths of gangling afterthought piping. Those rooms are palaces of the cockroach, shrines of the antediluvian ornament and haunts of makeshift necessities. The common verandah allows free intercourse of various types with occupants of other rooms, and also a view of the street below.

It is Saturday night. Australian banks and English counting-houses are closed; the port is idle; the local cinema is still alight, its crude posters hanging meekly under green neons; a few eating-joints are dishing up sausages and mash, mixed inedible grills dowsed in tomato sauce. The hotel bar emits a Fijian noise, compound of beer, Polynesian, English, and Antipodean drunkenness. At closing time the noise transfers itself with the bibbers to the street and murders sleep in all the bedrooms of the hotel. They all spill out— skippers of Pacific coasters, European dregs, merchant seamen, Lascar greasers, drinking Fijians with fine mops of brush-like hair and sarongs to just below the massive knee. They fight and smash bottles and rake off down the road to the corner where some garages breast the front. There they sit in drooping groups and fill their heads with the warm moist air coming off the sea, continuing desultorily the futile arguments of earlier on.

But Sunday morning—sun shines again on the island as if the heavens were grateful for a speck of land on which to pour their brilliance. Even the hungover air in the hotel is invigorated. In the shoddy streets of Suva only a few shops are open to catch stray tourists. By ten or so family groups of Fijians begin to appear; mother big and portly in mother-hubbard to her ankles and print frock on top of it to mid-calf, her proud head haloed in wiry brown hair sticking out radially from the scalp, her big breasts meriting the word deep, her bare solid feet reliably pacing along by husband in clean white sarong, white jacket, and confining tie. They have wonderfully generous features—large and spread and soft, with power and laughter built in, and a row of negroid teeth, and great hands that swing heavily at their sides. They are going to church. The children, too, all in white. Paterfamilias and mother and kids crocodiling along as if Victoria had never left the throne: which, in Fiji, she has not.

The bells ring over the tatty little township, echoing on the sides of docks and threading through the lattices of rusty cranes, penetrating into Hindu shops where Siva still fiercely reigns beside Victoria. Quietly and decorously the Fijians go padding along to Methodist Church, to Seventh Day Adventist, to Baptist, to the bells of 'Onward Christian Soldiers' coming sweetly and irrelevantly through palms, through haloes of Fijian hair, through massive Fijian skulls where Polynesian joy is now corralled as a frisking pony. Now the word of the Western God, carefully simplified and easier to get along with than the old spirits, comes out from the skinny throat of the white preacher and resounds on the gothic corrugated iron of the church. Now and then the Word is a bit tedious—but the organ booms out, surging somehow in your stomach and lifting up your heart. Just like the preacher said. You sing because you can't help singing, because it is good to open the big heart in your chest and sound out your feelings and let them carry up with the throbbing of the organ music.

' "No man is an island, entire of it self",' reflected the traveller as we sat in the back pews of the church. 'A Pacific of voluminous sound. . . .'

' "Never was isle so little",' I began. 'Do you recall? "Never was isle so little, never was sea so lone, but over the scud and the palm trees an English flag was flown." Kipling, after all, was a Victorian and he knew what was what in the Empire. It was he, tongue slightly in his cheek, who produced the definitive White Man's God.'

We sat on, curiously and happily there, feeling rather small-sized behind the broad backs of the Fijians, the traveller lost in the swell of their rich voices—right enough reason for attending to nothing more profound. We bowed our heads with them in the prayers and caught mischievous glances of children whose fingers fiddled with the gilt edges of Hymnals, and frowned properly at the pink tongue of a girl who was licking the pink edges of a Bible.

There was a simplicity there seldom dreamed of by me. The kind of simplicity which used to be called simple faith. It went in Kipling's day with putting pants on the natives of Fiji and other realms of Victoria's commercial empire, with the right sort of docility like that of cows in the hands of experienced milkers. It was and is part of the Word of the missionaries' God. Only believe and the white man will help you to help him to a better life. By copra, in Fiji, and sugar—which are nourishing things to both stomach and stock exchange.

Copra especially is the milk of the Pacific Islands. It is still pouring out of them into the West. Copra it is that leads, almost impells you, to study those maps which are mostly sea, and to consult the owners of boats. To see it you must sail to the large and also the small islands where it is the means of subsistence and where the old trade of the Pacific continues much as it did in the adventure books of boyhood.

By now the traveller and I were fully prepared for the charm and remembered glamour of such things to have worn down to the hard core of their reality. And this we found true. But you have to be prepared to discriminate between what is aesthetic reality and that other one which is the context of life in the place. The traveller had evolved a way of letting them alternate in his thoughts, as moods shift into one another.

' "Away with systems! Away with the corrupt world! Let us breathe the air of the enchanted island," ' he cried at this moment. But the categorical imperative was fading from his voice, because he knew he would have to reflect later on the other side of the picture.

'Perhaps you've got something,' I said to him, as we were sailing in the small copra boat between the foaming lips of the reef, heading for the sea-wastes.

'Remember Donne?' he mused. ' "I am two fools, I know, For loving, and for saying so. . . ." That's exactly me.'

On the boat all day, and day upon day, those fractious, compulsive things called time, space, energy, stop bothering you—even cease to be. You are always in the exact centre of a convex disc of sea, yet curiously unimportant for one so centrally placed in the visible world. Sail how you will you can't escape the position until some land comes up over the rim of the sea and ousts you—or vies with you until you join it and are once again in the perfect centre of the world.

The crew are only half a dozen—Fijians, Tongans, and one from the Island of Rotuma—working about the deck, chaffing everyone, sprawling in shifting shade, grinning with their rows of giant teeth as though they might eat you for fun. No land. No spot of cloud. Sequinned cheeks of the Pacific on which you are smaller and less consequential than a tear. A solitary bird sits on a post at the stern, waiting more intently than you and more instinctually for land. Some moments it does not feel safe to be there in the eye of the sea and under the vast blue cyclops of the sky. Yet we are safer than of old. We are compassed, powered, willingly set out on our voyage and decently manned: yet—the Pacific is so endless-wide—we feel, as they must have done, the flagrant appetite of this ocean for the specks which teeter over the blue of her blood.

As you sit all day typing and scribbling, the Rotuman—the assistant cook, he is—stands over you, cloth in hand, scratching under his loin-cloth, smiling but puzzled. He can't exactly place what it is you are doing—why, as he puts it, you should take your office on a boat. You learn from him about his home, the isolated island outside the main Fiji group. There is some annual festival in spring, a rite of spring accompanied by fluent drinking and abolition of work, free love, and a delightful paganism which feels so mythological that it is almost Mediterranean. Telling you all this his eyes take on the springtime of humanity, part of which sometimes appears in the eyes of a happy child, part in the face of a youth at the beginning of his first love. The traveller longs to have been born with a Rotuman brown skin. But . . .

'No work in my island,' the cook says suddenly. 'Many must go away. My brother. Two of my friends.' The worm in the heart of the rose.

Eating with the chunky Tongan captain and the Indian engineer in the four-by-four saloon, idly served by a Fijian as dark and smooth of face as the mask of an Egyptian king—day upon day sailed up with clear dawn regarding the wine-dark sea, with still heat of petrified noon, with softening dusk; nights followed, chattery with Polynesian voices on the forrard deck. Maybe there was one uninhabited island that passed by in all that time of sea. But no more. We were lost with the benighted mariners of former times, we could resurrect in ourselves their fears of nameless creatures swarming in the meaningless sea. There is time for thought, for fear, for speculation, in this burden of the desert of the sea. It is a melancholy of mine own, compounded of many simples, extracted from many objects, and indeed the sundry contemplation of my travels, which, by often rumination, wraps me in a most humorous sadness. Even at noon it came, with the multitudinous laughter of the sea all round. For those rich and various gems inlay the unadorned bosom of the deep, but glitter, you feel, with the baleful eyes of corpses floating there. We hungered for land, for those summer isles of Eden lying in dark purple spheres of sea.

One morning they appeared—little dots on the horizon line. But crazed and shrieking with promise of human life, with the society of men. How fragile is our little life! How tenuous our content! An air, something that was inexplicable, beamed out from those dots, and aboard we were immediately more jocular and at ease with ourselves. That severed loneliness, with which the traveller is benighted, vanished with the smell of men. And one more stratum in the long excavation of the mound of life was coming within the traveller's vision.

We came to land, the crew scrambling about the rigging and taking the covers off the hold. 'The isle is full of noises,' that's it, that's what we have

missed, 'sounds and sweet airs that give delight and hurt not.' Those lines
spring to the traveller's mind with charming congruence. A quay projects a
few yards from the sands, piled with long, stuffed sacks of copra. A gesture
of a derrick sticks up at its seaward end. A fairway of green turf lies between
flanks of coconut trees and ends in a wooden house and sagging verandah
to whose side is a line of sheds. A few men begin to move from the house and
huts and from the shade of wide shelves where copra is sun-drying. They
straggle towards the jetty.

The ship's boat plunges over the side and smacks the water, throwing
one of the crew, who was in it, into the sea and sparking off laughter in the
rest of us aboard as his pants come off and he clambers back aboard with a
herculean thrust of naked thighs and dog-shake of his woolly head. We drop
into the boat and set off for the quay; set foot on the island, set nose in its
copra air, stand talking, near to these islanders whose aura came out to us
over the Pacific. A lorry comes stumbling down a rough road from inland,
heaped with copra. The foreman is winding up the telephone which speaks
along that single strand of wire with the great house of the owner of the
island. He sends his cold regrets that he is too busy to see me today. From
apologetic looks I gather that he doesn't much want me on his island. I
wonder why—or I would have wondered, had I not already heard something about how it is run.

The islanders are loading the boat, the sacks emitting their heavy
pungent smell. The lorry is about to set off empty up the hill. I cadge a lift
while the foreman is busy elsewhere. We lurch off into the trees. Sun is
falling on their heads, splashing their slender trunks and the heads of
Indian labourers splitting coconuts and extracting the meat with long knives,
their children and women sometimes helping. It takes a long time to fill a
whole sack. Pay is very poor. Market price of copra is high. In long collecting sheds the nut is fragmented and set out in the draught to dry on tiers
of shelves, then shovelled off by a couple of old men in the thick shadows.
The sacks are heaved out into the light and thrust on the lorry.

Girls from the Fijian village nearby came out to see me round the corner
by the local store. They grinned suggestively, making personal comments
and forming into a two-row group automatically so that I would take their
picture. I preferred them as they arranged their wiry hair and titivated their
shabby toilettes, unsuspecting that I was recording them at that moment.
The worn-out cotton of their dresses moulded by long wearing to those
full cushiony bodies made them more nubile than they knew.

The foreman was angry when I returned to the shore—or frightened
might be a more accurate word. I am not supposed to have seen the local
store, run by the owner of the island, where a packet of cigarettes on sale to
the workpeople costs some pennies more than it does in the shops in Suva.
The islanders are loading the boat and our men from the ship are taking it

out and unloading the sacks into the hold. The islanders are not allowed to
leave the shore. The owner of the island is afraid of losing his labour force
in stowaways.

We saunter away from the activity at the quay, along the beach where
uprooted palms lie like dark leek roots ten feet in diameter, fuzzed like
Fijian hair. Here, as Byron put it, 'There is a rapture on the lonely shore
... by the deep sea, and the music of its roar.' And, having taken the psalmist's
wings of the morning, we are there. And the islanders are there, living out
their sad life in those uttermost parts of the sea with a sort of gaiety in spite
of circumstance. We are there with them only for the happy moment. We do
not belong there except in the projects of our imagination. So we can't know
about the islanders—or not much at any rate. In human terms you can understand most people. It is our histories that sever us and are hard to overcome.

The traveller prints his bare feet into the fine crust of the baked sand,
takes off his shirt to get the sting of the sun on his shoulders. It isn't hard to
know what goes on in his head at that moment. The rapture of the beach,
the siren voices of the islands seduce him from reason. But the echoes in
my head are hardly sirens. I hear the full swell of the hymns we listened to
the other day in the Suva church, now mingled with the long strophes of
the waves. That rapturous singing when the Fijians were given simply to
the happiness of expressing the instinctual happiness of human beings. You
could construct in them a medieval fervour for religion, a fervour in all
simplicity. You could construct the beginnings of any other fervour, as the
potter makes what he wills of his clay. It is sad to see it not done: sadder to
see the cold exploitation we practise with the blessing of religion and coconut-
oil consumers.

But it is hard to dwell on those serious matters when the shore is beneath
the feet and the palms wave gracefully in the heady air, when the sea beats
its eternal rhythm on the virgin shore like a lover on his mate. Distantly
there is a promontory and a few grass-thatched huts of the people where we
could see women going to and fro, and where some children are playing
among the piglets. A little cooking smoke comes from the huts. An old boat
is lying on its side. . . . But we had learned not to be deceived. These people
were the cogs in the coconut machine. All the barbarity and integrity of
their natural life—the way of living they had carved out for themselves since
they came to the islands—has been destroyed by us. We have taken away
their moral code and given them another which is like a suit that doesn't
fit: and we have given them enough substance to keep them working for
our benefit. We have given them the rights of land tenure, which were
in any case their own and not ours. We have given them our religious song
and taken away whatever song was in their lives. For all this they are rewarded
by being outnumbered by Indians whom we imported, and outwitted politically by Indians and Europeans alike. The tourists come now from Australia

and New Zealand and other safe comfortable places to see how delightful the natives are in their island paradise.

We were nearing the end of our journey. Why should it end in these islands? You can begin or end anywhere—if you remember that the end is only another beginning. No man is an island, entire of it self: but too many think they are. Even the romantic traveller agreed with me on that, now that we had gone so far together and learned so much from each other and from what we saw and felt in haphazard places. He had learned perhaps to accept more of my point of view than he would formerly have thought possible. And I had learned how sometimes it is essential to temper intelligence with emotion and still not let emotion run away with intelligence.

'Somehow, we must be able to pull it all together,' I said, while we were sitting there on that Fijian shore with the village conducting its life on the promontory as unconscious as we were conscious and self-conscious.

'How?' the traveller replied. 'Well . . . you have a go.'

It was beginning to be pulled together in my mind but . . .

'And in your heart, don't forget,' he cautioned me.

'Yes. There too. But all scrumbled. We really need our own place for a while—to get it all straightened out. Our own perspective.'

'Which will seem radically wrong when we get there, I suspect.'

'Probably. But everything settles. Like sediment. The trouble is to keep things lively and not like sediment in the corners of your self.'

'Everything is much too vast,' he replied. 'You're wasting your time trying to concentrate the world into essences.'

I didn't agree. If you are not frightened of recognizing it, there is an essence. It is people: of whom you are the merest unimportant fraction. To find them different from you and your own kind is only the superficial view. To think of them as an essence, and to feel yourself part of it. . . .

'Is the beginning of wisdom?' the traveller suggested. And perhaps he mocked me a little. I don't know.

A boy of maybe eight, naked and grinning, holding a string with a tiny kaleidoscopic fish threaded on it, came along the shore leaving his track in the sand. We called him to come, if he would, and talk to us. We did not understand each other's words, but he showed us that he had speared the fish from the reef. Running to that collection of huts on the point, he came back with his spear, and we went with him out on the reef. We learned from him how to drive the spear into the refracting water, delicately and precisely . . . or rather *he* had learned this; even with his patient teaching we made only unsuccessful attempts to emulate his skill.

None of us caught any more fish to add to his dinner. But the traveller and I caught once more the prize catch in life: that abundant happiness in people and their inexplicable hope.

# Index

# Photographs

## SINGAPORE, MALAYA, THAILAND

## BORNEO

## HONG KONG

1

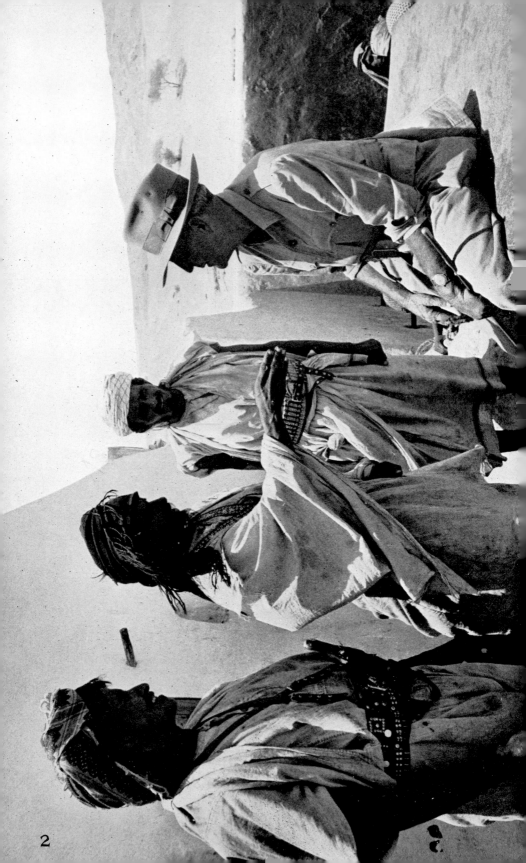

2

3

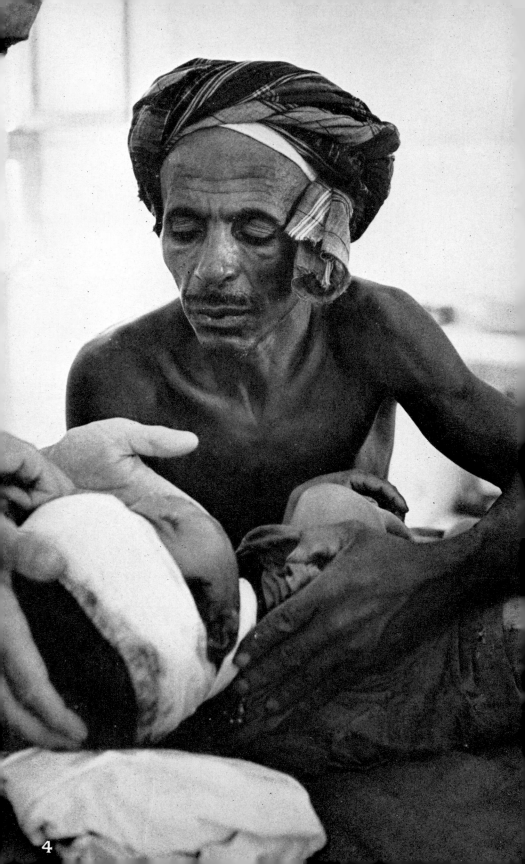

4

5

7

9

12

13

15

17

19

23

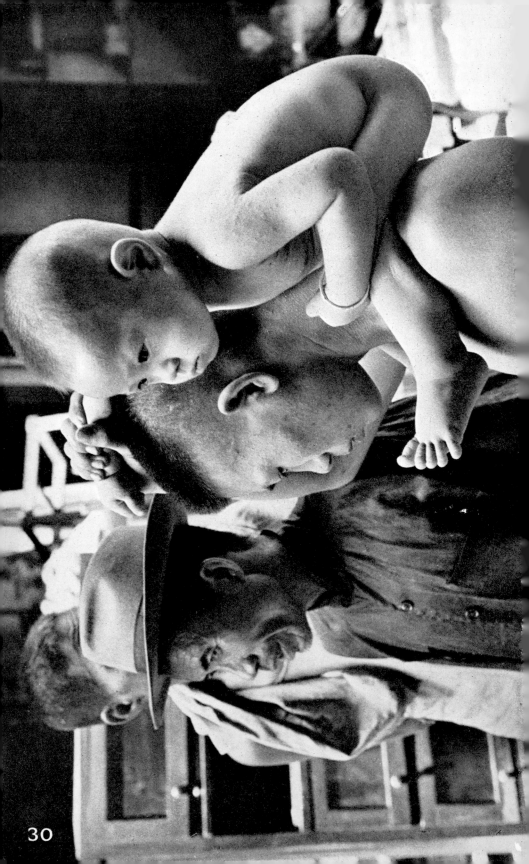